FERTILITY

AND

PLEASURE

FERTILITY

AND

PLEASURE

RITUAL

AND

SEXUAL VALUES

IN

TOKUGAWA JAPAN

WILLIAM R. LINDSEY

UNIVERSITY OF HAWAI'I PRESS
HONOLULU

12 11 10 09 08 07   6 5 4 3 2 1

Library of Congress Cataloging-in-Publication Data

Lindsey, William R., 1964–
    Fertility and pleasure : ritual and sexual values in Tokugawa
Japan / William R. Lindsey.
        p. cm.
    Includes bibliographical references and index.
    ISBN-13: 978-0-8248-3036-6 (hardcover : alk. paper)
    ISBN-10: 0-8248-3036-9 (hardcover : alk. paper)
    1. Sexual ethics—Japan—History. 2. Social values—Japan—History.
3. Women—Japan—Social conditions. 4. Sex role—Japan—History.
5. Japan—Social conditions—1600–1868. 6. Japan—Social life and
customs—1600–1868. I. Title.
    HQ18.J3L56 2007
    306.810952'09032—dc22

                                              2006022269

Designed by Liz Demeter

Printed by The Maple-Vail Book Manufacturing Group

To Mom

CONTENTS

ACKNOWLEDGMENTS

THIS BOOK is not the work of one person. Many people and organizations gave their support and advice, which transformed a raw idea into the book you now hold. Through the support of a postdoctoral fellowship for foreign researchers from the Japan Society for the Promotion of Science, I was able to put aside my teaching responsibilities and travel to Japan for research at the Institute for the Study of Japanese Folk Culture at Kanagawa University. I am deeply grateful to Sano Kenji for allowing me to participate at the institute and for encouraging me as both mentor and friend throughout my tenure there. I also wish to thank Takagi Tadashi of the Enkiridera Mantokuji Shiryōkan for his kindness and openness in sharing his research and knowledge to a curious guy who dropped by his museum one day. Long before this, I conducted initial research at the University of Tokyo with the support of a Fulbright Graduate Research Fellowship. Shimazono Susumu kindly made introductions for me, suggested ideas, and encouraged me to take full advantage of the school's libraries and archives at a time when the project was still in its infancy. Many people read this manuscript at different stages and offered valuable suggestions and criticisms, no one more so than Linda Penkower, who, with much energy and encouragement, was instrumental in helping me put together the initial draft. Likewise, Fred Clothey, Ann Jannetta, Evelyn Rawski, Tom Rimer, and peer reviewers gave their time and ideas to the manuscript, and it is an immensely better product because of their efforts. To the editors of the University of Hawai'i Press I extend a special note of thanks for their faith in the project. My departmental colleagues at the University of Kansas also deserve mention for their support of my efforts during my time away from teaching and for being good friends. Also, I am grateful to Mitani Yukihiko for encouraging me to use the fine and valuable sketches of his late father, Mitani Kazuma. Toyama Haruko, Ito Michiko, Takahashi Mariko, and other Japanese friends and colleagues have helped me immensely with sources and the Japanese language. Finally, I wish to give special thanks to Charles Hambrick, who many years ago introduced me to Japanese religion and became my first mentor.

ONE

INTRODUCTION

IN THE 1790S Kitagawa Utamaro (1750–1806) drew a portrait of the courtesan Hanaōgi, smiling as she dreams of her wedding procession and the start of a new life as a wife in a respectable household (fig.1). Employing a technique of visual allusion—a picture within a picture *(koma-e)*—to point to the unreality of the dream world, Utamaro makes clear that the woman's hope for a fabulous wedding is really a pipe dream.[1] While it was not unusual for courtesans to marry after their term of service had expired, their husbands were usually simple commoners, or, in some cases, habitués of the world of licensed pleasure such as artists and writers and those who dreamed of becoming so. The hope that a wealthy patron might pay off a woman's contract and take her as his wife was often an unrealized dream. Given his courtesan's dream of a formal processional wedding representing a ceremony of high social rank, we may agree with Utamaro that her dream will vanish upon waking.

Yet Utamaro produced something more. He sketched a minimalist metaphor of a ritual and symbolic reality in which many women—both wives and courtesans—participated as actors. His metaphor of a courtesan dreaming of her wedding hints at a congruity between the incongruous roles of wife and courtesan in the composition of Tokugawa society (1600–1867). Much of this composition was forged from the late seventeenth century when political, economic, and ideological processes produced distinct valuations of female sexuality that constructed the roles of wife and courtesan as disparate signifiers of sexuality. From Utamaro emerge two links central to this composition: values and rituals. Wives and courtesans lived under, if not always by, distinct and idealized values concerning the purpose of their sexuality. A courtesan's sexuality was

FIGURE I The courtesan Hanaōgi dreams of her wedding procession. From a Kitagawa Utamaro print. Courtesy of Les Museés royaux d'Art et d'Histoire, Brussels.

valued as a type of play to serve the sensual pleasures of clients; a wife's sexuality, while valued for the mutual pleasure it gave her and her husband, was also marked in the early years of a young woman's marriage by hopes of a purposeful fertility to provide an heir for the household. In addition, Utamaro's courtesan dreams not simply of being a wife, but of *becoming* a wife through a wedding ritual. In her hoped-for becoming, ritual accomplishes two things: one indicative of the young woman's own dream and the other in line with the artist's view of that dream. In her dream ritual serves as a bridge, a mediator, between the conflicting values of two intensely opposed female roles. Still, any bridge reveals the very gulf over which it spans; the presence of a mediator necessarily shows the unresolved differences between parties. In Utamaro's view of the courtesan's dream, ritual serves to make salient the gap marking divergent values and the constraint and behavioral expectations such values promoted.

This interplay between the artist and woman on what her dream wedding accomplishes—clarifying the disparity of values while also changing and reorienting the ritual player in the midst of such disparity—projects onto Tokugawa society the interplay between sexual values and rituals. Although the values that idealized the roles of wife and courtesan were highly disparate, the actual rituals, symbols, and popular practices in which women engaged exhibited a degree of similitude and parallelism that clouded the distilled clarity of values. This ritual activity is inseparable from the religious and social makeup of the time. Not only did this activity pull from the universe of symbols, but it also acted in and through society, and particularly within the context of a woman's, usually a daughter's, sexuality and her role in either the institution of the household or the pleasure quarter. Natal household, marriage household, and pleasure quarter sought to lay claim to a daughter's identity and sexuality. Amidst these claims of communities upon individuals, ritual served to transform roles and social identities, orient women to new communities, and help them face crises of social and even mortal dimensions; but ritual could also be used to express a woman's ambivalence toward her community and its values, create common worlds of immediate female experience underlying these values, or resist the values completely. The following discussion of rituals covers marriage, debut and first meeting of the courtesan with her clients, as well as pregnancy, betrothal, retirement from the quarters, and cutting ties. These rituals act as a type of narrative not because they tell the story of any one woman, but rather because they narrate the constant interplay between competing values, conflicting notions of female sexuality, the coexistence of institutions dependent on women's loyalty and sexuality, and the ritual responsibility women undertook in their participation in this narrative, as well as the religious underpinning of this interplay. Before beginning this narrative it is important first to place it against the dual background suggested by the courtesan's dream of her wedding: 1) contextualizing wives and courtesans in Tokugawa society, and 2) conceptualizing ritual and religion.

Wives, Courtesans, and Tokugawa Society

Utamaro wanted to convey that the courtesan's dream of becoming a wife is illusory. Her waking world of professional sexual play is a realm of activity antithetical to the behavior and role of the wife she becomes in her fantasy. Yet he also conveyed the constant connection Tokugawa society made between the two women as idealized, inverse images. Each image, through the negation of its qualities, necessarily implied the other. As sleep and wakefulness ultimately form two different experiences in the same individual, the courtesan and wife developed divergent but linked images in Tokugawa society. These images of night and day constituted part of a discourse concerning female sexuality. The root question of this discourse that the wife-courtesan dichotomy epitomized was this: is the purpose of female sexuality to serve the virilocal household through reproductive fertility, or is it to serve the commercial sex industry and its paying clients through nonreproductive pleasure? The ideal wife was obedient to her husband and in-laws and used her energy and skills to work toward the economic advancement of the household and her sexuality to produce an heir. This valuation formed *fertility values*. The ideal courtesan was sophisticated and spirited, an expert at pretending to love many men while loving none, and offered her sexuality for the economic advancement of the bordello holding her contract. This valuation constituted *pleasure values*. Other values existed, such as celibacy, which the Buddhist nun exemplified, and the sexual activities of many young villagers that were regulated more by local youth groups than they were by individual households. However, fertility and pleasure constituted a dichotomy of difference that profoundly shaped Tokugawa society and culture. Much of that shape developed from society affirming both sets of values, but doing so while seeking to keep one affirmation separate from the other. Arts and literature, urban spatial configuration, and political policies expressed much of this orientation of bounded affirmation. Further, Tokugawa society did not simply affirm these values, but also produced them through its labor needs, the growth of a national book market, and the rise of economic class distinctions among commoners. In the following paragraphs I describe some aspects of the affirmation and production of these values.

For painters and printmakers like Utamaro and authors such as the playwright Chikamatsu Monzaemon (1653–1724) and the novelist Ihara Saikaku (1642–1693), this orientation of bounded affirmation offered rich possibilities for animating their works with both tragic and humorous pathos. In his 1720 play *The Love Suicides at Amijima (Shinjū ten no amijima),* Chikamatsu uses the pull of a wife's love and loyalty and that of a courtesan for the same man to push the protagonist and his lover into the climax of double suicide. Saikaku, in his 1686 novel *The Life of an Amorous Woman (Kōshoku ichidai onna),* allows his anti-heroine to romp on both sides of the wife-courtesan divide, revealing the humor and pathos of her life choices.[2] Even musical instruments were not free of this orientation, at least in the early part of the period. The samisen was considered primarily an instrument appropriate only for entertainers of the pleasure quarters and for kabuki musicians. The koto was much preferred for training young women in the musical arts.[3]

Affirmation of female sexuality as constituting both fertility and pleasure values also contributed to the creation of a distinct social space in urban areas. The pleasure quarters—settings in several of Chikamatsu's and Saikaku's works—were districts segregated from the rest of urban space. Edo's famed quarter, the Yoshiwara, was walled off on all four sides with a single front gate marking its entrance. The Shinmachi of Osaka and the Shimabara of Kyoto, which with the Yoshiwara formed the country's three great quarters, were similarly segregated. Spatially configuring the urban landscape was not uniquely connected to prostitution. Demarcating space for pleasure in Edo was part of a broader spatial categorization that included the creation of holy sites and class-based residential areas housed in a hierarchy defined in terms of geographic locality and size.[4] Warriors *(bushi)* possessed more than two-thirds of residential space in the city, while temples and shrines—some with spacious grounds—and commoner housing split the remaining area.[5] The walls of the Yoshiwara formed a subdivision of sexualized space within the area where commoners resided. Although Edo's physical geography denied this spatial hierarchy the clean lines of perfect borders, there was an underlying order that measured each allotment of space using the same grid pattern as that of the imperial city of Kyoto.[6] This creation of social space, attentive to hierarchy, divisions of sacred, secular, and sexual activities, as well as to ancient political pedigree, reflects the insight that in Tokugawa Japan, "spatial and geographic discourses inhered in political practices and cultural forms."[7]

The pleasure quarters, along with theaters, formed one part of these spatial discourses. The national government, or shogunate *(bakufu)*, viewed prostitution and kabuki, which was a new and wildly popular form of theater, as "two wheels of the vehicle of pleasure" and thus necessary evils.[8] It realized that outlawing bordellos and theaters would essentially commit its limited resources to making arrests and meting out punishment for such public nuisances as gambling, drunkenness, and lewd behavior—all linked to sex and show businesses.[9] The *bakufu* was not unconcerned about such behavior, but of greater concern to authorities was how to limit and control, rather than eliminate, morally corrupt behavior. The *bakufu* decided on a policy that circumscribed the behavior of pleasure and sexual play through spatial restrictions and walls. Further, female providers of such play were restricted to residences within the enclosure, while their male customers could leave upon receipt of services. Requiring courtesans to live within the quarter was one of the conditions the government set in 1617 when it allowed the Yoshiwara to be built in the hustle and bustle of Edo.[10]

Men were the main players in the building and development of Edo in the first decades of the seventeenth century from a provincial castle town to the center of national government. Its swift growth into one of the largest cities in the world represents on an exaggerated scale the expansion of castle towns and markets throughout the country that had been taking place throughout the 1500s.[11] However, with a rapidly expanding population consisting largely of warriors, laborers, artisans, and entrepreneurial merchants, Edo was in its early decades effectively a city of men.[12] In fact, the demographics led the *bakufu* to occasionally employ Yoshiwara courtesans to serve as court attendants at formal functions during the first half of the seventeenth century. Women honored with these responsibilities abstained from sexual activity to purify themselves in preparation for their temporary duties.[13] In a male metropolis, however, prostitution proved ubiquitous. *Bordello Episodes (Ihon dōbō goen)* describes unlicensed bordellos quickly developing along the outskirts of Edo during these first decades to meet the demands of the city's unusual demographics.[14] This unregulated prostitution boom and its predictably attendant crimes and misdemeanors presented the kind of situation the government wanted to curb. By following the models of the earlier Shimabara and Shinmachi, the *bakufu* hoped the Yoshiwara and other authorized quarters would keep vice contained, allowing the government to regulate it and enjoy its benefits.

One such benefit was gaining a tax revenue. The ready attraction of additional tax revenue from prostitution, for example, lay behind a request from Edo magistrates in 1731 to have the government sanction areas of the city that had already developed heavy traffic in illegal prostitution. By spatially defining these as areas of public vice and bringing them under government regulation, the magistrates reasoned that taxes could be levied and collected and employment would consequently rise, since legal quarters required an abundant support staff of laborers, entertainers, waitresses, and cooks. Although the government eventually dismissed this proposal, it speaks to the readiness of municipal leaders to accept prostitution in order to share in its profitability.[15] Still, the very profitability that national and local governments sought to regulate through sanctioned public prostitution *(kōshō)* in turn encouraged economically competitive varieties of private prostitution *(shishō),* ranging from semi-organized public bath women *(yuna)* to "hidden prostitutes" *(kakushi baita)* such as streetwalkers and wives, in partnership with husbands, either willingly or through coercion opening their homes for business.[16]

Prostitution was widespread in both public and private forms. Indeed, the *bakufu* sanctioned at least twenty-four profitable and revenue-producing quarters across the country.[17] I focus, however, on the three great quarters in Edo, Osaka, and Kyoto, which were the institutional centers of pleasure values. Along with urban theater, they defined style and panache. A strict hierarchy among women in these quarters also defined the class, duties, and expectations placed upon them. Like any society, the quarters had haves, have-nots, and those in the middle. Women working at the lowest rung lived at the physical margins of the quarters and sold their bodies to many for minutes at a time. At the highest rungs, however, existed originally three ranks through which a woman might be promoted (from lowest to highest): *kakoi, tenjin,* and *tayū.*[18] Rankings and names changed throughout the period and the terminology varied somewhat in the different quarters, but the notion of a hierarchy of idealized skills and beauty remained critical to the world of courtesans. I use "courtesan" rather than "prostitute" to refer to those women possessing status unavailable to private prostitutes and beyond the reach of poor women scraping by on the margins of public prostitution. Additionally, Charles Bernheimer, in his work on literary and artistic depictions of prostitution in nineteenth-century France, stresses that "courtesan," unlike "prostitute," denotes a woman whose sexual services were reserved for men of some means and who was a public figure herself.[19] The Parisian courtesan's relation to moneyed men and her own public and institutional stature parallels that of the ranking women of the Tokugawa pleasure quarters, though with one important caveat. Parisian courtesans, unlike their Japanese sisters, offered their clients pleasure free of a political policy of physical segregation.

The policy of restricting prostitution within approved pleasure quarters contributed to the bounded affirmation of the fertility-pleasure discourse in at least two ways. First, by quartering nonreproductive sex, this policy gave a degree of institutional definition to sexual purpose, as seen from the male perspective, as an "either/or" proposition between play within the walls and activity more bound up with emotional and household duty beyond the walls. The regulation of public prostitution throughout the country was a product of early modern political organization, which Toyotomi Hideyoshi (1536–1598) commenced when he quartered Kyoto's sexual workers in 1589 as part of his attempt to bring order to his new rule.[20] This politically backed institutional segregation of nonreproductive sex altered an earlier social construction of women's sexuality and partnership with men, which some identify as the medieval ideal of a wife. According to this ideal a woman was both wife and sexual friend, both household partner and play partner. Segregated institutions of play separated her roles of mother and household manager from her role as her husband's sexual satisfier, leaving the latter function to be shared with the courtesan.[21] How much this medieval model of the wife was a cultural ideal or how much a simple matter of the vague structural nature of sexual relationships in medieval culture is not clear.[22] Still, in contrast, the early modern demarcation of female sexuality placed women in either the household or the bordello, idealized their roles as either wife or courtesan, and produced a discourse of sexuality as primarily serving either fertility or pleasure.

Second, institutional quartering recognized the courtesan's profession as a female occupation equal to other jobs in that it entailed a woman contractually working outside the home. Contracts of the period typically apply the term *hōkō* to public prostitution, which denotes paid, contractual labor covering a wide range of mainly urban jobs that commoner men and women filled.[23] Understanding Tokugawa prostitution as a form of contractual work connects with recent feminist approaches that analyze prostitution less as a type of oppression than as a type of work. In this analysis labor is the performance of self-interested economic activity that is rationally, if rarely freely, chosen. Wendy Chapkis terms this work "erotic labour." Like other forms of labor, erotic labor's value is contested in the fields of politics and culture, and within its own structure it provides, as with all types of labor, a hierarchy of social distinctions, statuses, and inequalities among its workers.[24] From Chapkis's description we may see the contours of Tokugawa prostitution—the coexistence of government-sanctioned and unlawful forms of prostitution, the attempts to redefine illegal districts as legal, and the use of hierarchical status to distinguish ranks—as a culturally specific example of erotic labor and its fields of contestation and hierarchy.

From the standpoint of erotic labor (with equal emphasis on both words), the fact that many late seventeenth- and early eighteenth-century texts cataloging occupations registered "courtesan" *(keisei, yūjo)* alongside other types of female labor is not surprising.[25] *A Record of Treasures for Women (Onna chōhōki),* which is a 1692 lifestyle guide for women and a central source of examination in this study, opens with an illustration depicting women of various classes, statuses, and occupations.[26] Along with courtesans, the text pictures a woman who is a courtesan manager or a bordello owner's wife,[27] a peasant woman, townswomen, widows,[28] a samurai wife, and an aristocratic woman.[29] This pictorial jumble of women, independent figures drawn without any background of appropriate social environment to delineate them, is indicative of a cultural anxiety toward the rise of contractual female labor. This anxiety reflected the understanding that working outside the household positioned women in an unbounded public sphere where they were sexually vulnerable, especially if they lacked the moral education and internal discipline necessary to comport themselves with prudence and wisdom.[30] In light of this anxiety the courtesan stood not simply as one occupation among others, but as the moral end result of labor performed outside the bounds of home and husband and without knowledge of correct social behavior and moral grounding. In this sense every unmarried daughter without such knowledge was in danger, especially if she worked, of, if not literally becoming a courtesan, then behaving in ways both sexual and social that would lead others to think of her as no better than a prostitute.

This anxiety was rooted in the economic environment that put many women in the workforce. Trends in the early modern political economy such as the growth of castle towns and large cities, urban migration, development and expansion of markets, rise of the merchant class, and the money economy hit their stride in the late seventeenth century, which the Genroku era (1688–1704) epitomizes with its prosperity and its celebration of the commoner classes. Young, unmarried women were an important element of this economy quite apart from prostitution per se. They found employment as maids in warrior and commoner households, as workers in cottage industries and textiles, and also in the service sectors of entertainment, food, and hospitality, which often overlapped with prostitution.[31] Promotion of fertility values—idealization of marriage into a man's household, of obedient and loyal behavior to that household, and of sexuality as purposeful fertility for that household—was born from the uneasy sense that young women, unattached to home or husband and untrained in right behaviors and moral grounding, needed protection against sexual exploitation while laboring outside the home.

Lifestyle guides and moral texts, many of which were originally published around the Genroku era and reissued throughout the period, promoted these fertility values. The rise of the printed book during the Tokugawa was critical to this process of promotion and dissemination. The same economic changes that produced anxiety about female labor also produced a means to a solution: a competitive, nationwide book market that churned out a variety of tomes including lifestyle guides and moral primers.[32] These texts, written in Japanese script *(kana)* as opposed to Chinese, formed a popular genre called *jokun,* or "women's training," which contributed to the seventeenth-century publishing boom.[33] These publications were intended for the edification of girls and young women and covered a range of topics such as moral values, proper deportment, home management, and general lifestyle matters. The quarters were also important in the growth of publishing. More than two hundred titles concerned with varying aspects of prostitution, from guides to the quarters and courtesan critiques to fiction, were published by the end of the seventeenth century.[34] Further, as letter writing was central to a courtesan's occupation, there was a need for books to satisfy her development as a literate professional.[35] Female managers, themselves retired courtesans, were the main teachers of reading and writing to young girls serving as child attendants to their sister courtesans. Literacy among courtesans indicates that while not all women could read and write, especially those living far from cities and their surrounding villages, all categories of women could do so.[36] Typically this literacy was functionally appropriate to their professional and personal aspirations.[37] Among daughters from families of commercial traders, for example, the ability to read and write was important not only for their participation in family businesses, but also in making them attractive as potential daughters-in-law.[38] Similarly, wealthy peasants invested significant time and resources to cultivate in their daughters both educational and cultural literacy gleaned from *jokun* books because they knew a family improved its own standing by grooming its daughters in the values, behavior, and cultural knowledge that *jokun* writings made available.[39]

By promoting these values, authors of *jokun* books hoped to prepare girls and young women for the moral and social responsibilities of marriage and the life of a wife and household manager. Lifestyle guides such as *A Record of Treasures for Women* are particularly interesting as a means for espousing these values. The guides filtered fertility values from their elite origins in the warrior household by making available to commoners and their daughters descriptions of daily and ritual life loosely based on samurai household codes. The Ogasawara and Ise, which were noted houses of ritual, developed these codes in the Muromachi period (1338–1573) to codify military training styles and ceremonial deportment among warrior households.[40] Lifestyle guides funneled fertility values less through moral didactics than through descriptions of rites, customs, and behaviors. Guides offered commoners a window through which they could view the world of elite ritual and etiquette, and then employ it in varying measures in their own lives. This borrowing acknowledged the period's schematized hierarchy. Hierarchy serves to place individuals and groups in varying positions of social worth for purposes of organization and control, and yet it also produces in people aspirations and strategies to acquire as much status as the hierarchy makes possible.[41] In this manner, guides like *A Record of Treasures for Women* were not published simply to show commoners an unattainable lifestyle reserved for those at the social top. Rather, they offered up the world of elite behaviors for commoners to seize as their own in acquiring forms of ritual and symbolic status that the given hierarchy defined as valuable. The commoners' appropriation of warrior culture has been dubbed "pseudo-samurai pretensions,"[42] but such so-called pretensions validated samurai culture as the primary operative field of status, and acted to recognize the hierarchy upon which that culture sat. In this context, *A Record of Treasures for Women* possesses a prescriptive quality in its idealization of warrior lifestyle vis-à-vis commoners and a descriptive quality in that it allowed commoner daughters and their families to appropriate elements of the samurai lifestyle as they saw fit. In this manner the guide and other representatives of its genre offered to commoners an important means to begin creating the "samuraization" of their own lives by narrowing through ritual and behaviors the social gap between them and the warrior class.[43]

A Record of Treasures for Women, which privileges Ogasawara ritual,[44] consists of five illustrated chapters describing categories of life experience considered the epitome of feminine knowledge and practice. These chapters cover 1) the historical and contemporary position of women, illness and behavior, a vocabulary list for proper speech, and appropriate makeup and hairstyles; 2) the wedding ritual; 3) pregnancy and birth rituals; 4) penmanship, poetry reading, the care of the sick, and the maintenance and cleaning of clothing; and 5) bridal and clothing items, character recognition for common words, chapter names from the *Tale of Genji*, seasonal celebrations, definitions of literary phrases and words, and styles of wrapping items in paper. Sections dealing with speech, characters, *Genji*, and literary words indicate both the text's assumption of female literacy and its educational function in developing that literacy.[45] *A Record of Treasures for Women* offered a "values education" to families wishing to instruct their daughters to some degree on a lifestyle grounded in moral knowledge of elite female values, practical knowledge of maintaining health and home, and ritual knowledge for guiding one toward the text's vision of womanhood: married, serving the household of one's husband and in-laws with skill and loyalty, and giving birth to an heir.

This vision assumed the household *(ie)* was the institutional hub of fertility values, just as the pleasure quarter was institutionally central to the vision of pleasure values. Fertility values had their origin in samurai family morality and reflected the institutional structure of that morality. The early modern *ie* that spread among the commoner population was a collection, large and small, of individuals—typically related by blood but not always—committed to a corporate identity. The individuals were more than simply a family under a roof; they were an ongoing enterprise that was as much gesellschaft as gemeinschaft, and they recognized their official headship, if not always actual leadership, as an inherited male position ideally passed on from father to eldest son, but which in practice would often position a younger sibling, an uncle, or an adoptee for headship.[46] A bride marrying into a middle-class or upper-class *ie* was expected to be loyal and industrious and possess organizational and educational skills to further the household economically; in addition, there was the hope she would provide an heir to succeed as head and continue the household for another generation.[47] This description of the *ie* is generic and requires historical and social qualifications. It was not a family system buttressing an ideology of nationalism, as it would later become in the Meiji period;[48] rather, it was a cultural ideal and economic unit that for the most part was not within the reach of the poor and propertyless. The Tokugawa *ie* was actually one pattern, albeit universal, among a patchwork of local family and inheritance patterns, some of which were matrilocal versions of the *ie;* it could be easily manipulated, especially on its points of virilocal marriage and agnatic inheritance, to fit the immediate, pressing needs of a household; and thus inheritance in the patrilineal *ie,* as was true of all Tokugawa inheritance patterns, was always more improvisational than mechanical. Still, as an economic and family unit, it constituted a growing norm—an *ie*-consciousness—among comfortable and confident rural and urban commoners whose relative economic stability encouraged institutional commitment to and identity with the household.[49] Consequently, for many such commoners the question of household and marriage—to which household they should send their daughter and from which household they should accept a daughter-in-law—became a major concern. Lifestyle guides and moral primers read by them and their daughters bolstered the significance of this concern by presenting the *ie* as institutionally central to the moral and social development of girls who would one day become wives in the *ie* of future husbands.

In measurable ways the daughters of these commoners were direct opposites of those whose families sold them to the quarters. Quartered prostitution depended on the hardships of poverty and family misfortune.[50] Buyers for the quarters often searched for girls and young women in economically vulnerable rural areas. One response to failed crops, market jolts, natural disasters, perennial poverty, and the sudden illness or death of a breadwinner was to release family members to become contractual wage laborers elsewhere, including discharging daughters to the erotic labor force. For example (albeit a later one), in 1900 half of the Yoshiwara's women were from areas that had recently experienced damaging floods, which suggests a historical precedent of families releasing daughters during grim times.[51] On the other side of the divide—one of real economic class interspersed within a social system that distinguished between peasant, artisan, and merchant—was an increasing number of rural and urban commoner families, with a growing *ie*-consciousness, that managed their economic destinies well, tied a household identity to that destiny, and wished to partake of the forms of social status available to them culturally and financially. Financial success bred a desire for social success—those pseudo-samurai pretensions—and the economic ability of wealthy and middle-class commoners enabled them to access education for their sons and daughters, employ tutors, and purchase cultured literature such as *jokun*.[52] Wealthy farmers, village headman families, and middle- and upper-class urbanites and those living in proximity to large and provincial cities constituted the primary readership of moral and ritual guides.[53]

Raising commoner status by improving a daughter's values, education, and ritual knowledge was central to Namura Jōhaku (d. ca. 1748), who wrote *A Record of Treasures for Women* under the penname Sōden Tadakishi.[54] In 1693, a year after he wrote his seminal guide, Namura also wrote a companion manual for sons titled *A Record of Treasures for Men (Nan chōhōki)*.[55] Although Namura's biography is meager, key elements of his time help us understand the intellectual milieu of his text and of himself as a writer.[56] We know he was a physician and was likely a student of Itō Jinsai (1627–1705).[57] Itō's vision of a good society specifically reflected the "assumptions, ethical concerns, and material interests most characteristic" of the commercially active townspeople.[58] His rejection of neo-Confucianism in favor of classical forms of Confucian ideas linked to Confucius and Mencius was largely meant as a critique of the warrior class's embrace and interpretation of neo-Confucian ideas to suit and favor its social position and political concerns over those of rising commoners.[59] In similar spirit, Namura wrote *A Record of Treasures for Women* as a positive means to assert the value of commoner life, particularly that of daughters becoming wives and mothers in their husbands' households. Namura was determined that these daughters have the same ritual skills, lifestyle knowledge, and social values historically deemed worthy only of warrior daughters. Because of its popularity, *A Record of Treasures for Women* was republished throughout the period, and its replication charts the changing concerns of the times. Such change is particularly evident in its final 1847 edition, which novelist and culture critic Takai Ranzan (1762–1838) edited before its publication and which includes extensive passages he inserted in the manuscript, though without any erasure of Namura's original text.[60] The historical significance of Takai's redactions is most apparent in the chapter on pregnancy, where his passages express later issues of nationalism and anti-Buddhism and ideas concerning obstetrics that were not relevant to Namura's time. At appropriate points in this study I refer to Takai's edition to clarify such configurations of historical concern and change.

Desire among families to raise the status of their daughters points to the broader issue of female social standing in the Tokugawa. The period has traditionally been considered the "dark age for women" *(onna ni totte ankoku jidai)*. In this view, the Tokugawa represents the historical nadir of female status and authority, a marked decline from preceding periods. This conclusion comes in part from a methodology focusing on laws and customs that locked women out of inheritance and on varieties of *jokun,* which, typical of the genre, directed their laser-like focus on women's moral development while idealizing virilocal marriage. Recent scholarship has reacted to this view by reevaluating the educational value of moral texts and by stressing narrower, often biographical, studies of women to show "the limited but real power and prerogatives of Tokugawa women."[61] Joyce Lebra, for example, has examined the life of a daughter whose skills and contributions to her sake-brewing family were so valuable that the family devised strategies, such as matrilocal marriage, to get around traditional customs barring women from participating in the brewing industry.[62]

In another vein, Jennifer Robertson recounts the missionary activities of female devotees of the bourgeois religious movement Shingaku, with particular focus on a former Buddhist nun, Jion-ni Kenka (1716–1778), who propagated the religion's teachings in the city of Edo.[63] Such research insists on adding the color and detail of real individuals' lives to any canvas that portrays female life as simply one of social inferiority. Still, as Anne Walthall cautions in her biographical study of Matsuo Taseko (1811–1894), an accomplished peasant woman, methodologies "privileging the individual over the collective" must be careful not to raise the subject's life above the fray of her time and place, to see her simply as an individual willing her life forward.[64] An individual history is arguably interesting precisely because it captures a life embedded in time and place that produces ironies of disjuncture and contradictions between self and peers and between individual achievements and culturally shared ideals. Thus in Robertson's study of Shingaku women, the drive and accomplishment of Jion-ni Kenka—a celibate, unmarried woman active outside the home—is in complete opposition to the ideal of the Shingaku woman as an obedient wife, whose faith tied her to husband and home. Likewise, the life of the business-savvy daughter in Lebra's work is remarkable because her career in the sake industry represents the exception rather than the rule, since the production of rice wine had become largely a male enterprise in the Tokugawa period, whereas in previous centuries brewing was traditionally women's work.[65]

In addition to earlier studies emphasizing broad structures of social marginalization and more recent research stressing portraits of choice-making individuals and their families, an examination of ritual practices brings an additional layer of understanding to Tokugawa female life. Ritual is both an objective structure of culture that acts upon individuals and a subjective practice by which ritual actors shape their social environment.[66] Ritual is both "structured and structuring."[67] This dual nature allows the investigator equal footing in the emphases of the above historical understandings: the stress on burdensome social inequalities and the stress on the strategies and choices individuals and their families employed within the limits allowed by Tokugawa society and their own stratagems. A focus on ritual allows for the consideration of the cultural ideals and social structures that defined the valuations and life patterns of a number of Tokugawa women, while it also reveals one way by which women gained the prerogative of communal status and, at times, even individual authority to alter that status. In short, the investigator of ritual can move between the discrete perspectives of Utamaro and his courtesan, or, in other words, between acknowledging discourses constructed on idealized sexual values and examining the employment of ritual by individuals as they affirmed, clouded, or resisted these values.

Conceiving Ritual and Religion

This study, at its root, is an examination of actions: women moving between households, into and out of quarters, marrying, dealing with pregnancy, and divorcing. These actions expressed communal values of fertility and pleasure as well as individual concerns of whether or not and to what degree to affirm these values. In chapter 2 I conceptualize the values of fertility and pleasure, their communal positions, and their ritual expression through the notion of a "value model." The model's triadic structure of values, institution, and rites puts forward fertility and pleasure as not simply abstracted discourses but as structured and enacted discourses. I divide women's actions into three broad types: entrance, placement, and exit. In chapter 3, "entrance" describes a daughter's marriage into the virilocal household and the rites by which a courtesan establishes a formal relationship with a client. "Placement" is concerned with ritual activity that not only takes place within an institution and exemplifies in some measure a woman's position there, but also places a woman within a range of gender-specific experiences that cut across social status and idealized roles. In chapter 4 I investigate pregnancy as placement. In chapter 5, "exit" describes a host of rituals meant to move a woman from one institution and role to another. Betrothal and bridal departure from a woman's natal household prior to her entrance into marriage, as well as retirement of a courtesan from her quarter, are ritually mediated moves. Wives and courtesans could also employ other strategies to create unapproved exits from the marriage household and quarter through the respective actions of divorce and escape. While some of these practices of entrance, placement, and exit may be fruitfully interpreted as rites of passage of some sort, I avoid examining them as a single class of ritual. Instead, I am interested in describing them as a ritual narrative structuring, like the scenes and acts of a play, a larger drama. That drama was played out through the cultural coexistence of contradictory sexual values and the needs—sometimes corresponding and sometimes conflicting—between collectivities and their individual female members.

While I write much about buddhas, *kami,* ancestors, and other symbols, religion as I conceive it for this particular study fits awkwardly in the categories of Buddhism, Shinto, Confucianism, and folk religion. Alone, of course, each is inadequate to the task; together they risk dividing the complex of human experience—those obligations and improvisations of making choices, facing challenges, and forcing changes—into a systematic artificiality that may miss as much as it captures. For this study, I focus on the individual and communal-centered ritual experiences of entrances, placement, and exits rather than on religious traditions per se, as such an approach has the greatest capacity for understanding the individual, collective, and cultural significance of those experiences. Tokugawa marriage is a case in point.

As a subject of religious inquiry it is difficult to locate the significance of Tokugawa marriage if one seeks to place it in terms of a tradition such as Shinto or Christianity. Before the start of the Meiji period (1868–1912), marriage ceremonies were household affairs. Family members were both ritual participants and ritual leaders; there were no priests, and the ritual locus was the house. The practice of Shinto weddings has hardly any more tradition behind it in Japan than a Christian-style ceremony, which is a popular option for many non-Christian Japanese brides and grooms today. Both ceremonies are creations of Japan's modern period. During the Meiji period, weddings were one of many celebratory rituals that came largely under the purview of a newly self-conscious, professional Shinto priesthood.[68] The starting point of the "traditional" ritual link between Shinto and weddings is arguably as late as 1900, when the crown prince and future Taishō emperor (1879–1926) married at the Grand Shrine of Ise in a *shinzen* (before *kami*) ceremony.[69] Modern Shinto nuptials—conducted before *kami,* in shrines, and by priests—developed broadly in imitation of Christian weddings (conducted before God, in churches, and by clergy). Further, in moving marriage into shrines, Shinto adapted many ritual steps and ceremonial displays from the etiquette and ritual styles that Tokugawa guides had popularized. This modern form of marriage before the *kami (shinzen kekkon)* is in contrast to Tokugawa forms of marriage, which scholars of folk studies term marriage before people *(jinzen kekkon)* and marriage in the home *(jitaku kekkon)*.[70] Similarly, *A Record of Treasures for Women* provides incredible detail about elite wedding rituals—what people should do, when they should do it, and where they should do it—but it says nothing of *kami* as being part of this rite. Although this does not mean that participants did not symbolically engage *kami* in wedding ceremonies, the text's emphasis on ritual activity itself is evidence of the importance of ritual as accomplishing or intending to accomplish something, which is itself a matter of significant concern to the collective or individual employing that ritual. In the remaining pages I examine these two points —the centrality of ritual and religion as a type of concern—in order to understand a level of significance in Tokugawa women's lives amidst competing values, roles, and their social collectives.

An important aspect to ritual's centrality is that it expresses ideals of the cultural order. Through ritual people may behave in ways that correspond to and affirm such ideals. Yet the cultural order is full of categories that also call on ritual to both affirm and transcend them.[71] In the cultural order of Tokugawa Japan, "daughter" was a salient example of such a category. A young woman affirmed the behavioral ideals of a daughter—most notably obeying and supporting her natal family's wishes and needs—by transcending the category of daughter. Waiting on the other side of that ritual transcendence—the person she was to become —were the categories of "wife" and "courtesan," each with its own cultural ideals of role identity and enactment. In this way ritual entails a paradox in that it acts to *affirm* one's present social identity as it also attempts to *transform* that identity and bring a new set of responsibilities and self-understanding to the ritual actor—but the two goals are often in tension and sometimes even left unresolved after the ritual.[72] The rites I examine exhibit this tension of affirmation and transformation. Sometimes it is explicit, sometimes implicit. It is most conspicuous in the rituals of entrance and exit. In these ritual moments the push and pull of a woman's social identity and transformation take center stage, particularly from the perspective of daughter/wife and daughter/courtesan. It is at the boundaries of these perspectives that the values and behaviors of fertility and pleasure play out against the institutional need of the household and bordello to incorporate outside women as loyal wives and courtesans.

The centrality of ritual in Tokugawa society, particularly when mediating social movement and changes in social roles, points to the Tokugawa as a "unitized society."[73] All societies are composed of smaller "units," such as families, workplaces, and schools, which are institutionalized, self-regulated to a lesser or greater extent, and oriented toward achieving a particular mission. A unitized society, however, stresses the social reality of each unit and its membership to such a high degree that identity outside of recognized units is considered anomic. In less unitized societies there are more opportunities for social interaction free of formalized role behavior, hierarchical order, and membership identity. In contrast, a strongly unitized society offers for the most part intensely private and highly public spheres of behavior and presentation that form a social experience with few arenas offering public presence absent formal role identity. This kind of society necessarily stresses rituals of entrance and exit because it sees space free of social units as space devoid of social meaning. Movement from one unit to another, from one prescribed role to another, takes on a dramatic sense of change and often depends on ritual to mediate it. The Tokugawa hence represents an intensely unitized society in this respect. Movement into and out of its units of natal household, marriage household, and bordello necessitated ritual activity of some kind, whether formal and celebratory (as in weddings and a courtesan's first meeting with clients), or private and marginal (as in strategies designed to force a divorce and attempt escape from the pleasure quarter).

What can be said of this ritual activity, regardless of its kind? Time, place, and symbol are prominent factors. Rituals tied to becoming and un-becoming a wife or courtesan, whether formal and ceremonial or ad-hoc and personal, entailed various notions of time such as astronomical, institutional, and personal.[74] The ritual practices I examine often overlap with these chronological categories. Once again, the wedding provides a good example. Marriage between two families took place after consultation with the ritual calendar and its astronomical calculations to ensure an auspicious day; the institution of the household, particularly that of the groom and his parents' house, underwent profound transition with the entrance of a new member whose role was critical to the continuation of the household; and as a rite of passage for both the groom and the bride, marriage meant a powerful change in personal identity. Cutting across these categories of time is "existential time."[75] Ritual moments emerging from existential time occurred when an individual confronted the specter of anomie shadowing her life. In this study, such existential crises include entering situations that challenge one's sense of moral reasoning and behavior, reaching the limit of one's physical strength and facing life's finitude, and being no longer able to give consent to events in one's life.[76] Ritual practice often addresses such crises. It suggested itself in the lives of some Tokugawa women through such experiences as creating a new social identity, confronting the inherent health risks of pregnancy, and cutting personal and institutional ties. Becoming a courtesan, for example, demanded that a daughter leave her family behind and bind her loyalty, energies, and sexuality to a different community—her bordello—under the culturally affirming guise that she morally fulfill her role as a good daughter by abandoning that role and accepting another in the world of prostitution. Pregnancy exposed a woman to the potential of illness and death, and many of the ritual behaviors surrounding it were meant to provide for a woman's deliverance from a dangerous situation as she faced her own finitude. Marriage and prostitution were not fixed experiences. Categories of the Tokugawa cultural order—wife and courtesan—that previously marked the "becoming" side of the "daughter" category could also be transcended in reverse. In the ritual version of "everything old becomes new again," a woman who found she could no longer tolerate being a certain man's wife or many men's courtesan could attempt, through a variety of strategic practices, to find a way out of the marriage household or bordello and, if possible, back to the role of a daughter or even that of another man's wife.

The place of ritual in these experiences was highly varied, ranging from the avenue of a pleasure quarter where a courtesan paraded to meet her client to the woman's body in which a fetus developed. Ritual place in such experiences is more than a given locale; rather, it is an active construct of human imagination and practice. The practice of ritual not only *takes place,* but more importantly *makes place.* That is, it maps out the boundaries of an environment, often idealized and hierarchical, within which ritual actors play out roles, relations, and situations typically revelatory of collective or individual concerns.[77] The importance of place in this view is less that of a "particular location" of ritual activity than a "social position" constructed through ritual activity.[78] The marriage of a bride and the first meeting of a courtesan with her client idealized human relations between women and men within the hierarchical structures of the household and pleasure quarter. They created the positions of wife and ranking courtesan and reflected the behavioral ideals of the values of fertility and pleasure. As a different kind of example, a variety of customs, taboos, and health practices attempted to establish the woman's body as an ideal place through which to ensure safe childbirth. On the underside of such hierarchy and ideals, activities of divorce and escape, which were linked to places as varied as divorce nunneries, sacred trees, and shrines of tutelary deities, show that strategies of ritual action could also be used to move oneself out of place, out of the hierarchy and structure of the household and bordello, and out of the social position of wife and courtesan created earlier by marriage and first meeting rites.

Ritual makes place social, malleable, positional, and an active creation, but further ritual also establishes "perspectival boundaries."[79] These boundaries comprise the varying perspectives and positions of ritual actors and their actions in the context of the rite. Ritual place, at minimum, is concerned with either affirming existing or creating new perspectival boundaries. We can concretize this notion in relation to Tokugawa Japan as a unitized society. Women's lives were marked by all sorts of perspectival boundaries such as pleasure quarter/household, natal household/marriage household, one's family/one's in-laws, wife/courtesan, not pregnant/pregnant, and—the most fundámental with regards to the tension between affirmation and transformation—daughter/wife-courtesan. All the particular localities of ritual activity in this study—natal household, marriage household, bordello, pregnant body, divorce nunnery, cutting-ties tree, and tutelary deity shrine—either guard existing boundaries or generate new spatial, personal, and experiential boundaries of varying perspectives from women as ritual actors. From this perspective, ritual place is "a generative center."[80] Wherever the place of ritual, it is that place in which activities are generated—whether through public ceremonies of celebration, cautionary practices of safe birth, or in shadowy plots of strategy to alter and better one's life—that places a woman either on one side of a perspectival border or mediates her crossing the border to the opposite side. In this study, ritual place has multiple frames. It may be a location (often social, though sometimes bodily), but it is always concerned with socially constructed positions and necessarily intensifies boundaries of identity, behaviors, values, and institutions.

Finally, an examination of rituals employed by Tokugawa women and their families also requires attention to ritual symbols and their meanings. There are three levels of meaning an interpreter may give to ritual symbols: the exegetical, the operational, and the positional.[81] Exegetical meanings are those that people involved in the ritual expressly understand and articulate. Operational meanings provide evidence as to how symbols function in the logic of the ritual itself and the impressions and responses they encourage. Positional meanings show how symbols relate to one another in the full web of cultural practices and belief. This study primarily examines ritual symbols through the operational and positional levels as they speak to larger functional and cultural meanings that are more attuned to historical analysis. Still, through commentary by Namura and Ise Sadatake (1717–1784), the eighteenth-century head of the Ise house of ritual, views of individuals concerning the exegetical meanings of ritual are also available. This is particularly evident when data point to open differences. An example in chapter 5 discusses the ritual controversy concerning the use of funerary symbolism in the rite of bridal departure. Namura finds it appropriate for idealizing a daughter's change in location, role, and, it is hoped, new sense of loyalty. Sadatake argues that funerary symbolism is in bad form and invites grave consequences by flagrantly mimicking death rites during such an auspicious occasion.

This difference between Namura and Sadatake reveals another interpretation of ritual symbols. One common assumption of how ritual symbols operate involves the idea of ritual as a system of symbols imbued with meanings accepted as true by participants and to which participants give intellectual consent. However, the gap between Namura and Sadatake concerning the "meaning" of funeral symbolism in wedding rites indicates that intangible elements such as mood, feeling, sense, and memory—in other words, the capacity of symbols to evoke rather than simply mean something—are part of a symbol's power too.[82] What does funeral symbolism evoke in a wedding? A somber but necessary separation of a daughter from her natal family reminiscent of the dead separating from life, or a jarring clash of emotional tones that raises a macabre specter in the midst of joy and life? The power of symbols lies as much in their ability to evoke something in us as in their ability to mean something to us. This helps us to configure ritual knowledge as being, at times, as much implicit as explicit, as much created and intuited as learned, and as much intentionally employed as customarily practiced. Through this configuration we gain not only an understanding of the larger fields of operational and positional meanings possessed by rituals and their symbols, but also a sense of the ability of ritual and its symbols to evoke something in individuals and their communities. Thus, for example, the transparent intention and effort on the part of the pleasure quarters to create nuptial rites between courtesans and clients through mimicry of wedding ritual reveals less the meaning of the wedding itself, which was antithetical to the values and economics of prostitution, and more the ability of the ritual through imitation to produce a range of evocations, from aesthetics and playful love to assertions of elite cultural proclivities.

The paradox and tension of ritual to attempt both affirmation and transformation of female roles underlies much of the following examination of rites of entrance, placement, and exit. These rituals are characterized by time that is often existential, by place that is frequently social and hierarchical (sometimes bodily and always perspectival), by symbols that possess referential as well as evocative power, and by concerns of the individual and her collective, although at times individual and group concerns may conflict. How do we best understand the concerns of the individual and the collectivity to which ritual activity responds? This question leads to the final issue of conceiving religion as a type of concern.

As with Tokugawa marriage as a religious subject, the ritual practices of wives and courtesans require a definition of religion that is functional and not simply derivative of religious traditions. A functional definition seeks to understand how any phenomenon under investigation fits and operates within a transparent designation of religion. Such a definition does not rely on assumptions that religion possesses an unambiguous social reality, as sectarian studies of traditions assert, nor that it has an essence that may be plumbed, as comparative studies of "the sacred" assume. A functional definition acknowledges that religious inquiry is not determined by the phenomena under investigation, but rather by the kinds of questions put to the phenomena that best function to extract what the investigator thinks is religiously significant.[83] Returning again to marriage helps in formulating a useful functional definition. Continuity of the *ie* became a matter of social, economic, and ritual concern for a growing number of commoners as the Tokugawa period progressed. Marriage was one such ritual concern, for it marked the re-creation of the family and household. As described in detail in *A Record of Treasures for Women,* marriage, we can say, exhibited a "righteous and urgent tone."[84] The tone reverberates with a host of hopes and anxieties such as household continuity, harmony between bride and in-laws, reorientation of a woman's sense of loyalty and identity, and her long-term health. Other experiences and their ritual expressions of the roles of wife and courtesan also exhibit these and other concerns, both communal and individual, as we will see throughout these pages. In short, these hopes and anxieties and their ritual expression reflect what I functionally term forms of ultimate concern.[85] There are other functional definitions of religion, and ultimate concern has potential drawbacks, as does any methodological definition.[86] Still, as a transparent designation of religion specifically intended to produce religious inquiry, particularly inquiry into phenomena not so easily placed within conventional categories, it has advantages, as, I think, the fullness of this study shows.

Among these advantages are the ability to 1) straddle competing conceptualizations of Japanese religion; 2) avoid religious and cultural essentialisms that obscure other methodological narratives; and 3) accept competing and conflicting claims of ultimate concern amongst groups and individuals. I want to touch upon these points briefly in closing. Contextualizing ultimate concern in the ritual world of wives and courtesans resonates typologically with several linked, sometimes even bifurcated, conceptualizations that have shaped the study of Japanese religion.[87] These include stressing matters of social and political history over matters of doctrine, gaining practical benefits over salvific assurance, and being attentive to diffused religion versus that of institutional forms. This study draws on the front links of these sets, but it does not exclude attention to the back links. Despite the methodological tendency in the study of Japanese religion to split these links, ultimate concern requires focus on all of them because the ritual lives of many Tokugawa women touched upon all of them. For example, such a split is explored in a dialogue between Jamie Hubbard and Neil McMullin concerning the role and value of doctrine in understanding Japan's religious history.[88] McMullin argues that overt attention to doctrine, which tends to favor notions of autonomous traditions, great men and great ideas of history, and clear demarcations of sacred and secular, risks overlooking interpretations of religious phenomena ritually and institutionally situated in cultural, political, and economic discourses.[89] Hubbard concurs with much of the critique. Nevertheless, he holds that doctrine possesses interpretive value if investigators are attentive to the role of doctrine in refiguring historical conditions in such ways that it "resonates ultimately for those who believe it."[90] Although the methodology threaded through the pages of this book is more in line with McMullin's view, Hubbard's defense of doctrine is valuable for understanding the power of doctrine to act in refiguring forms of ultimate concern particular to time, place, and people. In chapter 4, for example, I discuss a specific symbolization of pregnancy disseminated in *A Record of Treasures for Women.* This symbolization visually depicts the development of a fetus from ritual items and is teamed with corresponding buddhas for each month in the womb. The symbolic logic of these illustrations was rooted in particular doctrinal environments that were in development before the Tokugawa period, but during the Tokugawa that logic was refigured in lifestyle guides to express the ultimate concern of pregnant women for a safe birth and for conceptualizing the life inside them.

This refiguring of doctrinally based symbols to express the hope of a safe birth indicates another aspect of ultimate concern in Japanese religion. Concerns about one's life in terms of health, happy relationships, and wealth, and the avoidance of undesirable events and situations are central to understanding a range of religious activity in Japan characterized by the search for worldly or practical benefits *(genze riyaku).*[91] Seeking such benefits intensely validates life in this world and the ultimacy of its concerns. A daughter's marriage or debut as a courtesan, her pregnancy, and various forms of cutting human and institutional ties reveal the validation of seeking benefits for one's collectivity or for oneself. While I focus on practical benefits as definitive of one form of ultimate concern for this particular study, I avoid the temptation of upholding worldly benefits as definitive of Japanese religiosity. Focus on the search for benefits as one expression of ultimate concern is, as part of a functional definition of religion, intentional in its methodological transparency. The methodological point of using worldly benefits in this study is not to uncover something essential about Japanese religion—to create an unchanging and timeless religious "metanarrative" of past and present that overshadows other approaches and the important stories of Japanese religion they can tell.[92] Rather, the point is simply to put forward an approach that helps answer most fully the particular questions I ask in this study.

Putting forward a functional definition tied to practical benefits as a form of ultimate concern marks a valuable approach toward understanding the ritual practices of women and their social institutions because it can account for the dynamic of competing claims of ultimacy.[93] In the context of this study, competing claims could arise between the benefits looked for by a community and those an individual within that community hoped to realize, and the benefits different value-based communities sought. Not only did the household and bordello seek different benefits according to the ultimacy of their institutional needs and concerns, but each depended on a woman to serve a specific role that included defining her sexuality in terms of the values that benefited the institution's economic success and future maintenance. Gaining benefits of institutional success and continuity sometimes paralleled those benefits an individual member sought, but institutional and individual concerns could run afoul of each other when collectivity and member each made irreconcilable claims of ultimacy concerning benefits. The potential for such a clash to erupt into domestic disharmony and dispute was a palpable concern among *jokun* authors, who addressed it both directly and obliquely in their writings. The potential for conflict between communal and individual claims in the pleasure quarters also was ever present and was resolved or circumvented at times through strategies of escape. The heterogeneity of claims between collective and individual also existed on a wider sociological plane between the values of fertility and the values of pleasure. These values not only co-existed, but were also institutionally co-sanctioned. The voice they gave to Tokugawa society that reaches us today is one of full-throated tension and difference. Indeed, these contradictory values scream out the real heterogeneity that existed in that society despite popular conceptions of social and cultural uniformity. In this study their cry resounds, reverberating off a methodology of religion constructed from elements of ritual, practical benefits, and ultimate concern. These elements, far from muffling these values and social tensions under metanarrative blankets of cultural and religious essentialism, amplify the cacophony of a complex and heterogeneous society.[94]

The amplification of difference reminds us again of Utamaro's illustration. In the sense that his courtesan's dream of a wedding and his skepticism assert that ritual is about difference—whether bridging it (her dream) or exacerbating it (his skepticism)—its use by groups and individuals seeking benefits to their varied concerns amidst multiple discourses of sexual values is a portraiture of ritual that we will see throughout these pages.

TWO

VALUE MODELS

IN THE SUMMER of 1808, the granddaughter of Uesugi Yōzan (1746–1822), lord of the Yonezawa domain, married. Thinking that an appropriate farewell gift should employ ancient wisdom to guide her in her new life as a wife, Uesugi decided on an epistle based on a classic Chinese ethical treatise, *Precepts for Women*.[1] Rooting his letter in the moral themes of *Precepts*, he wrote in contemporary Japanese, penned an evocative title—*Young Leaves of a Peach (Momo no wakaba)*—and sent it off with his granddaughter when she left for her new home with her husband's family.[2] Uesugi's creation of an ethical guide on wifely conduct, bearing a title rife with suggestions of fertility, and his offering it as a gift to his granddaughter on the occasion of her marriage reveal noteworthy associations. With a single gift, he linked behavior (a wife's conduct), rites (marriage), institutional location (household), and a specific valuation of female sexuality (procreation). Tying ritual actions to forms of behavior practiced in the home, and based on a belief that a woman's sexuality had value in its procreative potential formed a model of womanhood that assumed position in the center of society. Alternatives to this model played out on the periphery, such as the celibacy of the nunnery and the pleasure of the urban quarters. The quarters especially cast a long and contrasting shadow on the center. Like the former, the quarters constituted a model of womanhood that linked ritual practice, ideals of behavior, institutional location, and an explicit valuation of sexuality.

"Model" is a noun and a verb. A value model incorporates both. As a noun, a value model functions as a model for ideal communal life—in other words, an ideal world. The human mind, books, and art have always been loci of ideal worlds. The *Mishnah,* the rabbinical attempt to construct a perfect Jewish world in the absence of an actual one due to the Diaspora and the destruction of the temple in Jerusalem, is a powerful example, in the history of religions, of an ideal world of mind and word. Similarly, texts like Uesugi's epistle and other forms of *jokun* produced their own ideal worlds—worlds of womanhood—to show not how life is really lived, but rather how life should be lived. From the periphery of pleasure also came texts and art that portrayed a very different but equally ideal world of womanhood. As a verb, a value model encourages a person to model her behavior and relations with others in her institutional collective on a set of values that is promoted as beneficial to the betterment of the person and her institution. Ritual practice played out against institutions, behaviors, and role identity is key to this modeling. No matter how dissimilar value models may be in comparison to one another or how they may compete against one another, they all embrace ritual practice and its confluent elements to promote a model of human relations based on values that are considered good and necessary for living life as it should be lived.

Uesugi offered his granddaughter more than plain prose. He gave her a guide to a world of ritual-based values that he believed were good and necessary for living properly in the world. With his guide his granddaughter would familiarize herself with her role as a wife, pattern her life on the community of her husband's household, and extend his family line by providing an heir while using her energy and skills to maintain his—and now also her—household. This was the value model of fertility. Parallel and peripheral to this, young women in the pleasure quarters were to orient themselves as courtesans, model their lives on the structures, rhythms, and morals of the quarter, and cultivate relationships with men founded on the principle of fulfilling male desires through the performance of ideal behavior in the context of play. This was the value model of pleasure.

We may begin to understand these value models better by examining a third Tokugawa model that promoted an ideal different from that of fertility and pleasure. Multiple models existed, from nunnery-based Buddhism and its advocacy of celibacy, to youth groups of men and women in villages that advocated their own ideals of sexual behavior. The Shinto priest Masuho Zankō (1655–1742) promoted yet another model and gave it a structure similar to that of fertility and pleasure: 1) the delineation of distinct values and forms of idealized behavior; 2) the identification of institutional place; and 3) the centrality of ritual.

A Typological Value Model: Masuho Zankō's Mutual Love

Masuho was a talented man of the pen who was equally at home expounding on his own understanding of Shinto as he was writing popular literature. He gained renown through public storytelling and preaching that he undertook, according to the contemporary observer Miwa Shissai (1669–1744), "to disseminate Shinto by whatever means he could."[3] In publicizing his teachings he incorporated a range of interpretive concepts and symbols from yin/yang to the agricultural village to write passionately about his own model of human and sexual association. He understood that shared and loving activity between men and women is divinely creative. Sexual activity between couples is part of yin and yang harmony *(in yō wagō)*, which is the primordial and sustaining energy of the cosmos. Convinced of the primacy of Shinto and its organic relation with Japan, Masuho drew sharp contrasts with Chinese notions of gender relations that he believed were infecting Japan.

He viewed these Chinese notions of gender relations as unnatural to the Japanese order. Such concepts included discriminating between husbands and wives *(fūfu betsu)* and relying on socially constructed artifices *(jinsaku)* for the establishment and expression of male and female relations. Masuho associated Japan with the natural pairing of men and women, along with the close affinity between humans and gods as both created and creators.[4] In this kinship there is no ultimate line dividing gods and human beings. The buddhas and *kami* that are part of the temporal world of form were born through the energy of yin and yang commingling via human sexual activity. These deities are concrete expressions of pure, absolute reality, which Masuho termed the original enlightenment of the buddhas *(hongaku no hotoke)* and the ultimate reality of the *kami (hosshō no kami)*.[5] As with all living things in the world, however, buddhas and *kami* come into being through sexual intercourse and subsequent birth. It is only birth in the world that gives them the opportunity to experience enlightenment and ultimate reality, to effect their divine powers, and to become accessible to humans as worthy of worship because they have achieved the status of enlightened, powerful beings. As Masuho puts it in the first chapter of his 1715 work, *A Comprehensive Mirror on the Way of Love (Endō tsugan)*, "It is because the buddhas and *kami* to whom we reverently pray in this world had fathers and mothers from whom they were born that we refer to them as buddhas and *kami* that have attained enlightenment."[6] In this way, sex between women and men inherently possesses a sacred component. By their own charging of yin and yang, loving couples participate in creation as much as they are products of it, or, as Masuho notes, "Buddhas, *kami,* and all sentient beings *(shujō)* are born from yin and yang, which is the root of all things."[7] He follows this up in the second chapter of the same work by borrowing from the myths of *The Chronicles of Japan (Nihongi),* which was compiled in 720. In his retelling Masuho emphasizes the fundamental, operative power of yin and yang and the sexual activity of the *kami* to produce the land of Japan and their own sacred kind. In an instructive choice, he avoids the fuller tale of the birth of Amaterasu, in which she emerges from the eye of Izanagi as he purifies himself, and instead alludes to a simpler account where she is born from the sexual union of Izanagi and his consort Izanami.[8] Men and women of all ages join this divine legacy whenever they come together sexually in mutual love. Such participation creates a world where pure distinctions between mortal and divine disappear and the world becomes a place of sacred symbiosis between humans and gods, between men and women.

China corrupted this natural harmony by constructing human artifices on which to model relations, such as subordinating the female role to that of the male. For Masuho, the equal coupling between husbands and wives was as evident as the natural harmony of creation itself. "Man and woman make a pair; there are no grades of high and low."[9] They are two wings of a bird.[10] This does not mean, however, that there is no difference between men and women as equal and loving beings. Like yin and yang they are complementary; in their love they make a pair. Love comes together perfectly, most holy, when compassion and kindness *(nasake),* which is the yang-male element, combine with sincerity *(makoto),* which is the yin-female element.[11] In Japan the divine and creative energy of yin and yang harmony found pure human realization. Men and women lived free of artificial constrictions of social grade, and thus lived as fully authentic human beings: divine co-creators with the gods in the continual process of creation.

Gender relations become highly sacralized and equalized in Masuho's model. Mutual love between a man and woman was fundamental to the creation of a husband and wife; it underlay the rites of marriage. Married couples were not merely spouses, but as participants in creation became a sacred divine-human body of husband and wife *(shinjin gōtai no fūfu).* "Upon falling in love a go-between is sought, harmony is established, and when the rites of marriage are undertaken there emerges the sacred divine-human body of husband and wife."[12] Further, Masuho identifies the agricultural village and its celebrations of planting and harvesting as the place and time when this harmonious energy of creative principle, gods, and humans merged most intensely.[13] He richly adorns his analysis of sacred love with pastoral descriptions of peasant men and women at work, happily toiling and singing together in the fields: "When the fifth month comes, an auspicious day for planting is chosen. The men go down to the paddies and set up the seedling beds and shout out happy songs. The women put make up on their faces, change clothes and put on their bamboo hats. Against the skin of their hips browned by sun they tie white waistcloths. Then they head down to the rice fields to plant the seedlings. They sing together in the paddies, making up lyrics of handsome men and women and the lovemaking they share as husbands and wives. Here in the village all men and women celebrate the *kami* of the mountain."[14]

Masuho's imaginative use of the village, agricultural work, and loving sexuality is similar to certain predilections of nativist thought.[15] Nativists identified the village as the locus in recovering a Japan free of not only the accretion of Chinese and Indian influence, but also of history itself—that is, history as a progression of political events always vulnerable to corruption and misdirection. The village, where peasants labored and loved, became for nativist thinkers "the living embodiment of creation, production, and reproduction" and a "sacred place located at the intersection of the hidden and visible worlds."[16] It is there that divine and human realms, the hidden and the visible, meshed most intimately. In the village, history could fold back upon itself as an "uneventful" and constant recurrence of *kami* and humans organically interacting through timeless customs of work and worship. The notion of eventless history for the nativist Hirata Atsutane (1776–1843) was one of life lived in the pure practices of the ancient way of the *kami*. He set this "cosmic narrative" of "real history" over that of eventful history, which is the narrative of political intrigues, slow social degradation, and the abandonment of ancient ways in the face of the foreign interference that had been affecting the Japanese way of life since the introduction of continental culture.[17] In Masuho's description of peasant lovers, and in the explicit rhetoric of later nativists, the quotidian life of the village made visible the hidden, made manifest the ultimately real, and made mundane the activities of labor and sex charged with divine emulation.

Against this idyllic backdrop of men and women working and loving, Masuho places Confucian conceptions of gender relations in lowest regard. Its hierarchical distinction separating a man and a woman cut the ties of love and mutual labor between them; it denied a couple its embrace of a divine legacy of creative equality, love, and sexuality. The pleasure quarters proved more problematic for Masuho. Despite its practice of pulling husbands away from wives, putting a wedge between their creative lovemaking, he concedes that love between clients and courtesans did genuinely arise. "Work is work and love is love. When a customer gets singled out [by a courtesan] it really gets the master [of the bordello] angry."[18] Still, he admits that such heartfelt love was not the way of the skilled courtesan, who had to be true to the way *(michi)* of her training and enact pure play, not feel pure love.[19] Being true to that training, being true to her professional self, meant being true to insincerity. Sincerity, which is the yin-female element in relation to the yang-male element of kindness, is necessary for creative love. Yet the pleasure of lovemaking that men sought in the quarters also had to be enjoyed with their wives, for whenever a man and woman took pleasure in their love they also took part in an ever-unfolding sacred creation.

Masuho's model is telling for several reasons. First, it signifies that how men and women ought to relate to one another was an unsettled question in the Tokugawa, with many competing answers, of which his was only one. The controvertible point of any answer was centered on values and their behavioral expression. With his model Masuho connected a behavior pattern expressed through sexual equality and shared toil with the value of mutual love. Second, models of relationships put forward a specific environment for behaviorally expressing these values. Masuho idealized the agricultural village as one such place. It marked the meeting place where men and women experienced the total meaning of his model, where love and sexual activity merged into a creative co-identity with the gods. Not all places are equal, however. Love, even when genuine, could not be realized in all its sacred power in a place such as the quarters, which claimed a different value system for women laboring as trained courtesans. Third, Masuho infused his model with abundant resources from the symbolic universe in order to idealize— or to create a sense of ultimate concern toward—his understanding of human relations. Fertility and pleasure, to which we now turn our attention, also reflect the same structure as Masuho's model: 1) affinity between values and behavior; 2) identification of distinct locales where these values are enacted; and 3) a patchwork of ritual practices and symbols clustered around these values that signal ultimate concern.

Values and Behaviors in Fertility and Pleasure

In the letter to his granddaughter, Uesugi addressed the fear of some brides of facing and enduring the emotional strain of moving into a new household. Among these anxieties was the fear of a weakened relationship with her own parents. Uesugi assured his granddaughter that her parents' happiness was in her hands. "Your father and mother will undoubtedly be happy and content in their hearts if they see upon your marriage into another household that you look after your parents-in-law, affectionately tend to your husband, and prosper with children."[20] In comforting language, he expressed the essentials of fertility as a sexual value: obedience to and identity with one's husband and his parents and, hopefully, the begetting of children for the continuation of the household. Obedience in marriage was the anchoring link in a chain of acquiescence: obedience to one's parents, to one's parents-in-law, to the need of the husband's household for descendants, and to the reverence of ancestors. A contemporary of Uesugi, Yashiro Hirokata (1758–1841), put the matter of linked obedience succinctly: "When we state the purpose of marriage, it is to consider with great care the ancestors, to do one's filial duty to parents, and to have descendants for inheritance."[21] While a young man found himself tied to the same expectations as a husband, Tokugawa social structure placed the burden of commitment on the woman and her role as a wife. The virilocal marriage system, which the prose of Yashiro assumes, was culturally normative by the Tokugawa period. A bride's move, however, was not simply a change of locale, but a change in mind, body, and soul. In mind she would place her loyalties with her husband's family; in body she would provide children as household heirs; in soul she would join her husband's ancestors and be worshiped as one of them by the children she brought into the world. The multiple avenues of obedience a bride walked when she entered her husband's home served to reorient her total being: her identity as a person, the value of her body, and the state of her soul.

Pleasure also envisaged its model woman. In describing the ideal courtesan in his 1682 novel, *The Life of an Amorous Man (Kōshoku ichidai otoko)*, Saikaku pens a conversation between the protagonist and friends pertaining to qualities a woman of rank must possess. They agree she must not only be physically attractive, but must also be accomplished in the arts of pleasing men and entrancing them with her talent and charm.

Such talents include holding her liquor well, singing prettily, being accomplished on the koto and samisen, graceful penmanship, accomplished hostess skills, a generous and self-sacrificing nature, and possession of deep compassion and sympathy.[22] Pleasure as a sexual value centered around satisfying men with a playful spirit, talent, and a confident, engaging personality. Satisfaction was not limited to sexual gratification, but included exciting all facets of the senses, including emotions and aesthetics.[23] In fact, Saikaku's fictional conversationalists deem accomplishment in sexual acts merely one talent among many for a courtesan. As a value, pleasure conveyed a principle of sensuous play toward men rather than simply advocating sex with men. The 1720 edition of *Who's Who Among Courtesans (Yūjo hyōbanki),* which is a contemporary description of popular prostitutes, expresses well this ideal of sensuous play. It describes one young woman, Otowa, as musically accomplished, able to hold her liquor as well as any man, and an excellent hostess brimming with charm and elegance.[24]

While obedience to a single male lay at the heart of fertility, pleasure demanded sensuous play with many men, thus requiring a courtesan to keep her feelings in check with regards to any one man. Masuho captured this ludic demand for pleasure when he argued that love, be it ever pure, is not suited to the role of the courtesan and her place in a quarter. The economic logic of prostitution required a woman to avoid offering real love to any one man, instead offering herself in playful love to several men. However, the pleasure value went further, stipulating that each client must remain an exclusive partner *(najimi)* of the courtesan with whom he had begun a relationship. Within the quarters there was a reverse ethic of obedience and monogamy. Although this reversal was a form of play, play in the quarters was serious business. It was a major economic enterprise and had a profound effect on Japan's cultural development in literature and art. Moreover, for a woman participating in this play, it was a serious commitment of her total self. Like her wifely counterpart, who had to orient herself to her new household, a woman moving into a quarter was also expected to reorient her mind, body, and soul. In mind she would place her loyalty in securing the prosperity of the house holding her contract; in body she would offer pleasure to numerous men; in soul she would participate in the celebratory ritual events of the quarter that linked her and her occupation to a sacred reality serving the worldly benefits of her walled-off community.

Advocates of fertility and pleasure put forward more than "values to live by." They promoted values of obedience and play as necessary to secure meaningful positions in the world women joined as either wives or courtesans. People do not simply *have* values; they *act out* values every day of their lives in concrete situations. Both fertility and pleasure recognized the importance of performed behaviors as critical in establishing values; each sought to incorporate behavioral patterns for women to use in guiding their actions with other people. Fertility advocated a behavior pattern steeped in modesty, attentiveness, and self-control for a woman who would develop her relationship with one man and his family. Pleasure emphasized an alluring, strong, and sophisticated spirit that would develop a woman's relationship with as many men as possible.

Vocabulary from the period reflects these different patterns of behavior. The exemplar of *jokun, The Greater Learning for Women (Onna daigaku)*, represents well the liberal use of specific vocabulary to describe ideal female actions most fitting to the household.[25] Conspicuous examples appearing throughout this study are *tsutsushimi* and *tashinami*. These terms incorporate notions of modesty, humility, self-control, prudence, and social refinement. *The Greater Learning for Women* makes clear the affinity between these qualities and obedience to one's husband.

> A wife must think of her husband as her lord and look up to him with humility *(tsutsushite)*. She must not make light of him. As a rule, the way of a woman is to follow people. In contrast to the husband, she should be docile in her facial expression, use of words, and in being politely humble; she should not falter in her endurance or be fickle in spirit. There must be no extravagance and unceremonious behavior. These things are the primary responsibilities of a woman. When a husband has something to teach his wife, she must not go against his teachings. When there is doubt in her mind concerning a matter, she should ask her husband and follow the advice he hands down. If he has something to ask his wife, she should answer clearly and correctly. To neglect answering is unceremonious. At times when he is angry, a wife must control herself and follow him. In a quarrel a wife must not go against her husband's will. A woman regards her husband as heaven. So as not to invite the punishment of heaven a wife must be careful not to disobey her husband.[26]

Authors of *jokun* tied obedience to modesty, self-control, and a sense of feminine refinement. They also linked these behavioral qualities to a solid sense of ceremony. I have translated as "unceremonious" the Japanese term *burei*. Although customarily rendered as "discourteous" or "rude," "unceremonious" captures the significance that fertility moralists placed on actions of modesty, discretion, and self-control. Opposite forms of conduct were not seen as unfortunate moments of rudeness, but as points of disjuncture between the individual and reality. It was not a break with reality in terms of simple existence, but rather with social reality as brought into existence through ceremonies. Traditionally in Japan there are three ceremonial occasions that most affect individual lives: recognition of adulthood, marriage, and the funeral. Collectively known as *kankonsōsai* (ceremonies of capping, marriage, and funeral), the term also implies any ceremony directed toward an individual rather than a collective body. Many of these ceremonies are meant to secure a space for the individual in an ordered community at a specific time in her life. That space holds meaning because it holds status, identity, and defined expectations of behavior. The writer of *The Greater Learning for Women* sought to diffuse ceremony from the exceptional moments into everyday behavior. He did this by defining obedience itself as ceremony and giving it the same function as ceremony: to create a space of social meaningfulness in a value-based community. Almost two centuries after *The Greater Learning for Women,* authors still expressed the idea of obedience as a form of ceremony. Egawa Tanan (1801–1855) wrote that the "way of respectful obedience is a woman's most valuable ceremony *(tairei)*."[27] *Tairei* (lit. "great ceremony"), which I render as "most valuable ceremony," refers both to an emperor's enthronement rites and to any ceremony, such as those among the *kankonsōsai* celebrations, that an individual deems as most important in her life. *Burei* in the fertility model implied immodest, self-centered behavior that broke the ceremony of obedience and risked displacing a woman from the meaningful space of social reality in her husband's household that she had created through her marriage rites and modest behavior.

Divorce was the most obvious form of displacement from the meaningful space of marriage and the community of the virilocal household. In their idealization of marriage, fertility moralists adapted from China the list of seven conditions a husband could invoke to divorce his wife: being unfilial toward his parents, not bearing a child, lewd behavior, jealousy, major illness, talking too much or talking immodestly, and stealing.[28] With the exception of illness and not bearing an heir, the conditions were tied to behavior that flagrantly challenged the ideals of modesty, self-control, and prudence. Childbirth was not unrelated to the question of obedience, either. With regards to the lack of an heir, *The Greater Learning for Women* includes a clause stating that if a wife's heart is in the right place, if her behavior is good, and if she has no jealousy, then she should not be subject to divorce. Instead, the household should adopt an heir or take in a concubine rather than humiliate such a morally grounded woman with a divorce.[29] Thus even in the idealization of fertility, certain realities of household life—primarily that childbirth was more anticipation than requirement and that a woman was judged less by commitment to motherhood than by commitment to a man and his household—come to light. The practice of obedient behavior and loyalty superseded all other concerns. Such behavior could even diminish the threat of losing one's place in the household in the face of failure to give birth to an heir. Exercising obedience, then, acted as ceremony. In other words, it allowed a woman to practice a set of behavioral expectations to create a meaningful space of identity and status that could secure and protect her position even amidst circumstances beyond her control that could bring about her displacement.

Like fertility, pleasure had its own defining vocabulary. Spirit, allure, and urbanity best typified a courtesan's comportment. These qualities are captured in the behavioral ideal called *iki*. Many scholars of Tokugawa urban culture, following Kuki Shūzō's (1888–1941) influential study of the aesthetics of *iki,* have commented on this behavior pattern and its relation to the world of play.[30] Seeing it, like Kuki, as a type of embodied aesthetic, these commentators have tended to examine *iki* as a cultural phenomenon originating in bustling cities among courtesans, dandies, artists, and entertainers—those most familiar with the quarters where *iki* was most intensively put on display. These commentators see *iki* as a property of historical culture and as possessing an objective quality open to structural examination, which has led to analyses that break it down into the smaller components of attitude and emotion, each with an equally independent and objective existence.[31] Such focus, however, ignores *iki* as a socially constructed behavior pattern. As much as it may have developed as a product of the culture of the urban floating world, it was also something that bordello owners, courtesans, and their managers actively honed and marketed for the business of play. In this market *iki* was invaluable in establishing a woman as a successful courtesan both in relation to her clients and as a way to secure her own rank and profitability in the quarters.

Tokugawa literature, especially those examples topically related to the quarters, is replete with descriptions of courtesans and their comportment of style and sophistication suggestive of *iki*. A passage in Saikaku's *The Life of an Amorous Man* (discussed earlier), is an excellent example. In the same scene mentioned above concerning a group of revelers discussing the traits of the ideal courtesan, the novel's main character, Yonosuke, asks his merry band who, among the courtesans they have known and heard about, might fit such a description. They answer in a single voice: Yūgiri. They continue,

> To a customer intent on throwing away his life and reputation because of love for her, she explains to him the ethical duties of society and home that are his life outside the quarters. When a client is caught in scandal, she always thinks of something to erase it. To one lost in love for her, she persuades him to cut his ties to her. Without diffidence she states her opinions to men of rank. She makes a married client come to an understanding for the reason behind his wife's jealousy of his dalliance. She even allows the fishmonger, Chōbei, to take her hand into his, and she always speaks pleasantly to the green grocer, Gorohachi, which brings him so much happiness. Yūgiri tosses no one aside.[32]

Yūgiri (1654–1678) was a courtesan of Osaka's Shinmachi. Although she died before the age of twenty-five, she had gained so much fame during her short life that later puppet plays *(jōruri)* and the kabuki stage produced testimonies of her person and qualities.[33] She was so important to her bordello owner, Ōgiya Shirobei, that when he elected to move his establishment from the Shimabara to Osaka in 1672 he made sure to bring along Yūgiri and her promising reputation of *iki*.[34] As Saikaku's band of bawdy brothers suggests, *iki* was a type of female idealization developed from and for the man's perspective.[35] And yet it was more than that. Ideal behavior is an act of modeling. When a courtesan molded her conduct to fit, as best she could, a model of communal excellence based on *iki*, she did far more than please men. She performed ceremony to create for herself meaningful space in the hierarchical social structure of the quarter. As obedience was construed as a "great ceremony," which allowed a woman to make meaningful space in the household through displays of modesty and obedience, a comparable process was available to a woman in the floating world. By skillfully employing *iki* in her associations with men, she too participated in ceremony—the ceremony of play. In his classic study of play, Johan Huizinga stresses that play is voluntary and free. Once play becomes bound by obligations and duties, it becomes a "cultural function"—in other words, a rite, a ceremony.[36] As play, a courtesan's relations with men necessarily demanded behavior that was neither voluntary nor free. The idealization of *iki* stemming from male bias was really just one side of the dual nature of play practiced in the pleasure quarters. For men, enjoying a courtesan's performance of *iki* was true play. They chose to play the game of sexual dalliance. For a courtesan, however, her performance of play was a duty. Her role required her to achieve an effective display of sophistication, compassion, and spirited discourse that men found alluring. The accomplishment of *iki* as the obligatory side of play made it a form of ceremony. As ceremony *iki* affected a woman's standing in her bordello and among her clients and colleagues, which also had a direct effect on her livelihood. Skillful performance of the ceremony of play could secure a woman the meaningful space of status, identity, and success that the quarters made available.

Institution

Masuho's model of human relations does not put forward the value of mutual love in an abstract context. One place where he locates that love is the agricultural village, dotted with rice paddies and shadowed by mountains. The locales institutionalizing the enactment of the values of fertility and pleasure were the household and the bordellos of the quarters. Returning once more to Uesugi's farewell letter, discussed at the beginning of this chapter, offers a helpful start in seeing the importance of place in the behavioral enactment of values. Uesugi urged his granddaughter always to remember this truth: the times and deeds of her life that would unfold in her future would do so not at the home of her birth but at the home of her marriage.

> As I have said before, it has always been that a woman's path is that of following her husband. Outside of those women serving their parents throughout their entire lives, a bride must be careful concerning how and toward whom she spends her emotions. She will be negligent in serving her parents-in-law if, as from the time of her birth, she follows the example of thinking only of her own parents. So will she also be negligent if all she knows that is good is the way of her own household. It is from desiring to do things according to the style of her own home *(waga ie no fū)* that she will never come to know her parents-in-law's will. Upon becoming a bride in the house of her husband, a woman must take orders from her mother-in-law and father-in-law and follow the household traditions *(kafū)* of her husband's family.[37]

For Uesugi's granddaughter, not only would her time be spent with her in-laws and her acts of obedience directed toward them, but such things would occur in a particular place: her marriage household. Of equal importance, moreover, is Uesugi's recognition of two correlated matters that greatly intruded upon the idea of place. One concerned behavior and the other the use of hierarchy. Uesugi's first insight is that not all households were the same, and behavior had to be modified appropriately to fit the expectations of one place over another. He recognized the potential for conflict between a bride's feelings for her natal household and her in-laws' wishes. A consistent theme in many examples of *jokun* is a backhanded acknowledgment of the ambivalence brides could experience when moving to their husbands' homes. By preemptively criticizing the feeling of attachment to one's own home, family, and accustomed ways of comporting herself, *jokun* writers exhibited sensitivity to the idea that a certain pattern of behavior could be carried out effectively only in a certain place. Unchanged behavior in a changed environment invited friction, strained relations, and put the institution at risk of becoming dysfunctional. Unchanged behavior, such as a wife's thinking only of her own parents, was misdirected obedience that could undermine, and thus threaten, the household's authority over its members. At times, such a threat had to be removed for the sake of the collective body. Thus among the seven conditions for divorce, removal of a disobedient or unfilial daughter-in-law was primary, taking precedence over the failure to produce an heir. Similarly, the quarters were also wary of unchanged behavior. Whereas total identity with one man was the foundation of obedience and the anchor of the household, the same behavior made a mockery of play. Since what were normal emotions and behaviors outside the quarters broke the rules of play, a non-playful relationship with a man could create a breach through which the competing reality of the outside could flood the quarters and threaten profits. As love for one man free of play could mean love free of charge, both *iki* and profits drowned in the emotional currents of the heart.

Both fertility and pleasure had measures to meet these threatening infractions of obedience and play. Among commoners the husband's household had broad, unilateral powers of divorce as one means of dealing with violations of obedience. If disobedience entailed adultery, then, depending on decisions by local authorities and the household, punishment could range from execution or bodily injury to imprisonment or banishment.[38] Bordello owners sometimes resorted to severe forms of corporal punishment. In *The Life of an Amorous Man,* Saikaku depicts such punishment in the Shimabara of a courtesan named Mikasa.[39] She falls in love with Yonosuke, the novel's protagonist. Worse, she refuses to follow the rules of play by declining to charge him for their time together despite her bordello owner's orders to do so. Her master thus reduces her rank to kitchen girl, forces her to wear simple cotton clothes, and sends her on humble errands to buy miso and tofu. He promises her that if she would simply renounce her love for Yonosuke, her high rank would be restored and she would no longer suffer from such humiliation. Mikasa refuses. The master resorts to tying her half naked to a willow tree in the November cold. The punishment comes to an end only when Yonosuke threatens the master by promising to kill himself in order to die with Mikasa and then haunt him for the rest of his life. Harsh forms of discipline, while available to authority figures in the quarters, as Mikasa's story shows, were generally not used on ranking women because their bodies and good spirits were central to the success of the bordello.[40] A courtesan's body possessed pecuniary value for her employer; it was a commodity that he, his wife, and the courtesan's female manager might decide to bruise, but it was not something they wanted to lose.

Physical punishment was not unique to the quarters. As a form of discipline it was an important element of control in the hierarchical- and institutional-based human relationships that made up much of Tokugawa social reality. Shop boys, Buddhist acolytes, apprentices, maids, menservants, and samurai retainers could typically expect painful physical consequences for misbehavior and failures in their responsibilities. The quarters possessed their own understanding and fears of such behavioral breaches and failures. Buyō Inshi, an observer of events in the latter half of the Tokugawa period, notes that various infractions could bring punishment to a Yoshiwara courtesan exhibiting behavior ill-suited to the institution of playful sexuality. Among such infractions were displaying overly effusive feelings for a particular client, spending one's leisure time with a customer, and positioning oneself to run away with a client and gain the "status of wife, concubine, or daughter" *(saishōjō bun)*.[41] The first two violations, Buyō notes, were suspected precursors of the third. Each on its own, however, potentially threatened to undercut the economic prosperity and authority structure of the bordello.

Uesugi's second insight concerning place is that it was structured through hierarchy, which a young woman could wisely use to her long-term advantage. A bride's natal home and her husband's home were usually similar in structure: they represented the same economic class, possessed the same hierarchy, and expected similar forms of behavior in their members. Fertility moralists, however, recognized that the institution of the household had to be understood beyond the mere fact of its social structure and hierarchy. They saw that meaning fully came only when a woman actively interacted with hierarchy rather than passively had it imposed on her. It is hierarchy itself that provided the social materials—status, role identity, and rules of behavior—necessary for a woman to establish a meaningful position. Again, Uesugi's insight arises from an uneasiness over possible conflict. A woman's interaction with the hierarchy of her husband's home established a different configuration of role, identity, and status than that which existed in her own home. It is the potential for conflict between these configurations in orienting a woman from daughter to bride that led Uesugi to stress to his granddaughter the need to abandon interacting in the style of her own home *(waga ie no fū)* in order to interact in the family traditions of her husband's home. He recognized that household hierarchy offered more than the imposition of itself on the individual. The virilocal household was, instead, a setting that offered her the opportunity to make her place. She could do so by utilizing its available structures of hierarchy, such as status, role identity, and behavior patterns. By "family traditions" of the husband's home Uesugi meant the use of this hierarchy. With this awareness of the household, Uesugi placed the institution in human-centric focus. For him, the household was not so much a place imposing hierarchy on a submissive person, but rather a place where people used that hierarchy to make their place, to make meaningful space. A pleasure quarter, too, was no different in this respect. With its hierarchical grades of courtesan and ideals of behavior, it also made available the hierarchical structure necessary for a woman to make her space.

A view of institutional place from the perspective of persons acting through hierarchy—that is, being active participants rather than passive subjects—has important implications. First, such a view puts focus on the actions people perform as members of a hierarchical institution. Second, it constantly connects these actions to establishing an individual's institutional position. These two corollaries are significant in approaching ritual action, which is the third component of the diagram of the fertility and pleasure models. Ritual as a form of action sought to transform a woman's status and identity and orient her to the new and changing social realities that were intruding upon her life. In so doing it delineated the coexistence of conflicting sexual values and their models, and by pulling together common symbols from the Tokugawa religious universe it gave each model an ideally ordered and distinct reality.

Ritual

Masuho's vision of love between men and women working together in the fields of a bucolic village may strike us as maudlin. However, it gives his model order, purpose, and a high degree of distinction over others. In short, Masuho infuses his sentimental creation with sacrality. His order allows him to put forward the literal godliness of love between men and women over a continental corruption of human relationships. He built this order from the multiple tones and notes of the Tokugawa symbolic universe such as yin and yang and *kami* and brought them to symphonic purpose with rites of first fruits offered to the mountain god by loving peasant men and women.

Masuho's sacred order is a composition in three parts. Two are an exercise each in discrimination and incorporation. The exercise in discrimination delineates elements of his model with counter-notions of human relations in other models. Masuho does not create his model on principles of relativism or in a state of incognizance to the world and its complexities. The very creation itself is a declaration that other value models exist apart from his, but participation in his makes men and women distinct—indeed, true to their humanity—from people participating in other models. As Durkheim first insisted, creating distinctions among things, setting off a community, a body of ideas, an object, or a vision from others is the elementary task of sacralization.[42] Masuho proved no different in his task. Values and behaviors in his model were highly attuned to asserting difference—setting themselves apart—from other values and behaviors. Mutual love and shared work among men and women easily contrasted with continental and Confucian ideals. And this contrast is exactly what he sought.

The second part is incorporation. Masuho brought together several elements of the symbolic universe in his order. Familiar with Yuiitsu Shinto, he readily acknowledged *kami*, buddhas, and, as the lynchpin of his model, the creative yin and yang life force. Yuiitsu had, since the fifteenth century under the energy of Yoshida Kanetomo (1434–1511), integrated elements of Shinto, esoteric Buddhism, and Confucianism within the framework of a unified, systematic Shinto, which it favored over other religious systems.[43] The tree metaphor was a favorite of Kanetomo's in expounding on the primacy of Shinto. Buddhism was the fruit, Confucianism and Daoism the trunk and branches, and Shinto the roots from which all gained sustenance.[44] It is not surprising, given this intellectual background employing both syncretism and distinctive rankings of teachings, that Masuho liberally used a variety of symbols to build a distinct model and favor it over others.

Masuho made yin and yang harmony the vital center of his model. However, the advocates of fertility also used the concept to serve their own model. Often using the metaphors of heaven and earth *(tenchi)*, as well as yin and yang, fertility moralists found the suggestion of harmonious complements indispensable in giving sacred order to their model. Unlike Masuho's explicitly anti-Confucian and anti-Chinese understanding of the male and female principles as complementary and *equal* in the creative process, promoters of fertility saw them as complementary and *unequal. Women's Imagawa (Onna imagawa),* an exemplar of *jokun* and a popular educational text, states the interpretation unequivocally: "Heaven is the yang principle *(yō)* and is strong; it is the way of the man. Earth is the yin principle *(in)* and is passive; it is the way of the woman. The yin principle follows the yang, and as this is the true principle underlying the universe, it stands to reason that the way of husband and wife, when compared to the order in the universe, is that the husband is like heaven and is revered. This, in short, is the way of heaven and earth."[45]

Masuho's exercise of incorporating symbols is one that other models carried out. This use of a common symbol to support different values brings to mind what Epictetus said long ago: "What disturbs and alarms man are not the things, but his opinions and fancies about the things."[46] The divergent opinions and values of Masuho and fertility moralists found expression in the same yin and yang concept of harmonious complements. The stress on the varied meanings of a thing points to its essential character as a symbol, which operates "in the human world of meaning," and its only worth is in vivifying, evoking, and mediating human meaning.[47] Its substantiality, its form, its material construction, if any, do not generate meaning. Only when people grasp something as animating values, sentiments, behaviors, and principles important to them (Epictetus's "opinions and fancies") does it act as a symbol and evoke and mean something.

Discriminating values, behaviors, and principles as well as *incorporating* common symbols into competing models of how life ideally should be lived is brought to full realization through forms of ritual, which constitutes the third part of Masuho's sacred order. He completed the vision of his model with the rite of village men and women offering the first fruits of the harvest to the mountain deity. Ritual is indispensable because it is at once able to embrace both the discrimination and incorporation that a value model mutually exercises. Fertility and pleasure depended on the rites of marriage and debut and first meeting to keep both discrimination of their values and incorporation of their symbolic worlds intact. These ceremonies achieved this because they created a controlled environment that intensified the divergent values of fertility and pleasure. At the same time, these celebrations of human relations gathered symbols from a common universe and shared the common task of transforming young women from daughters into women of different identities.

Controlling their environments of performance was an essential goal of these ceremonies. They mapped out and established place, space, time, things, and people in fixed worlds of order. Each created for its duration the ideal or very "model" of a value-oriented community in which full attention was focused on the perfect vivification of the collective's values. If just for a moment, reality as it should be was the only reality playing in weddings, debuts, and first meetings. At the same time, neither of these ritual environments was hermetically closed to the world and to competing or contradictory claims. Precisely by controlling its environment, a wedding or a debut made obvious to its participants that the world existing outside the performance was both palpably different and undeniably there. In this way, such ceremonies possessed a "gnostic dimension."[48] This bifurcation of ritual and real environments was a model's best method for marking the uniqueness of its values vis-à-vis other values coexisting in society. These socially transformative performances of the household and quarter, which I discuss in the next chapter, were events of sharp focus on the values of obedience and the hope of childbirth in one model and sexual play and status achievement in erotic labor in the other.

By controlling the ritual environment so as to present an ideal image of reality in a world that the ritual actors know is imperfect and complicated, celebrations of fertility and pleasure exercised their discriminatory half. At the same time, they also exercised incorporation by assimilating common symbols and ritual elements with human situations of personal change and role transformation. This symbolic and social character of the celebratory rituals of fertility and pleasure is telling of a society like the Tokugawa, marked as it was by growing complexity, such as the sanctioned coexistence of central and peripheral institutions that relied on ritual ceremonies both to express divergent values and to establish new human relationships between men and women necessary for the

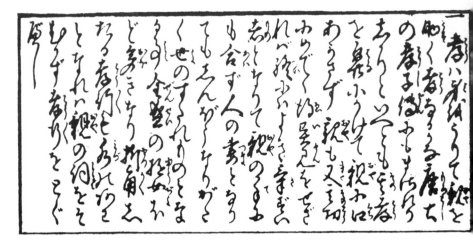

FIGURE 2 A filial daughter leaves her impoverished family to serve as a courtesan. From

maintenance of the collective good. (In addition, other practices like those centered around pregnancy, divorce, and escape—each exhibiting its own symbols and challenges of personal change—stood apart in varying degrees from fertility's and pleasure's idealized values and thus compounded the socio-ritual environment even more, as we will see.)

This ritual character of incorporation is conspicuous in the rites of marriage, debut, and first meeting. Fertility and pleasure pulled from the same religious universe, and each populated its model with a host of multivalent symbols, concepts, and rituals in their respective attempts to achieve distinct orders. Although critical in orienting a woman toward a new identity as either wife or courtesan, rituals in the home and quarter were fraught with a multiplicity of symbolic meanings that could induce ambivalence toward, as much as affirmation of, values and roles. In addition to incorporating elements from the symbolic universe, fertility and pleasure also incorporated women as outsiders. Both models opened their doors to, and really existed only because of, the same sociological fact: women on the move. Rituals of sexual values cannot be understood apart from this movement. Incorporating a woman into a new household as a bride or into a bordello as a courtesan presented to each institution the potential for disharmony. Part of this potential derived from women entering these institutions under a crisis-in-change. By this I mean the common human experience of facing a major life decision in which a person lacks full control. As discussed in chapter 1, one

The Greater Learning for Courtesans. Courtesy of Ōzorasha, Tokyo.

of the root existential crises often necessitating a ritual response is when one reaches the limit of one's ability to come to a morally satisfactory acceptance of a major life event. Confronting this "ethical paradox" relates to the crisis-in-change some women experienced when they left their homes to become brides or courtesans.[49] Fertility moralists were well aware of this ethical paradox and of the conflicting claims of ultimacy and disharmony it could produce between the need for a man's household to bring in a woman and her ambivalence toward dislocation and identity change. The common theme in *jokun* beseeching young women to submit to their husbands and in-laws and give their hearts to their new homes reveals this awareness of a bride's ethical paradox. On what side of a perspective boundary does her ultimate concern lie? Does she serve her parents and siblings or her in-laws and husband? Is she a daughter and sister or a daughter-in-law and wife? The pleasure model, too, was also sensitive to this ethical paradox. Is a woman a daughter loyally serving her parents or a courtesan loyally serving her bordello by satisfying the sexual needs of its clients?

On this question the pleasure model, like fertility, produced its own idealized writings describing women who resigned themselves to a new life. One example is *The Greater Learning for Courtesans (Yūjo daigaku).*[50] This text not only playfully alludes to the fertility classic, *The Greater Learning for Women,* in its title, but also borrows the important concept of filial piety *(kō)* to justify a daughter leaving her parents. One illustration, simply titled *Kō,* captures well this use of filial piety by the pleasure model (see fig. 2). A girl parts from her weeping mother as a buyer from the pleasure quarter looks on. He stands next to a palanquin with two indifferent porters waiting for her to enter the coach so they can transport her to the bordello. Tugging at their mother's kimono are the girl's two young siblings. The sketch portrays the sacrifice many daughters made to improve their families' shaky economic circumstances by following their parents' decision to sell them to the quarters. Such family strains are reflected in period literature, too, where the ethical paradox of *kō* can always be relied on to create dramatic tension. In the puppet play *The Treasury of Loyal Retainers (Chūshingura),* Okaru, having lost her position as lady-in-waiting due to the murder of her lord, resigns herself to her father's decision to sell her to a bordello in the Shimabara.[51] She departs for the city in the buyer's palanquin, leaving her small village and sobbing mother behind. Although they are highly emotionally charged portrayals, these scenes of daughters making sacrifices for their families' sake reveal a key element concerning ritual, symbol, and crisis-in-change. The concept of filial piety was only one (albeit important and universally recognized) of many concepts and symbols the Tokugawa symbolic universe made available. Fertility and pleasure models mutually incorporated and advocated *kō* to cope with the fact that among some women moving into the institutions of virilocal household and bordello were those bearing ambivalence, confusion, resentment, or resistance to the change in their lives.

The rituals that fertility and pleasure employed boldly asserted each model's starkly different attitudes toward female sexuality. Often they also created worlds oddly similar in their symbolic structures and in their need to take in women from the outside and behaviorally enact specific values. Ritual made the models at once unique and self-contained and simultaneously parallel and porous. It was the main method of separating one value model from another, and yet it also permitted other value models to share a degree of symbolic content and use these symbols to mediate similar human experiences. This character becomes clearer when rites of entrance into the worlds of fertility and pleasure take center stage in the next chapter.

THREE

ENTRANCE

FERTILITY AND PLEASURE models sought to guide female behavior in the marriage household and bordello. For each model, ritual was especially important in the celebratory incorporation of women into a new role and institution. In the fertility model the marriage ceremony ushered a woman into the wifely world; ceremonies marking a woman's debut as a courtesan and her first meeting with a client placed her in the role of courtesan. Although these rituals of celebration put the values of fertility and pleasure into sharp contrast, they also revealed a similitude of symbols, concepts, and human situations. Wedding ceremonialism was at the root of this similarity. A wedding in the fertility model sought to accomplish a number of things: reorient a woman's social identity, establish proper relations with her husband and his household, and charge her sexuality with a purposeful fertility. Marriage rites displayed in idealized form fertility's values of touting female obedience and loyalty to her new household and hoping for childbirth. Within the pleasure model a similar process was at work when a young woman debuted and when she ritually entered into an exclusive sexual partnership with a new client. Liberally borrowing elements from marriage rites, these ceremonies also created special relations between women and men while bringing to idealized form pleasure's values of feminine high spirits and sexual play. Still, within the pomp of these ceremonies lay potential problems that curbed each model's idealization. The celebratory rites themselves revealed this reality check. Wedding ceremonies allowed a bride's family to maintain symbolic ties to its daughter despite fertility's insistence that her identity be limited to that of simply wife, always obedient and hopefully fertile. In the quarters, rites of intimate relations proved no less problematic.

The incorporation of symbols and ritual forms taken directly from wedding ceremonies suggest a level of equivocation with pleasure's own values that a woman's identity be limited to that of an alluring and spirited sexual person with many lovers.

The parallels of pomp and problems faced by these two sets of entrances are the subject of this chapter. I first look at the religious motives and metaphors underlying idealizations of reorienting a woman's social identity and role. Still, these motives and metaphors indicate each model's symbolic acknowledgment that full incorporation of its women could be tenuous. Second, this hope for reorientation, accompanied by a sense of ambivalence toward fully achieving it, is best highlighted through finding historical windows through which to view the symbolic structure of the rituals. I describe these rites of entrance by first detailing the elite wedding ceremony portrayed in Namura's guide, *A Record of Treasures for Women*. Then I move on to the rites of debut and first meeting as a variety of period sources depict them. Before proceeding, though, I give a brief overview of the historical context of the normative marriage pattern and its alternatives.

Tokugawa Marriage in Historical Context

The form of marriage described in Namura's text, if less in elite details than in broad structure, was the culturally normative pattern celebrating the entrance of a bride into her groom's household. Several terms for this marriage appropriately focus on the bride: *yometori* (taking a bride), *yomeiri* (the entrance of a bride), and *yomemukae* (welcoming a bride). This pattern likely began among some early warrior families during the Heian period, particularly provincial families living far from the practices of the royal capital, Kyoto.[1] There, aristocrats practiced a complex system incorporating both matrilocal marriage and patrilineal descent of titles and ranks. A husband lived in his wife's home but inherited his own family's titles; a wife inherited her family's holdings independent of her husband.[2] This arrangement of co-residence and independent inheritance drew the female perspectival boundary of "daughter-wife" greatly toward the daughter's identity in terms of inheritance and natal family investment.[3] With the rise of the warrior class as the new elites in the medieval period, virilocal marriage slowly came to share center stage with—and eventually pushed to the margins—matrilocal marriage. Still, unlike the Tokugawa period, marriage at this time is difficult to describe outside of broad characterization. Patterns were in flux, likely variegated with locality and class, and, as several interpreters have noted, they defied clarification due to the vagaries of both marriage documents and the spousal relationship itself.[4] What is clearer is that since marriage was more of an inheritance arrangement than an emotional arrangement, the gradual rise of virilocality also roughly charted the slow decline of female inheritance throughout the Kamakura (1185–1333) and Muromachi periods. Much of this decline was due to chronic political unrest over the centuries that drove warrior families to opt for single inheritance to a son rather than divided inheritance as a means to concentrate household wealth in unstable times.[5] Whereas divided inheritance "nearly guaranteed property rights to daughters" and placed upon their shoulders the same responsibility of successful stewardship that their brothers carried, single inheritance made that earlier guarantee effectively null.[6] A family that maintained full inheritance rights for its son while giving its daughter in marriage with limited or no inheritance acted on a common strategy of protecting the household through single inheritance to the son and creating allies with another household through marrying off one's daughter. By following this common strategy a normative custom was born that redrew the female perspectival boundary toward a wife's identity. Although single inheritance to the eldest son was not codified into warrior law until the second century of the Tokugawa hegemony, in 1727 single inheritance, even if not always to the first son, had long been a household practice among most samurai families.[7] Further, codification of virilocal rites among Ise and Osagawara ritualists standardized *yometori* rites. With the emergence and gradual spread of the *ie* among the commoner population, options of single inheritance and virolocality also spread. It is this history that shaped much of Tokugawa marriage.

The form of Tokugawa marriage practices was multiple. The virilocal pattern of *yometori* shared in this multiplicity. People could perform the ceremony in a simple and economically frugal manner, or they might put on quite an elaborate show. Even the elite version of marriage described in Namura's *A Record of Treasures for Women* includes simpler variations that required only the consumption of some plucked barracuda and the sharing of sake between the couple.[8] In his book *Barbershop (Ukiyodoko)*, Shikitei Sanba (1776–1822) presents, through one of his characters, a description of preparations for a lower-class commoner wedding where a simple repast of tofu, dried bonito, and miso accompanied by tea and sake is quickly set out shortly before the bride arrives.[9]

In this way the widespread virilocality of *yometori* embraced the high and low, the ritually complex and ritually simple, and thus its perform-ance reflected both cultural centrality and class centrality.

Other marriage patterns existed. There is a wealth of research in Japan, both classic and contemporary, that delineates morphologically and charts historically these patterns in connection with the normative growth of the virilocal pattern.[10] Although beyond the scope of this study, in broad portrayal such patterns were alternatives to the Toku-gawa *yometori* by way of either local custom or family strategy. They fall under the terms *mukotori* and *mukoiri*. Each term describes movement of the son-in-law *(muko)* into the bride's residence for a period of time, which could range from temporary to permanent. There are two appli-cations of *mukotori* that are important in understanding *yometori* marriage and some of the alternatives to it that operated prior to and during the Tokugawa: First, *mukotori* is a synonym for the marriage pattern called *tsumadoi,* which literally means to "call on a wife." This duolocal pat-tern, defined by separate spousal residences and the husband's visitation to the wife's household, had been practiced in various forms through-out much of the country's history, and it was still customary among par-ticular groups in the Tokugawa.[11] Second, *mukotori* also describes the entrance of a son-in-law into a household. He marries, is adopted as the eldest son, and receives the family inheritance. This pattern, unlike the ancient matrilocality of the Heian period, was used largely as a strategy to ensure the household's continuity in the absence of a son or in the presence of a capable daughter whom the family did not want to lose as future manager.

Visitation marriage was based on the needs and customs of particular groups. One example is the need to maximize specialized female labor, such as that of women divers *(ama)*. Coastal villages whose economies were tied to divers typically practiced forms of *tsumadoi*. Since these women divers generated income for the families with whom they resided, the departure of a strong diver upon marriage was customarily delayed so that her family could enjoy the maximum fruit of her labors. It was not unusual for spouses to live apart for several years while the wife continued diving for her family, though the man would visit fre-quently. However, it was only after a diver finally moved into her hus-band's house that he could claim her labor and its income-generating potential.[12]

The second Tokugawa use of *mukotori* marriage describes a son-in-law's entrance into a woman's natal home. Like the first use mentioned above, it, too, was linked to economic issues, particularly single inheritance to a male heir, and suggests the improvisational character of household inheritance. Local customs sometimes dictated other forms of inheritance and household headship, such as a pattern favoring the eldest daughter.[13] However, this form of inheritance was typically meant to be temporary (as were most types of female inheritance), for the eldest daughter was also called to relinquish, at least nominally, her headship at some point to an entering groom.[14] Outside of custom, commoner women filled headship positions in the interim to secure the maintenance of the household until a permanent male head was acquired.[15] Contributing to the maintenance of her natal household and taking care of her parents could, if a woman and her parents so decided, trump any expectations to marry. The Tokugawa money economy allowed women to support their *ie* financially and avoid marriage—both *yometori* and *mukotori* patterns—altogether.[16] Whether embedded in local custom or simply an extemporized measure, *mukotori* represents a type of matrilocal marriage pattern in operation during the Tokugawa. In particular, the *mukotori* pattern as a strategy for households with only daughters or without a capable son was the most culturally salient type of matrilocality among commoners against the normative backdrop of virilocal marriage. The entering male, destined to be both son-in-law and adopted son, was called, appropriately, *mukoyōshi,* which combines the characters for "son-in-law" and "adopted child." The *mukoyōshi* shared certain similarities of discomfort with the incoming bride of the fertility model, such as being an outsider unfamiliar with the ways of the household. As an outsider, an adopted son-in-law could be pressured into writing out a writ of divorce for his wife and her family and leaving the household.[17] Being an outsider, however, at least held the promise of headship for an entering son-in-law. In this important sense, *mukotori,* unlike *yometori,* which emphasized incorporation of the outsider, emphasized adoption of the outsider with the full legal rights of an inheriting son.[18] As an adoption arrangement, it could bring to a family in search of a groom mixed feelings of awkwardness and relief. A sixteenth-century poem gives subtle expression to this in describing a bride's family crossing a small, rickety bridge to greet her groom, who will enter its house as both stranger and future head: "It is dangerous/But also makes us joyful/The log bridge/We cross in the evening/To welcome the groom."[19]

The *yometori* pattern also provided an incoming bride with a metaphorical bridge to cross, but hers was sturdy and strong, built as it was on a foundation of cultural assumptions that had firmed over time through ritual codification and then later through adaptation and dissemination by guides like *A Record of Treasures for Women*. This bridge also acted as a passage toward increased social status among commoners. Similar to the way money allowed merchants to purchase their own sense of status and worth in spite of their officially low social standing—often through participation in the materialistically driven culture of the quarters—the malleable complexity and cost of ritual ceremonialism allowed commoner families to participate vicariously in the elite lifestyle, ultimately making their own whatever parts they could afford and desired. Another indication of the cultural centrality of the *yometori* style is that the pleasure quarters broadly drew from its ritual pattern in creating rites of association between courtesans and clients. Because the ceremony was a mirror of social refinement, bordello owners avidly drew from it as well, adapting it to establish their own sense of elegance, decorum, and ceremony.

Motives and Metaphors

Fertility and pleasure relied on the ritual structure of *yometori* marriage to celebrate female entrance into the roles of wife and courtesan. They also relied on notions of motive and metaphor to speak to the necessity of entrance and about the women entering. Before discussing modes of motivation and metaphor, it is important first to consider the notion of motivation in general and in reference to Japanese religion. Wendy Holloway proposes the notion of "investment" to understand what motivates people to take up one identity over another in a society of competing discourses.[20] A sense or hope of economic security and social status, and whatever emotional contentment these things may bring, largely defines a person's decision to invest her identity in a specific discourse. The household and pleasure quarter offered hierarchy and social position to women for use in establishing security and status. As such, they were centers for investing one's identity. With investment in institutional hierarchy, there was also a hope, as Holloway's term suggests, of gaining something in return, such as the relative prestige and limited authority that long-term commitment to the roles of wife and courtesan potentially offered. For a bride, an investment in marriage could lead to co-management of the household and the potentially powerful position of mother-in-law; for a debuting courtesan, an investment in the higher ranks gave her status, prestige, and earning power. Still, "investment" as a motivation strongly assumes free choice and decision making.[21] In a highly schematized and unitized society like the Tokugawa, investing one's identity in an institution, role, and set of values was central to the very composition of society. At the same time, few people had the freedom to select their social identities in the ways that Holloway's interesting term implies. Indeed, when wives and courtesans did freely choose, it sometimes was, as we will see in chapter 5, the choice to divest themselves of their marriages and contracts by seeking divorce or escape from the quarters.

The question of motivation in Tokugawa society centered as much around meaningful interpretation in the absence of choice as around investment in the presence of choice. Much of the meaningful interpretation of motivation derived from the religious and moral universe. Winston Davis introduces two types of motivation that people bring with them in varying degrees to the maze of institutions, sacred services, and practical actions and assumptions Japanese religion makes available. He calls these "in order to" and "because" motives. The former cover a range of actions people may initiate *in order to* gain or secure something; these motivations are oriented toward "a desirable future state." The "because" motives emphasize responsive actions people may *perform* because feelings and convictions such as gratitude, guilt, and fear encourage them to do so; they are "determined by past lived experiences."[22]

The intersection of women's lives and Tokugawa religious thought and practice provides many illustrations of such motivations. An example of mixed motivations is the rite of *kōshin machi* (also called *kanoesaru machi* in an alternative reading of the characters). This was a defining practice among people belonging to the religious confraternity *(kō)* dedicated to the deity Kōshin. Since the second character of Kōshin's name may also be pronounced *saru,* meaning monkey, and designates a monkey day according to the sexagenary calendar, the presence of three monkeys frequently marks the deity's iconography. One covers its eyes, another its mouth, and one its ears. Together they represent the avoidance of evil and vice, which was a central goal in Kōshin devotionalism. Popular faith in the deity grew throughout the Tokugawa, and devotees erected large numbers of stone markers engraved with images of Kōshin and the three monkeys. Originally a Daoist divinity, the deity and its calendrical observances on *saru* days likely entered Japan from China during the early Heian period through the influence of diviners who were popular with the court due to their extensive knowledge of Chinese divinatory practices and texts. The rite, as it had developed throughout the centuries in interaction with Buddhism, required members of the confraternity to stay awake for the entire night on days of the monkey, which occur once in a sixty-day cycle. Devotees believed on this night that three worms *(sanshi)* existing in the body and capable of causing great harm if one let down her moral and spiritual guard reported the person's past conduct to the deity Taishakuten, who is charged with oversight of people's behavior in living up to the Buddha's teachings. If the worms freed themselves and reported misconduct to Taishakuten, then the person suffered the consequences of her behavior. Punishment often was in the form of physical illness. However, by staying awake to wait for dawn, purifying herself through listening to sūtras, observing taboos, and making offerings to Kōshin, a person could keep the worms from leaving her body.[23]

Divine punishment borne as physical malady was often manifested as a variety of diseases, including respiratory ailments. Further, period texts clearly state that illness of the lungs was a particular concern of women, and one method of prevention lay in practicing *kōshin machi* to blunt the disabling effect of the three worms. *A Manual for Female Longevity (Fujin kotobuki gusa),* a guide to women's health published at the time of Namura's text, explains that since "women may fall into a state of severe melancholy, they are vulnerable to lung disease. For ages it has been a tradition for women to observe the rites of Kōshin so as to avoid such sickness. They stay awake until the cock crows so the three worms will not leave their bodies to report misbehavior to Taishakuten and appeal to the deity to take action against their female hosts."[24] Sexual abstinence was the most important act of purity and devotion on this night. Other taboos against various types of contamination, such as pregnancy, mourning, and the consumption of certain foods, were observed on this night to preserve the devotees' purity. Violating taboos led to punishment. Not observing sexual abstinence, for example, was thought to lead to the conception of a child fated to become a notorious criminal.[25]

Women brought to their practice of *kōshin machi* a mixed bag of "because" and future-oriented "in order to" motivations. One participated in the rite to atone for and avoid punishment because of past moral lapses. Worship also protected a woman from contracting lung disease, to which she was congenitally vulnerable "because" she had been born female. Protecting oneself against the possibility of future illness—"in order to" remain healthy—was a major motivation. Abstaining from sexual relations acted as a motivator in order to avoid giving birth to a child destined for a life of crime. The link between sexuality and one's future life that influenced the "in order to" motives of *kōshin machi* is also expressed in literature. Chikamatsu used the eve of the observance as the setting for *Love Suicides on the Eve of the Koshin Festival (Shinjū yoi kōshin machi)*, which concerns the double suicide of a husband and wife, Hanbei and Ochiyo.[26] By placing the drama within the ritual time of *kōshin machi,* the playwright could heighten the sexual tension, both overt and subtle, running between his characters, such as the lust a group of samurai has for Hanbei's younger brother and the jealousy Hanbei's mother harbors toward Ochiyo. It is doubtful that Chikamatsu's audience missed his intentional juxtaposing of a holy night of abstinence and introspection with men's sexual desire for another man and an older woman's envy of her daughter-in-law. As Chikamatsu's characters intimate in their own flawed ways, mixed motives in the vigil for Kōshin were ultimately linked to one's participation with and behavior toward others. The nocturnal practice stressed improving ethical behavior in one's associations and atoning for past lapses. Atonement demanded the personal exercise of sexual regulation, which on the night of *kōshin machi* was an exercise in abstinence and purification. Failure to regulate sexual activity in accordance with the rite could prove dangerous to a woman's bodily health and bring social misfortune to her and her future children.

Like entering into worship on the night of Kōshin, entering into marriage brought both types of motivations into play, and both were inseparable from a woman's inclusion and conduct in the new web of human relations created by her marriage. The single most important motivation for marriage was that of duty to obligation. Returning briefly to Davis, he stresses that while both "because" and "in order to" motives are very active in the Japanese religious experience, "because" types incorporate a range of virtues central to Japanese society such as duty, loyalty, gratitude, and selflessness. These virtues are expressed through ideas of obligation and debt captured in the term *on,* meaning "benefit" and "favor." Acting on this sense of obligation and debt is called the "return of benefits or favors" *(hō on).*[27] Many religious activities that people perform in Japan are geared toward the idea of returning benefits. Throughout their lives people acknowledge a host of obligations and debts of gratitude to both humans and deities that they understand as having played a role in making them full persons: conceived beings having some relative degree of social identity and position, knowledge, skills, and health. Conversely, overcoming a paucity of these things or improving them also leads to actions that are stimulated by future-oriented, "in order to" motives. Although Tokugawa women entered very different models of sexual values when they became brides and courtesans, their motivations to enter such disparate roles often demanded adherence to the same moral base of realizing *on* and acting on it as a debt of gratitude.

MOTIVES AND METAPHORS IN FERTILITY

One outstanding debt of gratitude that has historically shaped family relations is that which children exhibit toward parents. Acknowledging this debt has been considered the basis of filial piety and the root of moral centeredness. The *jokun* genre intensely focused on a woman's need to pay this debt through her behavior. The *Women's Imagawa* includes the following in its list of twenty-two admonishments to women (see appendix A): "You forget the deep debt of gratitude you owe your father and mother, and you are negligent in the way of filial piety."[28] As construed through the fertility model, the best way for a daughter to repay this debt and express gratitude toward the life her parents gave her was to enter another household. Although it was a very complex exercise in gratitude, she was to show identity with and loyalty to her parents by affiliating herself with a new family. Further, she was to perform various actions within the hierarchy of this new family as a daughter-in-law as a means to express gratitude to her parents for rearing her in the proper way. The surest means to satisfy this complex duty of expressing gratitude to two families as both daughter and daughter-in-law was to provide the husband's household with an heir. It was in this hope that Uesugi wrote to his granddaughter that only she could make her parents happy by making her parents-in-law happy with conscientiousness, maturity, and children.

Although wedding ceremonies formally bound men and women in their mutual obligation to maintain family harmony and continue family lines, the fertility model focused sharply on women and their special obligations. They were not only the fertile carriers of a new generation, but also were new members entering homes dependent on their obedience to household authority and traditions. In his letter to his granddaughter Uesugi stressed that keeping peace with her new husband and his parents and avoiding what he refers to as *fundo sōshō* (resentful legal action), by which he probably meant divorce, was part of her debt of gratitude. "Intimacy between a husband and wife comes through devotion to harmony and through taking pleasure in one's debt of gratitude. Resentful legal action is no way of fulfilling that debt. When spousal devotion to their debts of gratitude *(ongi)* collapses, then the moral order of husband and wife is also rent."[29] Note that Uesugi acknowledged that damage to the moral order came about through *mutual* abandonment of a couple's duty to *on*. The implication of this is that moral order was still salvageable by at least the wife holding fast to her fulfillment of debt to both families, even in the midst of her husband failing in his duties as son and husband. The "because" motive for marriage put forth in duty to one's parents and parents-in-law through the obligations of *on* was satisfied most fully through successfully living by fertility values, namely committing oneself to her husband's household, caring for its members, and giving birth.

Marrying also carried "in order to" motives such as avoiding sickness. As with one of the motivations of *kōshin machi,* marriage was also one means of warding off the danger of lung disease by regulating a woman's sexual behavior through its monogamous structure. As a physician, Namura argues that one reason for the early marriage age of Japanese (sixteen and seventeen for boys and thirteen and fourteen for girls, according to him) is that parents worried about their children's, especially their daughters', moral and bodily well-being. They fretted about sexual misbehavior, which could make young girls vulnerable to depression and respiratory disease. To ward off these anxieties, parents tended to marry off their children early so as to put them in a structured environment that acted to curb improper sexual activity. Namura is critical of this practice. He felt that people so young would give birth to physically weak children.[30] Still, the logic of this parental prerogative is grounded in future-oriented motives. Like the sleepless rite of *kōshin machi,* marriage fixed one's identity and behavior in relation to others to a larger ethical universe. Failure to participate in the ritual structure of either—in other words, to act outside the ethical universe to which each is connected—could culminate in attacks on the body as a type of extracted justice. Further, just as Kōshin worship articulates ethical behavior in women's sexual relationships—in other words, the exercising of abstinence and purification—marriage rites articulate the values of fertility: obedient behavior and purposefully productive sexual activity over willfulness and concupiscence. Namura considered parents largely responsible for instilling these values in girls well before marriage. It was their task to make sure their daughters secured the status of position, as well as gained some security against sickness and ill luck, both of which marriage could provide. This is one set of future-oriented motivations that led daughters and their parents toward marriage. Failing in this responsibility could have grave consequences. In his text, Namura criticizes parents for not preparing their daughters well for marriage and putting the young women at risk of undermining their health. He cautions that parents can spoil their daughter throughout her girlhood by giving her more affection than they give their son. But when she matures and reaches marrying age, such doting parents, now realizing that they have wasted valuable time, attempt "suddenly to have her taught the arts of proper womanhood, straighten her nature and dampen her high spirits."[31] It is often too little too late, and the young woman thus enters her husband's household bewildered about how to respond to her new responsibilities as a daughter-in-law and wife. She may feel constrained by the expectations of her parents-in-law and, in reacting to this frustration, may act too eagerly to please her husband. In the end she succeeds only in straining relations among everyone in her new household. This failure in role and relations may sap her of bodily strength and encourage tuberculosis (*rōgai*).[32] Late or poor training of a daughter for the duties of a wife could actually bring about the very problems—the failure of health and the lack of social status—that marriage was intended to avoid. The flip side of Namura's criticism, however, is that attentive training started early should successfully satisfy the "in order to" motivations of parents and their daughters. Further, the "in order to" motives play back on the "because" motives, producing a cycle of motivation acting ideally to propel women into marriage and dictating successful conduct in the household.

The future-oriented motives of gaining status and avoiding sickness through marriage and proper comportment in the house of one's in-laws begin, as Namura stresses in his text, with the training a girl receives in her natal home. Her upbringing and her obedience to her parents to marry motivate a daughter to express her debt of gratitude to her parents through leaving her home and becoming a bride. The writer of *The Greater Learning for Women* was acutely aware of this cycle and recognized a daughter's parents as key to her success in the fertility model. He concludes his moral primer by admonishing parents to stop overspending on their daughters' weddings. Parents, he insists, do not raise girls by money and material valuables but by moral lessons and moral example.[33] Excessive expenditure on a wedding is proof that a daughter has not received from her parents the proper moral motivation for becoming a bride. These parents substitute money for morals, wealth for wisdom. Without morals, without wisdom, there is no base upon which a young woman may act in terms of the "because" motivation to repay the debt of gratitude to her parents for raising her with values. She has no debt because she was given no values. She enters into marriage ethically hand-icapped to act on the "in order to" motivation to comport herself properly to secure social and physical well-being as a wife.

The sacrality of human relations also finds expression in metaphor. Metaphor serves the task of sacrality well because it establishes correspondence between things of different classification and kind and intimates their similitude in terms of identity, certain qualities, or function. It is from this correspondence that ideas may be meaningfully and immediately comprehended. As Suzanne Langer states in her classic study of symbolism, metaphors are "our readiest instruments for abstracting concepts from the tumbling stream of actual impressions."[34] Amidst a tumbling stream of actual impressions concerning women and their socio-sexual relations in the period—ranging from the earthy relationships less bound by household authority that many lower-class commoners took part in and the play of women in the quarters to the celibacy of Buddhist nuns and the purposeful fertility of samurai and bourgeois commoners—*jokun* authors relied on certain metaphors to signify their vision of proper relations and advocate for purposeful fertility. "Heaven and earth," as we saw in the previous chapter, was a key metaphor in the fertility model for explaining proper gender relations. The metaphor responded well to the model's need to articulate the sacrality of structure that framed the marriage relation by creating a correspondence between principles of human association in this world and the cosmic principles of yin and yang that structure and maintain the universe.

In Namura's guide other metaphors appear that focus squarely on the promise and threat of woman as bride. Namura's introductory passage to his text, titled "Woman is the Beginning of Humankind" (Onna wa hito no hajimari no koto), commences with a selective retelling of Japan's mythical origins. The passage serves as a mythic history of womankind, tying contemporary women to the primordial woman, Izanami, and the most important of her children, Amaterasu. Like the dramatic structures of many sacred histories, Namura's own production marks its mythic vision with a pristine beginning, inevitable stumbles and challenges, and the promise of redemption. As a producer of myth, Namura chooses specific metaphors—Izanami and Amaterasu—to amplify his concern that a bride must aim to provide a harmonious life and generational continuity for her marriage household. Producers of myths have at hand, in the form of any available metaphor, an "empty signifier" in its pure potential. Creative control over mythological storyline demands that a producer fill the emptiness of each potential metaphor with meaning by choosing well the metaphorical form and content to create a persuasive image that speaks (so the producer hopes) an instinctive truth to the consumers of the myth.[35] In choosing Izanami and Amaterasu, Namura chooses as the form the life-giving goddess and as the content the cultivation of the right values and behaviors.

His production of these metaphors and the narrative in which he employs them leave little doubt as to what he hoped his audience would take away from their reading of the myth: that women should enter into marriage in the spirit of the original, divine women from whom all blessings flow. Namura's story of womankind shares many narrative similarities stressed in the myths of Ise Shinto. These myths, redacted largely from the *Nihongi,* were incorporated into the historical writings of Kitabatake Chikafusa (1293–1354), particularly his 1343 work titled *Records of the Legitimate Succession of the Divine Sovereigns (Jinnō shōtōki).*[36] Given Namura's breadth of cultural knowledge and education in Itō Jinsai's academy, he was likely familiar with the narrative assumptions of these influential writings, which, like his own, were forms of myths attempting to amplify the particular concerns of their producers.[37] In his own myth, however, Namura introduces Izanami and her male consort, Izanagi, as the first *kami* in a line of seven heavenly generations to possess gender distinctions.[38] The two *kami* enter into sexual union, from which Izanami produces a daughter and three sons. Namura ignores the identity of the sons altogether, but he identifies the daughter as Amaterasu and the "ancestress of all earthly deities *(chiji no mioya).*"[39] Along with the brothers' identities, Namura also omits from his narrative the death of Izanami upon giving birth to the fire god, the decomposition of her body in the underworld, the spontaneous and asexual birth of Amaterasu from Izanagi's act of ritual purification upon his escape from Izanami's putrefied grasp, and his charge to Amaterasu and her brothers, Tsukiyumi and Susanoo, to rule their respective realms. The signification of these metaphors (establishment of the imperial cult) and the particular narrative into which they are embedded in the *Nihongi* (removing Amaterasu's birth from sexual activity and linking such activity to death and pollution) complicate Namura's task as master of his own metaphors. As master, his solution is to ignore the form and content of these other metaphors and move forward in his particular task of favoring a vision of female life crafted on the idealized values and behaviors of fertility.

Toward this task of signifying fertility values and behaviors, Namura calls the creative sexual activity of Izanami and Izanagi *mitonomaguwai.* This ancient word appears in the *Nihongi* (also called the *Nihon shoki)* and the collection of myths compiled in 712 titled *A Chronicle of Ancient Matters (Kojiki)* as a description of the sexual union that was the climax of a circumambulation rite that Izanami and her consort performed around a pillar. In the *Nihongi* account, *mitonomaguwai* is made up of two ideograms meaning "to meet" and "join together."[40] Namura, while keeping the same reading, in his text replaces the first character (meaning "to meet") with one denoting "marriage," giving the meaning "to marry and join together." This word play and use of divine metaphors is the first intimation given that a woman's sexual activity, when practiced within the strictures of marriage, becomes purposeful action, like that of the *kami* and their creation of the earth and its multitude of gods. In Namura's narrative, however, time has eroded the moral resolve of women to act with purpose with regards to their sexuality and behavior toward others. The farther one lives chronologically from the mythic wellspring of the original mother and daughter, Izanami and Amaterasu, the more difficult it is for her to identify with the goddesses' divine standards. Mortal women of the ancient age *(jōdai no onna),* Namura puts forward, while not quite measuring up to the *kami* in the earlier time of the gods *(kamiyo),* were still close enough in terms of time to the original idea that their minds were obedient by nature and their hearts free of vice.[41] For contemporary women morally weakened through the degradation of time, though, Namura was convinced that they had to swim far upstream against the strong current of this sacred heritage.

As master of his own metaphors, Namura strategically chooses to change them in mid-passage. Buddhist images of demons and last days now begin to appear in his story. Through time women's hearts have become evil. Unlike when the world was new and women divine, the present world has grown old and is reaching its last age *(yo no sue ima no yo ni oyobi).*[42] In such a morally exhausted age women's hearts become wicked day by day *(onna no kokoro hibi ni ashiku nari).*[43] Namura portrays contemporary women, far removed from the pure spring of their divine origin, as floundering in the stagnant waters of moral bankruptcy. To create particular effect on this point of the long fall of woman, Namura borrows a well-used quote from the Hossō text *Jōyuishiki-ron:* "Women are messengers from hell, cut off from the seed of the Buddha. They have the countenance of a bodhisattva and the heart of a fierce demon *(yasha).*"[44] Buddhist demonology offers a plethora of otherworldly miscreants, and Namura's choice of *yasha,* a character originally from Indian mythology, is apt given the fertility values he is promoting in his text. *Yasha* that have been converted to the wisdom of the Buddha's message are fierce protectors of the dharma, but other *yasha,* the unconverted, roam in the forest and possess a wild and fierce nature that is violently threatening to social order; they have a particular craving for human flesh. Few metaphors are as appropriately demonic in advancing an apocalyptic vision in terms of the fertility model. It is in stark contrast to the model's emphasis on the ideal of passivity and obedience.

A perfect description of fertility's ideal, counter-figure to the *yasha* (and a reminder that fertility's concern is hardly a historical curiosity of a far-flung culture) is found in Virginia Woolf's own American metaphor of the "perfect" wife.

> You who come of a younger and happier generation may not have heard of her—you may not know what I mean by the Angel in the House. . . . She was intensely sympathetic. She was immensely charming. She was utterly unselfish. She excelled in the difficult arts of family life. She sacrificed herself daily. If there was chicken, she took the leg; if there was a draught, she sat in it—in short she was so constituted that she never had a mind or wish of her own, but preferred to sympathize always with the minds and wishes of others. Above all—I need not say it—she was pure.[45]

In contrast to the order such an angel's prudence, modesty, and selfless attentiveness brings to the household, the unconverted *yasha* (i.e., unconverted to the behavioral ideals of fertility) represents an ever-present danger to the household. The bride as *yasha* enters the given order of her groom's household as an outsider with as much potential, through her lack of proper behavior and fertility, to bring disorder and extinction to the household as she might bring order and generational continuity as an angel, a converted *yasha*—or, to return to Namura's metaphor, a goddess, a life-creating *kami.*[46]

What can parry the threat of the demon bride and pursue the promise of the goddess bride? For Namura it is the adjustment of a woman's mind to a state of pure integrity like that of the *kami* of the mythic past. He identifies the cultivation of the qualities of *tashinami* as central to this task. Pursuing these qualities—prudence, modesty, refinement, and attentiveness—establishes a mind of integrity *(kokoro shōjiki)* by which to live in the world with others. In a mind attentive to the qualities of *tashinami,* "the jealous spirit is no more, desires are few, and sympathy and sensitivity to others run deep."[47] According to Namura, internalizing the behavioral patterns of *tashinami* is no easy task in an age so removed from Izanami and Amaterasu, but nevertheless parents must not delay in cultivating such qualities in their daughter. Once such an untutored girl becomes a woman, indifferent to the moral restraints of humility and shame, she will think she has the world at her feet and will act only according to her own desires; unimpeded moral decline throughout her years of marriage will make a woman vulnerable to taunts and gossip behind her back. People may call her *kasha,* which is short for *kasha baba* (burning cart hag).[48] This term alludes to a Buddhist hell, ubiquitously depicted in many a mandala, in which sufferers must travel in a vehicle constantly in flames. This term was also used to designate older, powerful women in the pleasure quarter, typically managers and wives of bordello owners with reputations for abusing their charges, as it was hoped, due to their cruel behavior, that hellfire awaited them upon their deaths.[49]

Perhaps on this point of older, established women mistreating those who were younger and more vulnerable, Namura's use of *kasha* is not coincidental. A young woman who entered into the roles of wife and daughter-in-law, yet who was morally illiterate in the behavioral ideals *tashinami,* entered marriage not by way of the goddess but by the path of the *kasha baba.* With age and good fortune such a woman may very well, according to Namura, rise to the important position of mother-in-law and even de facto household manager, but years of self-centered behavior will surely bring, he metaphorically suggests, unhappiness to all with whom she is associated—and especially, at some point in time, her own daughter-in-law. With a mind of integrity forged in a firm sense of *tashinami,* however, then even in a degenerate world a daughter becomes more like a goddess of yore than a demon of the present age. This sacred story of womanhood, with which Namura opens *A Record of Treasures for Women,* ends appropriately on this note of redemptive hope in an honest mind and proper deportment.

MOTIVES AND METAPHORS IN PLEASURE

Like brides, daughters who became courtesans entered a place and role both strange to and demanding of them. The motivation for many entering the pleasure quarters as girls and young women was tied to the same moral bedrock as that of brides: loyalty and concern for parents and family. Here, repaying one's debt of gratitude was quite literal: the obligations of *on* were met through entering public prostitution. Similar to a daughter entering into marriage as a means of expressing her gratitude to her parents and discharging her filial duty, the obligation of financially benefiting one's parents and household was also a motivating fac-

tor behind many daughters who entered entertainment districts throughout Japan. As discussed in chapter 1, household poverty and urban
demands for erotic labor combined to draw women into the quarters.
For a woman with limited options to help her parents and family, a quarter's promise of regular pay and a set term of service may have made what
was a necessary decision also an ethically tolerable one of filial motivation. A comic haiku poem *(senryū)* put it like this: "Seeing your parents
ill, it is one's filial duty to enter a commoner's palanquin *(Yamu oya o
misute yotsude e noru kō)*."[50] The suggestion here is that conditions such
as the illness of parents and the economic insecurity of the household
motivated daughters and their parents to enter into contracts with buyers from the quarters—who were already waiting with palanquin and
porters on hand.

Acknowledging the debt to one's parents was the moral standard.
The fact that the "because" motive expressed through the moral principle of *on* could initiate participation in two competing value systems
shows that it acted as a type of "passive enablement."[51] This is a type of
intellectual passivity toward social change and the rise of ideologies that
is common to many religious groups and ideas in Japan and elsewhere.
This passivity allows religion a degree of malleability in order to change
with political and economic developments without altering its fundamental doctrinal rhetoric. Meiji-period Buddhists used many ideas of
the faith, such as the universality of suffering and the concept of no-self,
to throw their support behind efforts of industrialization and to explain
away its punishing consequences for workers. This religious justification
enabled priests to assert that their tradition was relevant to the modern-
ization efforts of the country at a time when Buddhism had come under
stiff criticism for being foreign and anti-modern. A similar exercise with
regards to disparate sexual values was also at play in the models of fertility and pleasure. Such idealized principles as filial piety were used to
legitimate vastly different values, institutions, and practices concerning
female sexuality. Whether acted on freely or as a result of parental coercion, duty to parents and to the household were viewed as expressions
of returning the benefits one had received as a daughter, which in part
enabled opposing forms of sexual practices and relationships to coexist
on the same moral ground.

Incorporation into the model of pleasure required the further motive
of a woman *in order to* secure future status within the hierarchy of her
bordello. Successfully managing her dealings with clients to create exclu-

sive relationships with them provided fame and position for herself and
a steady income for her employer's—and her own—coffers. She would
need this money to pay off her contract and terminate her employment.
If obedient behavior helped a bride create meaningful space in the fertility model, then the display of the behavior and attitudes of *iki*—sex
appeal, sophistication, intellect, and charm—could pay off handsomely
for a courtesan trying to gain standing and affirmation within the structure of the bordello. The pleasure quarters provided courtesans with a
hierarchical structure in which to act on their motivation to move up the
ranks and secure status, and they also encouraged the ceremonial behaviors of *iki* that were necessary to garner such standing.

Pleasure, like fertility, also produced contrasting metaphors that artic-
ulated the model's attempt to express the complex identity that women
took on when they took on the role of courtesan. In the world of pleasure, no metaphor was more powerful than that of the *tayū,* or the top-
class courtesan.[52] In the last chapter of his 1684 novel *The Second Life of
an Amorous Man (Kōshoku nidai otoko),* Saikaku describes a heavenly vision
of the *tayū* as a bodhisattva. He portrays many famed, late *tayū* of the
great quarters as having become bodhisattvas upon death and who are
now living in a Pure Land in which any man would hope to take refuge.
They are figures right out of Buddhist iconography. Light pours forth
from their bodies; an entourage of sister courtesans surrounds them like
protective deities. Adorning this Pure Land are bejeweled koto, golden
cups, silver bowls, and the finest incense and porcelain.[53] Saikaku's
description of the *tayū* as a bodhisattva may have been influenced by the
famous dream of Shinran (1173–1262) in the Rokkakudō, the six-sided
hall of Chōbōji in Kyoto, where he retreated for one hundred days of
contemplation in 1190 before cutting his ties to the Tendai school and
its monastic center on Mount Hiei.[54] On the ninety-fifth day of medi-
tation, Shinran dreamed of Kannon; the bodhisattva promised that if he
had to forsake celibacy, she would appear to him as a lovely woman,
marry him, allow him to enjoy sexual relations with her, and secure him
a place in the Pure Land upon his death.

The artist Suzuki Harunobu (1725–1770) also alludes to the bodhisattva mystique of ranking courtesans in a 1764 illustration from a series
depicting scenes in the Yoshiwara. Two rustic pilgrims on their first
journey to see the sights of Edo happen upon a courtesan and her young
attendant bedecked in their splendor. Assuming the woman to be an
incarnation of the bodhisattva Kannon accompanied by a heavenly assis-

tant, they bow their heads and place their palms together in worship of the seemingly divine pair.[55] Although the *tayū* as a class of individual courtesans disappeared from the Yoshiwara's ranking system in the middle 1700s, the metaphor and ideal of the perfect prostitute continued, as Harunobu's humorous and touching picture shows. The last *tayū*-ranked woman in the Yoshiwara appeared on the rolls in 1761; in the previous decade another term appeared, *oiran,* which would replace *tayū* and would come to denote the highest class of courtesan.[56] Like the primordial women of the fertility model, the *tayū* as the courtesan's courtesan best expressed the pleasure model's conception of female sexual value and purpose.

Tokugawa novelists and playwrights, like Namura, were also mythmakers, particularly of urban Japan's entertainment districts. Their fictionalized accounts of actual *tayū*-class courtesans commemorated these women long after their deaths and created paragons of perfection to which many could aspire but few could ever reach. They produced exemplars of these women through the dramatic technique of "double identity."[57] The concept of double identity is played out frequently on the stages of kabuki and bunraku. For example, the protagonist takes on a fictional identity and behavior, only to reveal his true self and purpose during the climax. Double identity produces imaginative narrative and surprising scenes by blurring the line between ideal characters and real people, between fictional worlds and the actual world, and by borrowing from or alluding to historical events and personages. Just as with the Osaka courtesan Yūgiri appearing in Saikaku's fiction, novelists and dramatists blended fiction and biography to give double identities to many courtesans such as Takao and Agemaki of the Yoshiwara and Yoshino of the Shimabara. Their reputations as great *tayū* live on so powerfully in plays and novels that some, such as Agemaki—the quick-thinking and loyal heroine in the play *Sukeroku*—are "known" almost exclusively from fiction. It is through these fictionalized representations of famous courtesans that the *tayū* as metaphor, and not simply as social rank, came to express pleasure's values both inside and outside the quarter. Agemaki was not simply beautiful, but also sagacious, sympathetic, spirited, and sophisticated in the ways and hearts of men. This spirit of *iki* that other women tried hard to cultivate came to her effortlessly. What was, in the end, skillfully learned behavior for most was her true self.

Saikaku, in his own use of double identity in *The Second Life of an*

Amorous Man, captures the first-class courtesan's effortless deportment and understanding of others. When the marriage of the dandy protagonist, Yonosuke, to Yoshino (1606–1643) is questioned by his female relatives for the shame it will bring them all, Yonosuke refuses Yoshino's initial pleas to end their relationship to save his ties to his family. Respecting his love for her, Yoshino decides to win over his relatives. Hosting a dinner party for them, she surprises the skeptical family members with her grace and intelligence. She astonishes them, in the end, with her real self. She performs everything expertly and with flair, from helping girls comb their hair to playing koto and reciting poetry, from performing the tea ceremony to talking with the womenfolk on topics as diverse as scandalous gossip and the vagaries of the world. So stunned are the relatives by the beauty of the courtesan's true self that they promptly demand that Yonosuke make her his wife.[58] Saikaku never met Yoshino. She died one year after his birth and forty-one years before the publication of the novel from which this episode is derived. So great was her fame, though, that even after four decades Saikaku could use this event to fictionalize her identity and establish her character as the embodiment of the perfect courtesan.

Idealization of the *tayū* also carried with it a negative assessment of courtesans. Her sophistication, intelligence, and charm were effortless. She was able to bridge the gap between displaying *iki* and displaying one's true self, between being the spirited courtesan that play demanded of her role and being simply herself. Given the idealization of the *tayū,* virtually all women of the quarters did not compare well to the metaphor. Their attempts to display the charms of *iki,* even if skillful, suggested insincerity. The play of style and allure demanded by their role made it difficult to bridge the gap between the playful prostitute and the sincere woman. From this gap emerges another metaphor: the fox. The relationship between women of pleasure and the fox is rich, and I address it further in chapter 5. As the opposing metaphor to that of the *tayū,* the fox is characterized by clever deception through the context of Yoshiwara courtesans and the deity Inari. In folklore the fox, whether for ill or good, was seen as a changeling or possessive agent, most often in female form, charged with powers of sexuality, seduction, and trickery. Here the fox, as opposed to Shinran's Kannon, puts sexual desire and its changing appearance to ignoble use. Courtesans, with their professional demands to play to the imaginations and emotional desires of their clients, were attributed with popular vulpine qualities. A woman might be called a "fox without a tail" *(o no nai kitsune)*. Another term, *kitsune ochi,* refers both to a fox leaving the body of the person it has possessed and to a courtesan taking leave of both her client and his money after rendering her services.[59] As we will see in chapter 5, a woman not only tricked her client out of his money but sometimes tried to trick her owner out of his legal possession of her through prayers and schemes of escape.

The perception of a courtesan as a type of trickster or changeling—deceiving a man into believing that she is reaching out for his companionship and not his purse or fooling her owner into seeing a loyal laborer and not a woman plotting to escape or giving her heart to one man—was often contained in the verb *bakasu,* meaning "to trick, enchant, or confuse." A *senryū* of the time compares both courtesan and kabuki actor as equal masters in the art of creating illusion. "Change happens on two streets; tricks happen on five streets *(Bakeru no ga nichō bakasu ga gochō nari)*."[60] Edo's theater district was confined to two streets. Further, all theaters featured only male actors, some of whom specialized in female roles *(onnagata),* many of which were courtesans. Such actors "changed" into women on stage and created the illusion of being female. The Yoshiwara was made up of five streets where courtesans lived and plied their trade in "tricking" men's emotions and perceptions with their abilities in *iki.* Together these seven streets made up Edo's pleasure districts, where play, both theatrical and sexual, provided fantasy worlds of escape from the moral rigors and daily toil of normal society. On these seven streets men acted like courtesans and courtesans acted like lovers by turning on their skills to alter, if only for the length of a play or a visit, their audiences' perception of reality.

Motive and metaphor vivified the models of fertility and pleasure. Duty to parents and household and the need to secure one's position in part motivated daughters to become wives and courtesans. Metaphors of fertility and pleasure such as Izanami and the *tayū* also cast the shadows of demons and changelings. These motives and metaphors also indicate that both models shared a degree of ambivalence toward the presence and status of women that each was attempting to incorporate. Daughters who were motivated to enter unfamiliar places were—as the linked metaphors of goddess-demon and *tayū*-fox suggest—both promises of and threats to the success of their new homes and relations. By attempting to act on the promise and evade the threat, the process of incorporating daughters was activated though entrance rites of marriage and first meeting.

Brides of Fertility and Brides of Pleasure

Daughters entering into exclusive relationships with men either in the household or the pleasure quarters did so as "brides." The pleasure model borrowed heavily and playfully from the nuptial ceremony of fertility in establishing its own rites of intimate association, including the person of the bride. A bride in the household activated her relationship with one man through *yometori*-style marriage; a bride in the quarters entered into her many relationships one man at a time through rites of first meeting. These rites gave each bride a stake in the institutional status available to her to develop her role as fully as possible in service to either the household or bordello. Further, as the metaphors of fertile goddess and first-class courtesan indicate, bridal rites from the idealized perspective of the models acted to transform women from daughters to brides of fertility and brides of pleasure by charging their sexual relations with men with a sense of institutional ultimate concern toward household posterity and bordello prosperity. From this basis of ultimate concern, the symbolic and behavioral trajectory of each entrance rite aimed at orienting a woman's sexuality toward either the production of a child or a profit. In each rite, marriage and first meeting, this trajectory traveled in two stages: 1) procession to the ceremony and 2) the formalization and consummation of relations.

PROCESSIONS OF FERTILITY AND PLEASURE

Entering into relations with a new husband or client required a woman to be a type of traveler. Travel in the Tokugawa period gained popularity with the peace of the times, the construction of roads built to accommodate commercial growth, and a growing class of economically comfortable commoners seeking leisure, sights, and spiritual renewal. The Tōkaidō, connecting the cities of Edo, Kyoto, and Osaka, gained fame not only as a trade highway but also as a road of sightseeing and pilgrimage. Guidebooks such as *Famous Sites along the Tōkaidō (Tōkaidō meishoki)* were widely published and detailed famous sites along the highway, largely temples, shrines, and pilgrimage centers.[61] For tourists and pilgrims, traveling to distant places was an excursion of possibilities, a time of leaving behind the normal order of the household, village, or city ward. Along the way there existed the threat of meeting thieves or con artists, the anticipation of touring sacred sites, the potential for religious encounters of insight and curing, and the simple hope of pleasant experiences common to any traveler. For some male travelers, securing a brief sexual encounter with a woman, such as an inn girl or waitress working in the gray area of public labor and private prostitution, was another possibility.[62]

Daughters on the way to their weddings and first meetings traveled on the road as well. Their trips were also excursions of possibilities. For a bride traveling to a largely unknown household there was the possibility of new relations and obligations, including perhaps having sex for the first time, securing her place and identity in the household, and likely becoming a mother. For a courtesan traveling to meet a new client there was, along with the absolute certainty of a sexual encounter—just another in a string of countless assignations—the possibility of gaining greater prestige with another paying customer who has committed himself to her and her bordello, of perhaps finding a suitably agreeable man to whom she was not averse to giving her sexual favors, and, if she were a dreamer, of meeting someone who might one day pay her contract and take her as his wife. A bride's trip was the wedding procession that led her from her natal home to her husband's household. A courtesan's trip was a slow parade with her entourage through the streets of her quarter as her client awaited her arrival at a teahouse.

The definitive act of *yometori* marriage was the wedding procession of a bride moving from the house of her birth to the house where she would ideally give birth to an heir. Before she departed on her journey, another series of rites was concluded at her household and established her betrothal. The actual wedding ceremony following her arrival at the groom's house was performed later. The practice of both betrothal and nuptial rites was commonly understood to constitute a wedding, and even abbreviated, simple ceremonies generally reflected this divided pattern.[63] The journey between the two rites moved a woman away from one side of the daughter/wife perspectival boundary toward the other side. For this crossing *A Record of Treasures for Women* briefly describes the use of palanquins for carrying the bride. Passage between households involved both male and female representatives of the bride's family. Women, particularly older women such as the bride's mother or other female relative, however, did not just represent the family, but were also the spiritual protectors of the bride. Travel between households, between shedding a known past and attempting to create an unknown future, was a time of high liminality, of possible danger to the fertile potentiality of the bride.[64] The illustration in Namura's text depicting a procession reveals the men trudging ahead with eyes and heads straight, but the three women walk within arm's length of the palanquin with their eyes on it rather than the road (see fig. 3).[65] Other period illustrations of processions typically show women close to the palanquin.[66] Older women, their institutional standing and sexuality already long established, stood immune to that which threatened the young woman in the palanquin. She was the embodied question mark of social and sexual identity. In her palanquin she sat no longer as a daughter but not yet as a wife, no longer as a virgin in her parent's home but not yet as a sexual partner in her husband's household. Her unsettled status regarding her role and body raised dangers to her fertility and health that demanded symbolic remedies to avert the perils and impurities lurking in the bride's shadow.

This type of female mediation in weddings, which the presence of older women suggests, is seen most conspicuously in the figure of the ritual specialist called *katsurame*. These women were active mainly in western Japan, particularly in the area around Kyoto and Osaka, during the medieval and early modern periods. Although claiming a long line of ecstatic ritual specialization reaching back to the legendary reign of the empress Jingū (r. 201–269), *katsurame* both expanded and altered their ritual functions throughout their history. They produced various records to legitimate new ritual tasks with stamps of either antiquity or authority.[67] Their Jingū records "proved" both antiquity and authority when *katsurame* began performing rituals of safe birth and selling amulets. Their most distinguishing feature was a long, white head wrap, which is said to be derived from the belly wrap that Jingū wore while pregnant with her son and future emperor, Ōjin (r. 270–310).[68] By the early seventeenth century *katsurame* were active in providing a range of ritual performances at weddings, such as singing celebratory songs, performing purification rituals, and leading bridal processions from one household to the other.[69] In their function as professional ritual specialists, they represent a broad range of ritual technicians who wandered the land prior to and during the Tokugawa period. Many of them were peripatetic and offered to individuals, families, and communities services of divination, exorcism, and purification.[70]

A household could employ other women to function similarly to protect the bride and her fertility at the outset of the procession. Ise Sadatake states in his explication of wedding ritual that the fear of demons (*akuma*) bringing harm to the bride during her procession led some families to employ female specialists whose task was to clear the bridal pathway of evil spirits and demons (*akumabarai*). Sadatake describes the spe-

FIGURE 3 Illustration of a wedding procession from the 1692 edition of *A Record of Treasures for Women*. Courtesy of Tōyoko Gakuen Joshi Tanki Daigaku Josei Bunka Kenkyūjo, Tokyo.

cialist as an ecstatic and colorful character who is "tall in stature with a face of frightening countenance, and her hair, dyed or decorated, hangs loosely askew."[71] Although he points out that the Ise House has never called for the attendance of such a person, he acknowledges that it is currently a popular custom with some.[72]

Another way a family might try to keep a departing daughter safe on the way to marriage was to have her travel with a doll, typically fashioned from paper or cotton, which was used commonly as a ritual substitute to protect children from illness and malevolent forces.[73] Dolls functioned to protect the bride on a journey that was considered potentially hazardous. In addition to protecting traveling brides, dolls might also constitute one part of a bride's trousseau that she brought with her into marriage in anticipation of soon bearing children and using them to protect her offspring.[74] Namura, for example, lists such a doll among over one hundred items a bride might bring to marriage.[75] Outside of this list Namura makes no mention of such dolls, but Takai, in his 1847 edition, includes an entire paragraph on the custom of dolls as ritual substitutes. He ties this custom to the ancient activity of the *kami,* an editorial flourish of nationalistic concern, but he also describes the practice of girls keeping these small figurines close to their bodies, tucked in their clothes, until they marry.[76] Paralleling the health aspects of marriage discussed above as one type of religious motive, Takai suggests that upon marriage a young woman is no longer in need of the doll's protective power to keep away illness and ill luck. With marriage a woman reaches a social, physiological, and spiritual stage of development in life that liberates her from the vulnerability to the reckless behavior of youth, childhood illnesses, and baleful spirits that prey on the young. The concerned parents whom Namura criticizes, those who with the best intentions but the worst judgment rushed their children into marriage, reflected in their worry this understanding of marriage and the protection it offered. But to everything there is a season, and until her parents properly trained her for marriage, a girl had to depend on good parenting, prayers to the buddhas and gods for good health, and protective dolls. Even in the procession toward marriage that season had not yet turned, and on a road full of dangers to their health and fertility a number of brides kept their dolls close until the journey finally ended at new households, where they assumed a new identity and responsibilities.

The wedding procession was both a utilitarian and symbolic exercise grounded in the necessities of the *yometori* pattern so central to the fertility model. The pattern's virilocality demanded that the bride move to the groom's home, but the model's concern, and those of the two families, for her health and fertility also required spiritual protection of them while she was on the road. It was important to protect the bride in order to deliver her with her health and fertility intact. The procession was an orderly march into conflict: protection of a bride's body against the potential for spiritual aggression toward it. This battle between fertility and destructive forces for the bride's bodily and spiritual health reflected the metaphors of the life-giving goddess (Izanami and Amaterasu) and life-devouring demon *(yasha)* that Namura lays out in his text's sacred history of women. Each bride in her procession, in her liminality of being neither a daughter nor daughter-in-law, stood at the intersection of this sacred history. She was poised in her palanquin between godliness and demonism, fecundity and emptiness, obedience and willfulness, and a household's highest hope and its deepest fear. What protective female escorts and dolls ultimately delivered to the groom's family—a goddess or demon—would be uncovered only in the course of time and in accordance with the family's own judgment of the bride.

Processions in the pleasure quarters were also important in marking paths toward formal relations between women and their clients. Called *dōchū,* which means "during travel," these processions led a courtesan from her bordello to the house of assignation where she would meet her waiting client, and the term itself may have originated from the journeys of palace officials between Kyoto and Edo. In the Yoshiwara, which had two streets named Kyoto and Edo, the parading of a courtesan between these avenues was a visual pun that reflected the stateliness of her short journey.[77] The *Yoshiwara Compendium (Yoshiwara taizen)* claims that the procession between the streets of Kyoto and Edo was designed to emulate the mood of a lengthy and important journey, such as official business travel between the two cities.[78] In the same manner that economic and other considerations influenced the degree of display and richness in wedding processions, a courtesan's *dōchū* varied depending on her rank, the desire and wealth of her client, and the particular occasion for the procession. For clients able to afford a relationship with a woman of the *tayū* class or commit their finances to sponsoring the debut of a young woman into the top ranks, the processional display of a woman parading with her full retinue in tow was quite impressive.

Such display was also a treat for bystanders. The public and popular nature of the *dōchū* moved it beyond the realm of purposeful walking to a type of *misemono:* an enjoyable and unusual spectacle that broke with the monotony of everyday life.[79] A courtesan, as the star of her own *dōchū,* became a figure of the extraordinary. She and her entourage walked with stately purpose past crowds of people stopping to catch a glimpse of her, including perhaps a future client. While entertaining to watch, it was a dignified procession; it was not a circus parade. A courtesan held her head erect and looked straight ahead to avoid catching the eye of friends or colleagues and calling out to them, thus breaking the seriousness of the moment.[80] A significant feature of the procession was the courtesan's choreography. The pleasure quarters of Edo, Osaka, and Kyoto all used similar styles of ceremonial walking based on a slow, arching swing of the foot outward from the side of the body and then leisurely planted forward.[81] This manner of walking contributed to the public spectacle of the procession as *misemono* by slowing the gait of a courtesan and intensifying attention on her body and its movements. In this way a courtesan effected *misemono:* with each swing of the foot and turn of the ankle she registered a small kick to the consciousness of ordinary life.

As in a bridal procession, women were conspicuous in a courtesan's procession (see fig. 4). In the *dōchū,* however, their role was to create the sense of spectacle necessary in effecting *misemono.* Male laborers participated, but only as porters carrying lanterns printed with the name of the courtesan's bordello or a long umbrella used to shade a parading courtesan. In the eighteenth century, large processions included musicians and geisha playing supporting roles as entertainers for the client and his friends. Even small *dōchū* included female attendants escorting the courtesan to her appointment. Whereas the fertility model emphasized the use of older women in the bride's procession, the pleasure model did just the opposite in the courtesan's: female escorts in the quarters were younger than the courtesan—her teenage apprentices and child attendants. The only older woman involved who was professionally related to the courtesan was her manager, typically a retired courtesan herself. Unlike the bridal procession, with its concern for guarding a woman's sexuality to serve a single man and his family, the pleasure procession was a celebration of female sexuality in service to any man willing to pay the price to enrich a bordello's coffers. Made up of females of different ranks, professional development, ages, and sexual potential, the *dōchū* formed, in effect, a lineage and learning curve of carnal pleasure.

A courtesan's style and attitude while participating in the procession reflect the importance the ceremony held for the pleasure model. It was one of many forms of play integral to and perfected by the quarters, but as play it was far from frivolous. For the client, the *dōchū* stimulated his desire by sharpening the erotic anticipation, while it also confirmed his status within the unabashed materialism of the quarter: what his money could buy was on public display for all to see. For the courtesan, it may also have been an erotic moment—a choreography of exhibitionism—but it was definitely, as with her client, public confirmation of her status within the hierarchy of the quarter. In the nineteenth century, when the Yoshiwara was well in decline from its earlier and more glamorous days, only the top courtesan of a bordello formally paraded to her appointment with her client.[82] In this way, as the *dōchū* became less common, it also became ever more a symbol of status reserved only for a precious few women within the entire quarter.

Symbolically the *dōchū* acted as a type of bridal procession: it was the celebratory movement of a woman into a formalized relation with a man and with institutional hierarchy. Further, this movement placed a courtesan in a moment of liminality while on the road to her future. Like the bride standing at the intersection of the fertile goddess and destructive demon, the prostitute paraded to her own intersection of the pleasure model's contrasting metaphors of the bodhisattva-like *tayū* and the deceptive fox, of the extraordinarily sincere and empathetic woman and

FIGURE 4 A courtesan parades with her entourage. From an original reproduction of Kitagawa Utamaro's illustration by Mitani Kazuma. Courtesy of Rippū Shobō, Tokyo.

the merely coy and clever courtesan. In the moment of the *dōchū*, the act publicly acknowledging her high status as a first-rank courtesan, she and her sexuality were on parade for the benefit of one particular man waiting to formalize ties with her and her alone. She marched for no one else; she was one man's bride—if only on that day. The next day she would parade for yet another client desiring to create faithful bonds with only her.

RITES OF MARRIAGE AND FIRST MEETING

Ritually similar processions of fertility and pleasure put the values of the competing models into sharp relief. The rites of marriage and first meeting continued this process of ritual incorporation and value discrimination. The ceremony in the groom's household effectively functioned as a fertility rite. As Sadatake prosaically puts it, "Marriage ceremonies are for the purpose of giving birth to a child."[83] From the fertility model's perspective, the ceremony sought to possess a bride's fertility and activate it, and incorporate her into the purposeful activities of the household. Paralleling this was the rite of first meeting in the quarters, which brought into sexual play a skewed imitation of marriage rites. This was not play meant to mock wedding ritual, but rather to co-opt its normative meaning, turn it on its head, and drain all notions of fertility from relations between a courtesan and her clients.

Marriage Rites

Post-procession rites were made up of four steps: 1) transfer of her possessions; 2) the sharing of sacred wine; 3) change of bridal clothes; and 4) consummation of relations. The first step in marriage rites was the transfer of the bridal trousseau from the woman's house to her groom's residence and its display. These articles made up a large part of her dowry *(jisan zaisan),* and as such they functioned as a public display of material goods that would remain independent of a bride's new household's communal wealth. In a society where women were largely excluded from property inheritance, a woman's trousseau of portable possessions came to take on great significance as one of the few things to which a woman could lay legal claim. Acting as her dowry, its items were hers and would remain so regardless of the future of her marriage. If the bride's household employed porters to deliver the trousseau, the men might receive a payment from the groom's family called *niwasen*.[84] It was not payment for the dowry itself. The requirement for the groom's family to pay for the transport of the dowry to display it gives meaning to the dowry in terms of the bride's identity between two families. *Niwasen* also refers to a charge paid for the temporary safe storage of luggage until it can be collected at a later date. By paying the porters and displaying the bride's items, the groom's family acknowledged its duty to keep the dowry safe. Further, the point of the display was to put the articles, whose security had now been promised, in the most conspicuous place so that a bride's family might show, through material and sometimes expensive and cherished objects, that its daughter, though now absent from her home, was still valuable to the family. The dowry represented throughout a woman's tenure in her husband's home constant and tangible proof of identity and connection to her natal home. Labeling each piece of the dowry with a daughter's name and matching it with a receipt was one kind of practice that conspicuously put forward that identity. Her family kept the receipt as evidence of ownership.[85] A husband who tried to pawn parts of her dowry as his own possessions committed a gross breach of decorum, and this action constituted one of the few circumstances under which a woman's family, if it so chose, could initiate divorce.[86] If a husband chose to divorce his wife, which he could do at will, then she would have the necessary receipts to prove her original ownership of the articles and extract them from the household wealth of her husband's family. In divorce, the general meaning of *niwasen* overshadowed the narrow ritual denotation. The groom's family, having temporarily, as it turned out, been entrusted with the dowry, was now obligated to release it to its owner. Paying to protect and display nontransferable property as part of the marriage ritual signified that the orientation of a bride's identity and allegiance to her husband's household, so fundamental to *yome-tori* marriage and the values of the fertility model, was actually partial and conditional.

Families of brides could take advantage of this stage of the wedding ceremony to the extent that their purses allowed. As mentioned earlier in this chapter, the author of *The Greater Learning for Women* bemoans in his closing words the fact that too many parents spent far more money on their girls' material comforts in marriage than time on their moral development. "Parents today give their daughters so many articles of clothes, furniture, and such when sending them off into marriage. It is better instead that parents teach well every article of this primer because it is treasure that will serve their daughters throughout their lives."[87] The writer understood the possession and display of material goods to be inherently problematic in achieving full incorporation of a daughter into another household. We get a sense of the potential composition of such goods in the list Namura provides (see appendix A). Some of the articles in the list are simply items of daily use, such as nail clippers and razors; others are expensive furniture pieces. Some are functionally useful while also holding significant feminine identity, such as sewing and weaving utensils. There are several articles necessary for writing, and there are items for entertainment, such as games and musical instruments. Although the list is highly specific, it is an ideal suggestion. Namura's guide does not demand an all-or-nothing performance of the ritual steps it outlines. Instead, it offers commoner families an adaptable ideal based on their own choices and resources in employing the ritual giving and displaying of expensive articles to state their connection, support, and love for their daughters.

One item on Namura's list is of great import to the meaning of the ceremony as a celebratory transfer of a woman's fertility. If a bride's identity and loyalty to her husband's household were not fully transferable, as her dowry and its display suggested, then the control of her fertility most surely was. The prime symbol of this, a box of shells called *kaioke*, is at the top of Namura's list. In acknowledging its import he states, "The *kaioke* is to be conveyed with the greatest decorum among all items transferred."[88] It was typically a hexagonal container, beautifully lacquered and painted, and, as an aesthetic piece, was no doubt as stunning as any other example of finery and furniture a bride might take with her into the groom's house. Similar to his commentary on protective dolls, Takai redacts, in the 1847 text, the origins of the *kaioke*, which is absent in Namura's original.[89] This inclusion of the genesis of the shell box was not original to Takai's text, as guides in the eighteenth century similarly explicated the beginnings of the container and provided illustrations of the box and women amusing themselves with its contents.[90] These illustrations show the game of shell combining *(kaiawase)*, which was a type of parlor game popular during the Heian and Kamakura periods.[91] The two components of the game, clam shells *(kai)* and their storage box *(oke)*, matured into one of a range of cultural pursuits like poetry, tea ceremony, and horticulture that, once the province of the social elite in earlier periods, became the cultural property of bourgeois commoners in the Tokugawa.[92] Playing the shell-matching game and possessing a shell box were emphatic expressions of such cultural aesthetics in part due to the shells being crafted objects of beauty and cultural allusion.[93]

For example, written on one half-shell were the opening verses of a poem, with the closing verses inscribed on its matching half. The separated shells were then matched to complete the poem. Women placed them in the lacquered box one on top of the other so that they would fit snugly, filling the vessel. A young woman in possession of a shell box displayed a sense of refinement and cultural sophistication. Yet the game of shell matching was an activity that courtesans pursued as cultured women too, as Harunobu, in his 1770 illustrated series on courtesan life, shows in a sketch of two young apprentices matching and admiring shells in their spare time.[94]

The shells were not only signs of social refinement, but were also potent symbols of female fertility. Shells and their stylized container symbolized on many levels the transfer of a bride's fertility for use in the husband's household. With their rounded shapes and crevices, the similarity of shells to external female sex organs is obvious, and *kai* was a crude slang for female genitalia.[95] Further, *kai* not only means "shell," but is also a homophone meaning "to open" when applied to a different ideogram. The pun conveys the fact that shells, as housing living creatures, perfectly present fertility's duality in the *yometori* ceremony. Protecting that which lives inside them, shells can tightly close. They can also be opened, offering up their living morsels for the sustenance of others. A daughter's fertile body acted in the same manner. Having been nurtured at home and protected on the road during the bridal procession, her fertility came to the groom's household firmly shut away. Once under the control of her husband's family, her fertility could be opened through a combination of symbolic and physical acts that would ideally eventually offer up an heir and the promise of new life for the family.

Shells symbolize the full meaning of fertility as incorporating both chastity and sexual activity. In the fertility model, chastity ultimately meant obedience to the household and sexual activity for purposeful procreativity. The transfer of a shell box was not simply the transfer of fertility, but a dialogue between families. It was a statement by the bride's family that its daughter was chaste *and* fertile and that her fertility could be used for the continuation of the groom's family line. Acceptance of the vessel was a groom's family's acknowledgment of the bride's chastity and its possession of her chastity for fertility.[96] Each set of matching half-shells that a daughter so carefully placed atop one another to fill her vessel reflected the relational ideal of a wife being in harmonious union with her husband (*fūfu wagō*). The threat to household order that each bride carried with her through her own potential willfulness, viewed by the fertility model as demonic, was symbolically put away with each set of shells nestled in perfect alignment. The liminal images of goddess and demon that intersected and blurred the identity of the bride during her procession sharpened, with the transfer of the shell box, into a single, pointed metaphor of the bride as fertility goddess. Yet as part of her dowry, it was in her control. Should the marriage fracture, she could take her box and her fertility to her natal home. However, the product of that fertility—a child—would customarily remain in the husband's household as a rightful member.[97] While the container of shells represented a woman's possession of her own fertility, as surely as she possessed all other items she had brought with her into marriage, it also represented her lack of control over the production of her fertility.

With the transfer of the bride her fertility was now placed in the service of her husband's family. However, her fertility still required ritual charging along with that of her groom. Triggering her fertility was completed through sharing sips of sacred wine with her groom that altered her identity and sexuality to that of a wife, whose body was to serve a single household through its energy and sexuality. Long considered the ambrosia of the gods, this exchange of sake has carried symbolic significance throughout much of Japanese cultural history. Sharing sake as a root act of communion trickled through the patchwork of ceremonies and their configurations that made up Tokugawa marriage—*mukotori* and *yometori,* high class and low, ritually complex and simple—and even first meeting rites in the quarters. Accordingly, ritual manuals such as Namura's placed great emphasis on the act because it not only signaled unity between a bride and her new household, but also indicated her fertility as an active force in her new household.

Namura describes a rite where the bride and groom sit before two bottles of rice wine. Decorative folded paper depicting a female butterfly sits atop one bottle, and a male butterfly decorates the other. The symbolic meaning of butterflies as creatures of metamorphosis is clear in the context of a wedding, where a bride and groom undertake rites of transformation. There are other symbolic associations between butterflies and couples coming together in union. Sadatake comments that butterflies flutter out with the sun to sip the morning dew from the surface of leaves and grass, and then spend the rest of the day flitting here and there among one another. He likens this to the warmth and good feelings people have for each other when drinking sake together. When the bride and groom sip rice wine, it is hoped that, like the playful butterflies with their fill of dew, the couple will find similar happiness and harmony.[98]

Sadatake then offers another explanation for the use of paper butterflies. The decorative folds also represent silkworm moths. Such creatures not only create silk strands in their larval stage, but also, once matured into moths, become prolific reproducers. For Sadatake they are a perfect metaphor for celebrating the hope of an heir.[99]

Namura and Sadatake also give a different order to this drinking rite. Namura, who bases his order on the Ogasawara name in ritual, advises the bride to put the cup of sake to her lips before her groom does; Sadatake, as the head of the Ise House, states the opposite. Outside of this, the two concur on much symbolic activity centered around charging the bride's and groom's sexuality. The bride drinks from the male vessel and the groom from the female vessel. The paper butterflies, once removed from their bottle tops, are placed side by side, with the female facing up and the male facing down, which is suggestive of coital positioning. The bride and groom sip the wine from their cups three times. This triple sipping is then repeated two more times. In total, the bride and groom sip wine nine times in three rounds of drinking, with each round requiring three sips, which is the standard structure in modern Shinto nuptial ceremonies. The idea of sexual union that both ritualists advance through the wine exchange is controlled, purposeful, and productive. Through this character it advances the ultimate concern of the fertility model for establishing household harmony and the single household identity of bride and groom, and for sacralizing anticipated sexual activity and reproduction. Within this broad consensus, though, Sadatake raises a point of difference concerning which participant should partake of the wine first. He argues for the groom with an exegesis of the myth where Izanami speaks before Izanagi in a nuptial ceremony preceding their first attempt to procreate. As a result of this ritual oversight, their sexual union produced a leech child. Only when they corrected the order of speech could they properly procreate. For Sadatake any celebration *(iwai)* was an act of worshiping *kami,* and thus the sake rite was an offering in the worship of the primordial couple, Izanagi and Izanami.[100] Through this linkage, the exchange of wine between a bride and her groom implied an exchange of wine between them and the divine pair, thus connecting the ritually ideal present with the pristine past. The bride and groom's identification with Izanami and Izanagi sacralized both their marital and imminent sexual union and required them to identify with the same ritual precedent of the gods.

Namura's guide, as well as Osagawara House ritual, makes no mention of *kami* in the context of the bride and groom sharing ceremonial sake. Namura, as his myth of womanhood shows, was ready to create sacrality through the introduction of divine symbols, but the absence of such explicit symbolization in his description of marriage rites speaks to another perspective in viewing sacrality. In the absence of *kami,* the presence of people as ritual actors became the central focus. This centrality of human ritual actors is what the term "marriage before people" captures against the modern practice of "marriage before the *kami.*" It is not a difference between secular and sacred, but an acknowledgment that what expresses a group's sense of the sacred, its ultimate concern, need not be reduced to the presence of deities. In this sense, the varieties of Tokugawa marriage broadly concurred, through the root act of sharing wine, that what was ultimately important in the ritual moment was the act of joining a new collective with a new identity, a new set of responsibilities and obligations, and a commitment to making the concerns of that collective one's own.

After making this commitment, sealed with sake, the bride changed her clothes. This change is called *ironaoshi,* meaning "correcting colors." Although Namura specifies that these clothes should be part of the betrothal gift exchange between the families that occurred in the bride's home as part of the pre-processional rites, he does not specify any particular color.[101] Shades of red in the bride's outfit were typical.[102] A bride's change from her white ceremonial kimono to a conventional one flushed with red spoke not only to a celebratory event (white and red typically signify an auspicious occasion in Japanese culture), but also directly to her social and sexual transformation. She arrived at the groom's house as a potential, albeit inactive, force of social and sexual identity. She came dressed in white—colorless, as it were, and thus a neutral material by which her new family could "dye" her into the household's ways.[103] White is also a color associated with death. As we see in chapter 5, death was a potent, if controversial, part of marriage symbolism at the pre-processional stage, suggesting that the bride had symbolically died to one family in order to be born again into another family. She might have come with her shell box, which acted as a sign of both her untapped fertility and the promise of being a harmonious match for her new home. She came, in the symbolic end, as both a dead virgin daughter and a newborn fertile wife. The red-tinted kimono the bride now wore signaled her near-complete transformation. In *ironaoshi* a bride changed her colors from white to red, and by doing so signaled a change in her identity from that of dead virgin daughter to fertile wife, from a daughter blanched of one household's traditions to a wife dyed in those of another.

She was no longer the ceremonial outsider but symbolically an incorporated daughter-in-law ready to give her time and effort to the affairs of her new household. At this point, the bride offered small gifts to her parents-in-law and other members of the groom's family, thanking them for accepting her as a household member.[104] Although now symbolically incorporated into the household, consummation of the relationship still awaited.

Namura advises that consummation be preceded by another round of wine drinking later in the evening.[105] Additional consumption of wine outside the ceremony proper had its ritual detractors. Sadatake criticizes a second round of drinking, termed *toko sakazuki*. Literally meaning "bed sake," it took place in the room where the couple would sleep.[106] Sadatake acknowledges the practice with scorn. He states that it has no antiquity behind it but admits it has become quite fashionable in his time. He stresses that the Ise House never performed it and that "good people" do not take part in it.[107] Namura is silent about the setting of this second sake exchange and does not use the term *toko sakazuki,* but he clearly places this second round of drinking as ritually proper.

Namura also recommends that the shell box be placed in the couple's bedroom.[108] Already a powerful symbol of sexual transfer and wifely harmony in the home, the box and shells may also have served as a type of potent amulet to help secure physical intimacy for the couple and reproductive success for the bride. In addition, he advises that the couple lie down with their pillows and heads pointing north.[109] Along with this northward alignment, other bodily positions sometimes preceded sexual union. Some forms of rites called for the couple to lie in postures like that of the paper butterflies from the wine rite.[110] In other words, the bride would lie on her back while the groom lay on his stomach. The custom of lying with heads facing north was not unique to Namura' ritual guidance. It was likely a common wedding night tradition. Under any other, ordinary circumstance such a sleeping position would be considered indecent, a violation of taboo, as it resembles the placement of the dead, whose bodies were laid out with heads pointing north. A wedding night, however, was certainly not an ordinary circumstance. *A Dictionary of Popular Language (Rigen shūran),* which Ōta Zensai (1759–1829) compiled between 1797 and the time of his death, states, "Pointing pillows to the north is either for the dead or the wedding night. Outside of these situations, it is taboo *(imu).*"[111]

A wedding, as Ōta's dictionary makes clear, shared with death the same extraordinary quality, a time set apart from time. It was an occasion of identity transformation for the couple collectively, but far more profoundly for the bride, whose transformation took place in another household. From the exit rites performed at her home on the day of departure, where death symbolism was at times prominent, to the entrance rites at the groom's home, which sought to possess and promote her fertility, a bride experienced symbolic death as a daughter together with her rebirth as a fertile wife. Tying themes of death and fertility with identities of daughter and wife came to its final and full conclusion with actual sexual relations on the wedding night in a room laid out for the "dead." Symbolically, at least, death and daughter vanished in the night, leaving only the household's desire for fertility and a wife to rise with the morning sun.

First Meeting and Debut

In the quarters a courtesan's procession concluded with her arrival at the house of assignation where her client awaited her. Ranking women made such processions to meet their clients many times throughout their careers. Certain occasions, however, held great import. A first meeting with a new client was one such occasion; another was a teen's debut through the sponsorship of a senior sister courtesan. Because of the status it conveyed, sponsorship of a debutante was a responsibility a ranking courtesan attempted to take on at least once in her career.[112] Sponsorship was time consuming and expensive; a courtesan had to plan the celebration and find a sponsoring patron, ideally from her own customer base, to pay for much of the event. Successfully carrying off a debut party, however, earned her significant prestige, praise, and promotion in rank. Ideally, the debutante was an attendant of the sponsoring courtesan. In her debut she was officially promoted from the ranks of attendant girls to that of the high tier, along with the social prestige and economic burden of maintaining her own entourage.

First meeting and debut rituals were a reflection of those performed for marriage ceremonies. The debut ceremony in particular, which was a young woman's first public official meeting with a client in her new role as a first-class courtesan, was a rich prototype upon which all other future rites of first meeting were based. Although the time frame of a debut ceremony spanned a number of days, much of it was given over to the execution of a large *dōchū*. The new courtesan paraded down the boulevards of the quarter with her senior sponsor, her entourage, and support staff.[113] Procession days were often scheduled to coincide as much as possible with the festival calendar of the pleasure quarters. As *misemono*, parades of debuting courtesans contributed to the energy and celebration of fete days. Further, it was considered favorable for the debutante to be presented to the public by her bordello on auspicious days. Beyond the parading, the common stages in first meeting rites for both debuting and senior courtesans were 1) the display of her trousseau, 2) the meeting with the client, and 3) the consummation of relations.

Reception and display of a trousseau was central to a young woman's new rank. Just as the display of a bride's dowry was meant as a "debut" of a woman as wife, exhibiting a courtesan's trousseau was significant in her own debut to her community. The *Yoshiwara Compendium* lists the gifts that a debutante might receive (see appendix B).[114] Some of these items, particularly furniture, articles of daily use, games, and objects of cultural refinement, are similar to those listed in Namura's guide. Among the courtesan's trousseau's unique articles was bedding. For a debuting courtesan, the first gift of bedding from a client was essential for a successful coming-out celebration, and for a courtesan already working in the upper tiers, additional presents of futons and quilts from clients marked her for further promotion. Bedding functioned similarly to the ceremonial use of a bride's shell box in articulating a particular valuation of female sexuality and in serving as an aesthetic symbol of status and ritual object of transfer. Just as the matching shells intensified the significance of a bride's sexuality within the limits of fertility and obedience, bedding focused a courtesan's sexuality within the limits of carnal pleasure. Futons and quilts were the public signs of an exclusive relationship between her and her client. Only the client presenting the bedding had the right to its use when he was with her. The accumulation of futons and quilts, typically expensive and sometimes even finely embroidered, signaled status, as it not only indicated the number of clients one woman held but also the wealth of these men. Like a bride's shell box, bedding was also a ritual object of transfer. Upon receiving the bedding, the client's preferred teahouse of assignation would then place it on public display either outside the building or in the latticed parlor. The day for its transfer to the courtesan's room was often timed to fall on a major festival day, to take advantage of the energy and crowds such days provided.[115]

Kitagawa Utamaro portrays this rite in one of his illustrations depicting events in the Yoshiwara. In an open parlor a young female attendant blows on a horn to announce the viewing of the bedding (see fig. 5). The rite of displaying futons, pillows, and such is called *tsumi yagu* (piling up of bedding). To the girl's right is the pile of new bedding. Behind her are stacked boxes of noodles and cups of sake to be distributed to patrons of the teahouse who will come to view the bedding and offer their congratulations to the courtesan. On the other side of the parlor, a lower-ranking courtesan prepares small gifts to be handed out to customers in appreciation of their patronage. Another young attendant lifts a roll of cloth on which is printed a pattern called *hiyoku mon,* symbolizing the happy coupling of a man and woman. In the quarters the *hiyoku mon* pattern designated the courtesan and client an exclusive pair.[116]

The word *hiyoku* connotes two things joined as one, just like the wings of a bird adjoining its body; it is also part of the term *hiyoku zuka* —a "happy couple grave." In the pleasure quarters this referred to the double suicide of a woman and her "true" lover—the man who occupied her heart and existed outside the circle of her "play" lovers. Often, real lovers committed the desperate act of double suicide in the hopes that they could gain emotionally in the next world that which had been socially out of reach in this world—the status of husband and wife.[117]

FIGURE 5 A courtesan and her assistants prepare for the display of new bedding. From an original reproduction of Kitagawa Utamaro's illustration by Mitani Kazuma. Courtesy of Rippū Shobō, Tokyo.

Trapped between love and contractual labor, double suicide was sometimes the only way a woman and her lover could fulfill their love, especially if paying off her contract were a financial impossibility. In his double-suicide plays Chikamatsu uses the literary device of the lovers' journey *(michiyuki)* to portray the flight of lovers preceding their deaths. With the inevitability of self-annihilation upon them, the couple creates a new and ideal world from the one they are fleeing by sharing moving expressions of love and envisioning on their path the paradise of another world awaiting them upon death.[118]

Returning to the world of play and profit, a courtesan's "play" lovers gave not their hearts, but bedding instead. Like the shell box marking the transfer of a bride's sexuality to a single household, bedding indicated a client giving his sexuality, loyalty, and money to a single courtesan and her bordello. Still, the celebratory exhibition of a debuting courtesan's personal and professional accessories suggested a critique of pleasure's own values of polygamous play. This criticism is analogous to the way the public display of a bride's dowry questioned fertility's promotion of obedience to a single household. The juxtaposition of bedding, which was for the exclusive use of a single client, with other accouterments central to a courtesan's career, which would be used with all the men in her future, raised the question of a courtesan's relational identity. This question arose not in spite of pleasure's idealization of female sexuality but because of it. By whittling away a woman's identity to that of a wife, for example, fertility did not settle the issue of claims to a bride's identity. Instead, fertility's own rites, as expressed through the public display of the dowry, forced into the open the unsettled nature of a woman's identity as still that of a daughter whose material possessions belonged to her and her family. Similarly, pleasure's parody of marriage rites necessitated its own question of identity in its exhibition of debuting gifts. Was a woman the "bride" of one man or of all? The question became even more pointed in the career of a courtesan as she collected even more "exclusive" bedding.

As the fertility model awkwardly insisted that a woman be the wife of one and the daughter of none, the pleasure model's uneasy answer to the question of identity was that a courtesan be both the bride of one and the bride of all. The pleasure model depended on the language and imagery of marriage relations in order to express its vision of human association and sexual values that stood in stark and deliberate contrast to the ideals embraced by marriage and fertility. *The Greater Learning for*

Courtesans lists eighteen principles and precepts for women to follow in the quarters (see appendix B). The fourth principle effectively uses marriage language to reject fertility values while articulating a courtesan's one-and-all bridal identity. "A courtesan is different from a faithful wife *(teijo),* for she has many husbands and is praised by the number of pillows she piles up."[119]

Marriage, however necessary its use and however playful its application, was an odd ritual format for use in casting human relations among courtesans and clients. Marriage ideally represented that which the pleasure model feared most: sincere feelings between two people and an identity that they form as an exclusive pair. Such feelings tugged on the mask of *iki,* risked turning erotic play into true love, and threatened the flow of cash into a bordello as a woman focused her thoughts and energies wholly on one man rather than playfully on many. Love for one man was as hazardous to the pleasure model as a bride's unapologetic emotions for her natal family were to the fertility model. Bordellos played up the "game" of love and marriage in employing debut and first meeting rites, but they sometimes had to deal with the problem of real love. Love broke the rules of play and threatened its order with the possibility of profitable women fleeing with their men or committing double suicide, or of a client falling in love with a woman from another bordello and taking his heart—and his money—down the street.

Still, like bourgeois commoner society, the quarters looked to marriage ritual as a means not only for performing a particular action to produce a particular result, but also for sharing in the status the ceremony offered. Being self-conscious places of style and glamour, the quarters borrowed from *yometori* rites to bedeck themselves in the aesthetics and prestige of the ritual that was offered as culturally normative. Debuting, which was effectively the first and grandest of many future first-meeting ceremonies, was the most elaborate and emulative of *yometori* marriage ritual. Saikaku describes in detail a debut ceremony in the Shimabara.[120] His novel's protagonist, Yonosuke, heads with friends to the quarter to see the debut of the newest *tayū,* a young woman named Yoshizaki. Their visit follows their participation in the popular annual memorial service for the Buddhist saint Kūkai at his signature temple and noted sight, Tōji.[121] People, Yonosuke's group among them, throng the Shimabara's streets, splitting their time between sacred and sensual pursuits during one of Kyoto's major fete days. Saikaku's portrayal of the ceremony begins with the bordello owner and his wife taking their seats in the parlor of the teahouse as household representatives. The parlor is filled with food and gifts, the latter from Yoshizaki's male sponsor. Saikaku lists lacquered shelves, an incense box, paper and writing box, smoking kit, kimono, and, most important, "sleepwear and bedding piled up in small mountains."[122] These small mountains of futons, quilts, pillows, and nightwear constituted the bedding that would later be put on public display. In a debut it was common to exhibit the debutante's first mound of bedding in the ceremony itself. Amidst these piles of finery and food, the client takes his seat and waits for Yoshizaki's entrance following her procession. In debut and first-meeting rites the client sat in a subordinate seat as he waited for his "bride" to enter and take her place in the seat of honor, which would typically be in front of the parlor's ornamental alcove *(tokonoma)*. In Saikaku's description, two teenage assistants, each carrying a candle, lead the young *tayū* into the parlor. An entourage of girl attendants and teenage apprentices, from whose ranks the new *tayū* has risen, sits on either side of her as she takes her seat in the teahouse's place of honor.[123] Debut and first-meeting rites made a high-paying client a small presence in the ritual, often seating him close to the edge of the parlor, while the young woman sat near the parlor's alcove.[124] Utagawa Kuninao (1793–1854) illustrates this ceremonial placement in an 1831 work. In his portrayal, the woman, gilded with a thick, richly brocaded kimono and long hairpins typical of prostitutes in the latter half of the Tokugawa period, has entered the parlor to take her position near the alcove (fig. 6). Encased in her elaborate and imposing costume, she looms over all the attendees. Her client is a distant observer and is nearly irrelevant to the ritual, which centers less on the creation of a couple and more on the presence of the courtesan. To paraphrase *The Greater Learning for Courtesans,* a courtesan has many husbands, and thus in a ceremony of first meeting a client becomes merely another face in the crowd, another pillow on the mound.

Saikaku also captures the rite's complete focus on the courtesan. His passage concentrates exclusively on the pageantry of the *tayū* and her train of attendants; the male protagonists are diminished by the extravagance of the ceremony. Saikaku's description not only reveals the courtesan's high status, but also suggests hyperbolic imagery, like his more explicit identification of the *tayū* with a bodhisattva discussed earlier, of the first-class courtesan's sacred aura. Sitting in the middle of a line of attendants, in front of whom has been placed rich, offertory foods and splendid fabrics and gifts, the allusion Saikaku puts forward is that of a goddess icon set among lesser statuettes on a temple's altar filled with offerings of flowers and candles. Set apart and distinguished from her client, the courtesan alone, like a bodhisattva icon amidst its worshipers, is at the center of the ceremony.[125]

What becomes immediately apparent in Utagawa's and Saikaku's depictions is the contention that the ritual body, acting on the simple phrase "Stand up straight!" can embrace an entire universe of meaning.[126] The courtesan's dominant and honored position, in contrast to her client's diminished presence in the proceedings, signifies her relation with her own sexuality and her high status vis-à-vis her clients. In opposition to the sexuality of the bride—fertility transferred into the possession of her husband's family—the courtesan's sexuality of pleasure is her own possession. As an erotic laborer, she "rents" her sexuality out for the financial boon it brings her bordello, but she never transfers it to any man for sole ownership. A client's temporary access to her sexuality requires his monogamous commitment to her, which is also a commitment to share her with her other "husbands."

This ritual commitment of a man to a "polygamous" woman is sealed

FIGURE 6 A courtesan and client have their first meeting. From an original reproduction of Utagawa Kuninao's illustration by Mitani Kazuma. Courtesy of Rippū Shobō, Tokyo.

with the exchange of rice wine. In Saikaku's description of the debut of a *tayū*, the exchange of wine is completed in the same style as marriage: she and her sponsor sip three cups of sake three times.[127] Non-debut first-meeting rites were simpler, but they typically stressed, like the humblest wedding, the sharing of wine.[128] By sharing a sip of wine a woman and her client signified not the activation of her sexuality as fertility, but rather the use of her sexuality as pleasure for him as her latest *najimi* (a courtesan's monogamous partner). Marking his *najimi* status with the drinking rite, the man superficially became analogous to the bride of marriage ceremonies. Like the bride, the burden of faithfulness was his alone. In the pleasure model, a *najimi* who fell for another bordello's courtesan was the definition of infidelity. Such a relationship spoke of the emotions of the heart and stopped the client's flow of money into the bordello's coffers and into the purse of his courtesan, to whom he vowed loyalty. The world of pleasure despised the show of nonplayful emotions because it invariably led to the loss of money. The master, the courtesan, and her young entourage were all tied financially to each client, and the man's loyalty equaled financial gain as much as his adultery equaled loss. A client behaving in such a fashion could bring upon himself humiliating punishment and coerced repentance. A courtesan's girl attendants might capture him on the street and haul him back to the bordello for an accounting of his adulterous actions by the bordello master.[129] Play, especially when its rules were broken, was not all fun and games.

With the exchange of wine accomplished, marking the playful uniting of a courtesan and client, Saikaku remarks that the debut rite takes on an air of *ironaoshi (ironaoshi o fuzei arite)*.[130] As described earlier, *ironaoshi* signaled a crossover point for the bride where she changed her white kimono for one tinged with color. The mood of the wedding rite changed from formal action to less prescribed behavior as the focus of the day eventually narrowed to the confines of the couple alone together in their sleeping quarters. Although a courtesan did not change her kimono during the ceremony, the gathering in the parlor took on a festive air after the drinking of sake. During this reception party the new *najimi* would toss his money for the courtesan's attendants and staff to catch and stuff in their pockets. The payment for the staff's work in preparing for the ritual and bringing it to fruition is called *niwasen*.[131] This term may have been taken directly from the vocabulary of weddings where, as explained earlier, the husband's family paid bridal representatives for transporting her luggage and dowry. What Saikaku identifies with his remark concerning *ironaoshi* is not a change of clothes, but a change in style, setting, and relationship that a wedding's *ironaoshi* stage similarly marked. It is a change of tone from formality to frivolity, a change, at some point in the night, of venue from parlor to courtesan's room, and a change of relation from simply woman and man to ranking courtesan and *najimi*.

Consummation followed debut. A sponsor received what he had generously paid for and had been anticipating in the days leading up to the final rite. First meeting did not always end with consummation. Once a young woman firmly secured her position as a top courtesan, she took on a certain official charisma and could command more authority over her erotic labor, although it was always subordinate to the monetary decisions of the bordello owner holding her contract. Outside of an owner's intervention, she might withhold sex from a new client until as late as the third meeting. A comic haiku of the period makes this point, while also leaving no doubt that play defined the relationship. "The third meeting is all about pretending to fall in love" *(Sankaime yotsubodo horeta mane o suru).*[132] Making clients wait until the third visit before they could pretend to love as they finally made love possessed the economic logic of easy profiteering. Initial meetings between a courtesan and each of her *najimi* partners entailed for the client significant entertainment expenses that he paid directly to the teahouse and bordello incidental of any sexual activity. In this sense, even the absence of consummation could signal the quarters' drive for good times and profits.

In the drive of the household and quarter to incorporate women into positions of wife and courtesan—positions where their skills and sexuality were institutionally critical—each reached for the same culturally normative and celebratory ritual structure that *yometori* provided because each had something big to celebrate with respect to its values. In the household a woman and man coming together signaled a new member joining the household and committing her loyalty, energy, and fertility to advance the household's daily tasks of maintenance and the future hopes of generational succession. In a quarter a woman and man—one man among many—coming together signaled a new source of revenue for her and her bordello. Yet the celebratory structure of marriage and first meeting, as well as the metaphors of bride and courtesan, quietly murmured with ambivalence as to how fully these rites could incorporate women and their identities, let alone their hearts and minds, in the marriage household and bordello. Marriage signified being dyed in the ways of a new household and a productive fertility, but it also signified the continuing ties with natal family and the anxiety of household disharmony. First meeting signified securing institutional rank and the expert display of a profitable playfulness with the emotion of love, but it also signified, by the broad use of marriage ritual, that such play could go too far and become real and unprofitable. With the consummation of each relationship the celebration concluded. What remained in the long days ahead was to see how well a woman measured up to the celebration of her institution's values.

FOUR

PLACEMENT

RITES OF MARRIAGE and debut/first meeting shared another characteristic beyond broad ritual patterning: culmination through the same act.
Each value model, however, interpreted the sex act with a different
understanding of its ideal purpose and the quality of relationship it signified. Along with the personal satisfaction that a wife and her husband
may have gained from it, which strengthened their bonds, household
sexual activity was also valued for its productive potential, and it signified through the use of her body a woman's obedience to the need of
generational continuity. The quarters valued sex for the profits it secured
from clients seeking sensual pleasures that courtesans stimulated skillfully
as part of their professional labor. Nevertheless, in households and bordellos sexual activity could lead to—regardless of valuations applied to
it and attempts to interrupt and control it—conception and pregnancy.
Despite their differences in values, the two models' common need for
female sexuality could lead to the same female condition: a belly swollen
with child.

In the face of this common biology and in spite of disparate values,
it is impossible to place pregnancy in the home and in the quarter in tidy
opposition within the context of the antithetical practices of birth and
abortion/infanticide. Fertility and pleasure models diverged on the ideal
of sexual purpose—to have a baby or to have an enjoyable time—but
acts of birth and child rearing, of abortion and infanticide cannot be
placed neatly on opposite sides of the divide. Fertility values promoted
sexuality as serving procreative needs, but households practiced infanticide; pleasure values cheered on sexuality as nonreproductive play, but
courtesans sometimes gave birth despite the preference to avoid pregnan-

cies completely. Occurring from the needs of fertility and the consequences of pleasure, pregnancy was a phenomenon of significant ambivalence in terms of such idealized values. As a uniquely female experience, pregnancy transcended both models and their values. Symbols and practices linked it to broad cultural notions of both gender and religion that escaped each model's narrow, idealized definitions of women. Although a woman's pregnancy *took place* within a specific institution, pregnancy also *placed* her within an experience free of strictly bound, highly disparate institutional values and roles. In other words, the symbols and rituals that constructed pregnancy as a meaning-filled phenomenon placed a woman within wider cultural conceptions and practices of being female, constituting a category of experience that in practice lay beyond the idealized rhetorical grasp of fertility and pleasure.

To enlarge upon this view, I first argue that pregnancy was a socially ambivalent phenomenon that evaded institutional containment and singular assumptions of purpose and outcome. Pregnancy took place in a home in need of an heir or in a bordello with rarely any need for a child; it could be terminated in either home or bordello through birth or abortion, through rearing, adoption, or infanticide. Second, I examine a particular and popular form of symbolization that mediated pregnancy's meaning through several fields of ambivalence, such as birth and death, divine and human, and the mother's body and the fetal body. Third, following upon the symbolic link between the bodies of mother and fetus, I turn to a variety of prenatal and birth practices that pregnant women and their caretakers employed as the bodies of mother and fetus together faced the dangers inherent in the pregnancy experience.

Ambivalence of Pregnancy

Infanticide as one response to birth was a salient expression of the multiple paths pregnancy could take, the conflicting considerations it entailed, and thus the ambivalence it possessed. Infanticide has also attracted scholarly attention for several years. Much of this attention has focused on the question of the practice's larger effects on the flattening of population growth from the early 1700s until the mid-1800s.[1] Still, focus on the choice of infanticide as a form of "deliberate control" over fertility has overshadowed influential factors of "unconscious control," which included extended breastfeeding of one child at a time and spousal separation due to employment opportunities in urban areas.[2] Such opportunities also attracted many young, single women to the labor market, and this occupational decision could thus shorten their fertile years to those remaining only after completion of their work contracts.[3] Women working into their late twenties under erotic labor contracts epitomized this trend. It is fair to say that infanticide was likely one of several, rather than the decisive, factor affecting population stagnation during the latter half of the period. Still, it was a salient practice and, along with abortion and the dangers that went with it, was as much a part of the experience of pregnancy as childbirth itself.

A variety of historical sources shed light on this dark underside of pregnancy. In the 1850s Utagawa Kunisada (1786–1864) created a graphic depiction of pregnancy diagnosis and abortion in the Yoshiwara (fig. 7). This is part of a set of illustrations portraying life behind the glittering facade of pleasure called *Day and Night in the Quarter (Kuruwa no akekure)*. In figure 7, the courtesan's manager and the bordello owner's wife prepare to carry out an abortion, which was the typical response to pregnancy in the quarters. One woman readies an abortifacient that she will apply directly into the courtesan's uterus using an insertional device similar to long chopsticks, while the other looks upon the pregnant woman's prone body—tied and gagged in anticipation of pain she will experi-

FIGURE 7 A bordello wife and manager prepare to abort a courtesan's pregnancy. From an original reproduction of Utagawa Kunisada's illustration by Mitani Kazuma. Courtesy of Rippū Shobō, Tokyo.

ence. Some abortionists orally administered abortifacients while others, as in Utagawa's depiction, inserted the mixture directly into the womb. Insertional instruments ranged from chopsticks to barley stalks.[4] A common element in most compounds was mercury, and the remaining elements were made up mainly of plant materials such as roots, leaves, and seeds.[5] *A Library of Obstetrics from the Chūjō School (Chūjōryū sanka zenshū)* describes procedures and pharmaceuticals for carrying out an abortion.[6] One such description of an abortifacient and application is similar to Utagawa's visual record; it calls for a powdered compound containing 50 percent betel nut combined with boiled mint leaves and a small amount of mercury. A technician dips a penetrating instrument into the concoction and then inserts it into the woman's uterus, piercing and killing the fetus to induce bodily breakdown.[7]

Abortion was risky to a woman's life due to postoperative infection, physical trauma, and the introduction of harmful elements into the body, most notably mercury. Infanticide, outside of the inherent dangers of giving birth, was a safer option. In partial response to concerns of population stagnation in the latter half of the period, however, many domains stepped up rhetoric and policies to make it also an illegal option.[8] Infanticide was often conducted immediately after birth through strangulation or suffocation. The question of the child's fate, "to be kept or 'sent back'" *(oku ka, kaesu ka),* was a standard query that a midwife posed after successfully accomplishing delivery. The midwife typically did not ask the mother, unless she was the senior voice in the household, but instead directed the question to the mother-in-law or the household's male head.[9] As the presence of the manager and wife in Utagawa's illustration indicates, the institutional judgment to terminate life typically fell outside the authority and emotions of the pregnant woman if she was not among her institution's primary decision makers.

The anti-infanticide text *Poems Admonishing Child Abandonment (Sutego kyōkai no uta)* graphically portrays this. In an illustration, a midwife strangles a newborn while in another room a husband and young son attend to the exhausted mother, whose tired smile suggests she is unaware of her baby's fate. This captures the dual role of the midwife. She helped bring the child into the world, and she was often responsible for taking the child out of the world. The text's author, Giten, was abbot of Tokuōji in Izumo. His publication belongs to a latter-period genre of voluminous writings exhorting women and their families not to practice abandonment, abortion, and infanticide.[10] Among his admonishments is a warning to families not to kill infant girls lest they risk experiencing the fate of karmic retribution: never securing daughters-in-law for their sons, whom they spared.[11]

Fear of karma or not, the institutional needs of the household or bordello—needs that its leadership determined—decided life or death in the matter of pregnancy. In this way, household and quarter varied little in qualitative practice despite being worlds apart in their spatial segregation and sexual values. Both sought to regulate the quality of collective life by reducing, when necessary, the quantity of individual lives that were totally dependent on the their active working women, both wives and courtesans—potential mothers all.

Just as abortion/infanticide as *practice* rather than as *valuation* proved similar in households and pleasure quarters, childbirth acted in parallel fashion. Strands of evidence suggest that while childbirth was certainly not the norm in the quarters, it was not so anomalous as to defy institutional appropriation. One of the most revered inherited names among Yoshiwara courtesans was "Takao," of whom there were eleven belonging to the Miura House, one of the most prominent bordellos in the quarter.[12] Often, a unique phrase or term adjoined the name to signify something biographically definitive—be it factual or legendary—about each woman and her historical place in the lineage. Anecdotes tied to these sobriquets were created and became part of the lore of the courtesan long after her passing. Takao I, a seventeenth-century courtesan, possessed several names. One was "Komochi Takao," meaning "Takao with child." Among many of the tales and sketches tied to her was the spectacle of her *dōchū,* which included a wet nurse and the child.[13] In the eighteenth century, Takao VI also gained the title Komochi Takao, raising her child in the parlor of the bordello before finally marrying some years later.[14] As an inherited name, *komochi* suggests that pregnancy and childbirth could at times be incorporated into the identity of a courtesan. Perhaps this sobriquet even carried some eroticism, as it intimated a crossing of borders, an awkward and enticing embodiment of courtesan and mother in one woman.

The institutional attitude toward childbirth, though, was one not of eroticism but of criticism. Pregnancy marred the veneer of glamour and slowed the operation of sexual services by removing a woman from her contractual labor. Another illustration from *Day and Night in the Quarter* strikingly reveals this attitude. Utagawa depicts a manager beating one of her charges, whose swollen belly shows the reason for the abuse. Discipline of courtesans represented the period's acceptance of physical punishment for mistakes made by those who labored at the low end of a rigid hierarchy. Utagawa's illustrated violence also captures why some who thought that managers were cruel hoped the women were destined for a painful purgatory of fire in a burning cart. Still, the harshness of the punishment indicates that a courtesan's pregnancy was viewed as an occupational mistake entailing unacceptable costs: the house owner's profits, the manager's reputation, and the courtesan's own health, if she were beaten or forced to have an abortion. To avoid such costly mistakes courtesans used various forms of birth control. Some used folded paper *(tsumegami)* as a pessary.[15] Others applied a moxa cautery below the navel, as moxa burning, often used to help ease pain, was also believed to possess preventive qualities, thus women in the quarters burned it on the belly as a form of contraception. In another one of his sketches from *Day and Night in the Quarter,* Utagawa depicts a woman receiving a moxa application to ward off pregnancy and other potential hazards. Moxa burning was considered effective for an entire year if applied for two days on the second day of the second month.[16]

In spite of the punishment and unreliable contraceptives, pregnancy that culminated in childbirth had some limited acceptance and institutionalization in the quarters. All mistakes were not erased; costs were sometimes accepted. Several *senryū* highlight the institutional, if reluctant, recognition of women bringing their pregnancies to term. "There's nothing else to do except raise [the baby] at Minowa" *(Naki ni shimo arazu Minowa de sodatesase).*[17] Another states, "When [a courtesan's] breasts become dark it is time to coop her up in Minowa" *(Chichi ga kuroku natte Minowa e chikkyo sase).*[18] Minowa was the area where the Yoshiwara and institutions closely tied to it were located. One institution was an isolation residence where courtesans recovered from illness and aborted pregnancies and also gave birth.[19] Torii Kiyomine (1787–1868), in an 1812 work, idyllically portrays a courtesan breastfeeding her new arrival in Minowa (fig. 8). A ranking woman's child attendants customarily accompanied her to Minowa, suggesting that the institution was meant primarily for courtesans whose labor was highly valued for its ability to enrich their bordellos.[20] The crucial factor for the decision makers in a bordello, in deciding whether to force a courtesan to have an abortion (as Utagawa depicts) or to house her in Minowa (as Torii shows), was the direction in which her status and money-making potential tipped the scales of risk and profit.

Once born, a courtesan's infant could be given in adoption. The humor book *A Single Harpoon (Ichi no mori)* describes an adoption transfer between a birth-mother courtesan and a townsman's childless wife.

The passage also uses the situation to poke fun both at the obsession with trends that many courtesans possessed as part of their cultivation of *iki* and at their supposed naïveté of the "real" world outside the quarters. Upon seeing the baby, the townsman's wife decides immediately to adopt and tells the young courtesan how happy the little one will make her. Pleased at the wife's contentment, the birth mother nevertheless expresses apologetic frustration at the tiny infant's ruddy complexion, as the reddish hue does not even come close to the current color of the day—tea green.[21] Although adoption was the likely fate of any child born in a quarter, not all children were considered out of place in pleasure's values. Rather than depending entirely on buying young girls from poor families, bordellos may have occasionally made professional business decisions to take girls born in the quarters and train them as child attendants and future courtesans.[22] As one *senryū* states, "Child attendants are divided among bloodlines [of fathers] that no one knows" *(Hito koso shiranu chi o waketa kamuro nari)*.[23] Another makes a similar point: "There's no other possibility except to raise [her] as a child attendant" *(Naki ni shimo arazu kamuro ni tsukaete sodate)*.[24] Boys, too, might be kept rather than given away, in order to serve the quarters in various capacities such as male entertainers *(otoko geisha)*.[25]

FIGURE 8 A courtesan tends to her baby at Minowa. From an original reproduction of Torii Kiyomine's illustration by Mitani Kazuma. Courtesy of Rippū Shobō, Tokyo.

Practices of childbirth/childrearing and abortion/infanticide existed in both the household and bordello to serve each institution's goal of improving its economic existence and maintaining its long-term welfare. Depending on circumstances and needs, the presence or absence of children could serve that goal. This is not to say that the household and bordello were indifferent to pregnancy. Clearly pregnancy mattered as either a hoped-for (household) or problematic (household and bordello) event that forced institutional decision makers to address it. Still, as a uniquely female experience, pregnancy itself and the institutional responses to it did not produce a sharply qualitative difference of practice, nor did it become definitive of value distinctions between fertility and pleasure. The underlying rhetoric of each model—"a wife does not serve two husbands" and "a courtesan has many husbands"—emphasized the structure of institutional human relationships between a woman and her man (or men) as the locus of values. The production and nonproduction of children, while idealized respectively in fertility and pleasure models, was both derivative of and subsumed under these relationships. The experience of being pregnant derived not from being a social role, but from being a woman in a sexual relationship. Pregnancy placed both young wives and courtesans, women of approximately the same age, in the same situation of having to face bodily dangers and even death and of having to give birth, abort, or accept the institutional decisions of infanticide and adoption. Further pregnancy placed women within a host of assumptions about how to understand their bodies so as to come out of the experience, for their own sake and that of the institutions depending on them, alive and healthy.

Many such factors concerning how best to understand the experience of pregnancy are at work in Namura's mind. As a physician of the late seventeenth century, he highlighted as most significant the inherent health of a woman and how well she maintained it in terms of conscientious behavior. These issues, which I examine in the last section of this chapter, form the bulk of Namura's pregnancy chapter. He also notes in his work, however, that a divine dimension is at play that defies full comprehension by human reason and, in the end, demands an attitude of acceptance and faith. He states that simple observation of social reality proves that people on the lowest rungs of society (iyashiki mono) are able to have many children while elite families are often beset with troubles in reproducing heirs and, in the end, resort to using concubines. This situation is not related to the workings of karma (shukuen naki koto).[26] If karma were a factor, Namura seems to imply, then easy reproduction as a sign of karmic blessing would be reversed. Karmic logic should favor those of high rather than low status so that spiritual principle and social reality coincide. To accept this paradox, he alludes to Buddhist literature and the mood of *mappō* (the last age of Buddhist law) by employing the phrase *masse jokuran* (the last age in a state of defilement) to describe the confused spiritual environment and its effects on pregnancy. He pushes this allusion and creates parallels between the buddhas and social elites and between hungry ghosts (denizens of one of Buddhism's suffering realms) and the masses of poor. In this age of defilement the seeds of the buddhas *(hotoke no tane)* have disappeared while the seeds of hungry ghosts *(gaki no tane)* have become ever numerous. In this upside-down world, those living in deprivation—"this world's hungry ghost hell" *(kono yo no jigoku gaki)*—easily have many children, while society's best —"this world's paradise" *(kono yo no gokuraku)*—remain childless.[27]

Namura's analysis of this paradox suggests that *mappō* thought, so intensely identified with the medieval ethos, was still in popular operation, at least through allusion and metaphor, during the first half of the Tokugawa—a time of economic expansion and social order. His reliance on the mood of *mappō* to make sense of contemporary reality echoes Hubbard's insistence, sounded in chapter 1, that doctrine matters in understanding the multifarious nature of religion in Japanese history. Hubbard's point about the power of doctrine to resonate deeply in times of plenty as well as in times of deprivation helps us gain some sense of Namura's description of a world turned on its karmic head. The doctor exhorts women lucky enough to become pregnant in this environment of spiritual deprivation to offer thanks to the buddhas and *kami*. This thankfulness in turn, he adds, leads to easy birth and a wise child.[28]

In the end, though, Namura was a physician, a professional dedicated to caring for the human body through an expertise in knowledge and practice. Accordingly, he did not rest his advice concerning pregnancy on faith alone. With a specialist's confidence he moved to assert his expertise within the central medical paradigm of his age. This paradigm understood the human body not as an isolated bundle of biological logic—a logic that placed the body on the path of either health or harm based on its own internal destiny—but rather as a responsive field of interrelations made up of beings and their behavior. Into this paradigm Namura pushed his understanding of pregnancy as an experience of interrelated bodies and behavioral expectations, centering around the initiative of the mother and resonating inward and outward between her body, her unborn child, and a divine dimension. This relationship was operative on levels of symbolization and practice.

Symbolization of Pregnancy

Pregnancy encompassed conflicting possibilities of threat and promise to persons and institutions. It signaled the possibility of a child's death as much as life, of institutional decline as much as prosperity, of a woman's lapse into illness or worse as much as her healthy recovery. Further, it brought to the forefront forms of symbolization that exemplified the depth of its ambivalence, most emphatically in its embrace of life and death. A simple example is *chishigo,* which was a systematic, determinative notion of time meant to roughly gauge, based on a person's birth, the length of her life. Literally meaning "knowing the time of death," *chishigo* indicated the term of one's life through divination based on the calendar and its ordering of days both through a cycle of ordinal numbers and a sexagenary cycle. Namura provides an example of *chishigo*.[29] It cautions that giving birth on days with certain matches between both cycles risks resulting in the child's early death. For example, giving birth on a designated day of the rat whose ordinal number also contains a one, two, nine, or zero indicates the child may die early in life.

The assumption suggested in *chishigo* that the shadow of death and the light of life claim equal portions of pregnancy's meaning appears in more exemplary ways. One documented traditional element of pregnancy is the understanding that fetuses and young children are not fully human. It is only until the completion of rites of passage—typically marking the ages of three, five, and seven years and known as *shichi-go-san*—that the child breaks its connection to the divine realm and enters the human community as a full partner.[30] Being between gods and humans places fetuses and young children in a state of liminality from where they move either forward toward the human realm or backward toward the land of *kami* and buddhas. Forward movement means birth and acceptance of the child into this world. Reverse movement is the result of a miscarriage, abortive techniques, infanticide, or early death by natural causes or accident that pulls the child back into the other world to wait for another birth opportunity.[31]

A Record of Treasures for Women offers a visual view of fetal life suggesting this kind of liminality—and much more. Inside the mother's body, the child takes form in an environment—the womb—that is not simply a passageway from divine to human, but a field of activity locating the ultimate unity of both divine and human dimensions. From this view of the womb pregnancy exhibits not only the oft-noted *diachronic move* from divine to human, but also a *synchronic moment* of unified divine and human identity in the fetal body. The text depicts this human-divine status of fetal development through ten illustrations juxtaposing Buddhist divinities and the fetus over ten months of in-utero development. These illustrations were reprinted (with minor alterations, such as addition of a full head of hair to the fetus) with Namura's text several times throughout the period, including Takai's 1847 edition (figs. 9 and 10). This type of pictorial genre is called "depictions of ten months in the womb" *(tainai totsuki no zu)*. Some versions are filled with divinities while others have no sacred referents at all. Throughout the Tokugawa period all kinds of ten-month pictures were produced for any number of purposes: religious preaching, safe birth devotionalism, medical views of corporeal fetal development, and even criticism of Buddhism. In this way the genre became a canvas upon which different groups at different points in the period drew their particular concerns of religion, medicine, and social criticism. Indeed, Namura's pregnancy chapter, and in particular its ten-month illustrations, subsumed all of these concerns throughout the middle and late Tokugawa period. This is especially apparent when we compare the original 1692 guide with Takai's redacted version. Takai inserts an updated version of the original illustrations along with a competing set of pictures (not shown here) stripped of divinities. I return to the 1847 text later in this section, but now the older pictures need examination.

NAMURA'S 1692 TEXT

In Namura's 1692 version, the fetus' first four months of existence are represented by various ritual paraphernalia. In the fifth month the fetus finally takes human form and remains largely unchanged throughout the remaining months. In the tenth month the body turns upside down to descend from the womb. Above each monthly depiction is a picture of a corresponding Buddhist divinity. The deities form the first ten of thirteen figures that make up the esoteric pantheon. Represented in the womb illustrations from the first month to the tenth are Fudō Myōō, Shaka, Monju, Fugen, Jizō, Miroku, Yakushi, Kannon, Seishi, and Amida. As part of a larger pantheon of thirteen Buddhist deities *(jūsan*

FIGURE 9 Depiction of the first five months of fetal formation and guardian buddhas. From the 1847 edition of *A Record of Treasures for Women*. Courtesy of Ōzorasha, Tokyo.

FIGURE 10 Depiction of the latter five months of fetal formation and guardian buddhas. From the 1847 edition of *A Record of Treasures for Women*. Courtesy of Ōzorasha, Tokyo.

butsu), the group has symbolically centered on death and memorial rites for hundreds of years.[32] Despite this connection between Buddhism and funerary culture, which by Namura's time had blossomed ritually and institutionally, he makes no note of esoteric Buddhism, death, or enlightenment. His use of symbols, which in monastic Buddhism signified death and esoteric visions of ultimate reality, to understand pregnancy and phenomenal life is testament to the malleability of Buddhist symbolism and the popular expansion it had achieved by his time. Further, his illustrations are not unique. *A Record of Treasures for Women* represents a late and popular derivation of the genre. Similar illustrations, for example, were published a half century or more earlier through a story called *The Original Ground of Kumano (Kumano no gohonji),* which was one version of a popular medieval tale.[33] As these visual precedents indicate, the symbolic overlap of death / life and ultimate/phenomenal connects Namura's mid-Tokugawa view of pregnancy to an earlier history of Buddhist thought concerning fetal status and buddhahood. Although Namura leaves this history unarticulated, as a compiler he was aware of symbols coming from this religious current that were then available for him to use. Much of this current flowed from earlier texts like versions of the Kumano tale and an important syncretic Buddhist writing, *Unity of the Three Wisdoms (Sanken itchi sho).*[34] This work, which I discuss below, offers an evocative description of fetal buddhahood. It likely influenced the later Kumano story, which in turn acted as a bridge for these symbols to cross into Tokugawa lifestyle guides. Namura's illustrations and redactions represent a popular diffusion of this religious history into the wider stream of Tokugawa culture.

Two key symbolic characteristics stand out from the illustrations. First, by incorporating symbols of death memorial, pregnancy acts as the symbolic inverse of death. Second, in identifying fetal status with deities and ritual items, the text's symbolization of pregnancy reveals two tendencies of reality construction in Japanese religious history that had reached full maturity by Namura's time: 1) to bring order to the jumbled sacred universe by creating links between the plethora of deities and between deities and human-created spaces and objects, and 2) to valorize phenomenal existence through radical identity with ultimate existence.

As for the first characteristic, the ten divinities of fetal gestation represent the same buddhas in death symbolism, where they are known as the ten kings *(jū ō).* Originally the kings came from China as rulers of an underworld where the souls of the dead received judgment from each of ten presiding officials. This underworld—a purgatorial system that mirrored the worldly bureaucracy of imperial China—developed around the seventh century but was not described in textual detail until the ninth-century publication of a text called *Scripture on the Ten Kings (Shi wang jing)*. Sometime between 1000 and 1300 in Japan a text influenced by *Scripture on the Ten Kings* was written titled *The Scripture on Jizō and the Ten Kings (Jizō jū ō kyō)*. A novel feature of this text is its pairing of the ten Chinese kings with the ten esoteric Buddhist divinities.[35] This linkage of kings and buddhas derived from the kind of reality construction I mentioned earlier that seeks to create an ordered symbolic universe by establishing connections among a tumble of unrelated deities, places, and things. The most explicit example of this is *honji suijaku,* which is a combinatory paradigm typically linking particular buddhas as numinous reality *(honji)* with *kami* as the manifest traces of that reality *(suijaku),* which in turn was the "linchpin" of the cultic, ritual, and symbolic order of much of Japanese religion until the Meiji period.[36] By the fourteenth century the ten kings, in their Buddhist transformation, plus the additional three deities completing the pantheon of thirteen buddhas, were becoming an integral part of Japan's developing funerary and memorial culture as symbols of the periodic thirteen services for the dead *(jūsan kaiki)*.[37]

As the illustrations in Namura's text indicate, the buddhas representing the passage into death also mirror the passage into life. As with particular junctures in death memorial, each divinity corresponds with the fetus at a particular time during gestation.[38] Fudō guides the dead in the first seven days after death; he also presides over the first month of gestation. Likewise, Amida establishes identity with the soul of the dead in the third year of memorial as well as with the fetus during its last moments in the womb. Although the symbolization of birth and death mirrored one another, a caveat is necessary when considering the illustrations and the pairing of birth and death. Texts and guides aimed at women and their concerns disseminated a variety of similar fetus-Buddhist divinity illustrations, particularly in the first half of the Tokugawa, before latter-period developments in obstetrics and criticism of Buddhism emerged in full to alter the genre. However, the correspondence of deities with gestation never matched the cultural hold of the correspondence of deities with death memorial.[39] Part of the reason for this disparity is that death ritual became the operative realm of a professional priesthood in the Tokugawa period. Although periodic memorial rites, the corresponding thirteen buddhas, and the use of memorial tablets began to achieve popularity around the fourteenth century, death and ancestor ritual was still largely a concern and practice of families. In 1640 the government required all families to register with a Buddhist temple. This in turn moved the authority of death ritual out of the house and into the temple.[40] Unlike death rites, rituals of pregnancy and birth never came under the control of temple authority; they remained bound to the home throughout the Tokugawa. It was not until the late nineteenth century that Shinto gained ritual relevancy by remapping birth and other kinds of celebrations such as marriage, which family and village authority had traditionally managed, to fall within its institutional borders. Still, practices of birth, if not pregnancy, mirrored death to some extent. Most obvious are those attentive to the corporeal bodies of newborns and corpses meant to stabilize each body's new ontological status. Examples of this are washing the newborn *(ubuyu)* and washing the corpse *(yukan)*, cutting an infant's hair *(ubugezori)* and tonsuring the dead *(teihatsu)*, dressing a newborn in its first clothes *(ubugi)* and dressing the corpse *(shinishō-zoku)*.[41]

The second symbolic characteristic of the illustrations juxtaposing the bodies of buddhas and fetus reflects onto the womb a complex background of two paradigmatic religious inclinations. One, to which I have already referred—namely the variety of ordering patterns by means of linking deities and other symbols—may be broadly considered under the rubric of *honji suijaku*. The other is *hongaku shisō* (original enlightenment thought), which is a medieval trend in Buddhism that put forward a new way of imagining the status and meaning of phenomenal life. The history of these processes of classification and imagining is too complex and significant in its own right to be reduced to the purpose of this study.[42] However, in the following paragraphs I tease out some of their strands from the evocative depiction of life in the womb that is described in *Unity of the Three Wisdoms*.

Unity of the Three Wisdoms is not the first Japanese description of life in the womb. A very early depiction is found in *Essentials of Medicine (Ishinhō)*, which was published in 984 and is one of Japan's oldest medical manuscripts.[43] Tanba Yasuyori (912–995) compiled its thirty volumes from Chinese and Korean texts, and, accordingly, continental interpretative concepts become key in correlating monthly fetal gestation with development of gross anatomy and life essence. One such concept is the five operative elements *(gogyō)*. Just as these elements interact with all patterns of change and difference in the universe, so do they act with the ten-month pattern of fetal growth. Other key conceptions include the five viscera *(gozō)*, the six internal organs *(roppu)*, and the notion of life force *(ki)*. *Unity of the Three Wisdoms* explains the monthly formation of fetal physicality somewhat similarly to interpretations of gross bodily development in *Essentials of Medicine*. The former also employs concepts of the five operative elements and yin/yang to tie intercourse and conception to the patterned processes of the universe. As a product of a later time, however, a time when the spread and development of Buddhism in the medieval period had taken deep root and swelled the boundaries of Japan's symbolic universe, *Unity of the Three Wisdoms* reinterpreted the womb primarily through esoteric symbols and the paradigms of the combinatory *honji suijaku* and original enlightenment thought.[44] By bearing hard toward esoteric symbolism and Buddhist paradigms of reality construction, it redefines the womb as a "pre-samsaric pocket universe."[45] In this new view, the fetal body not only physically develops in tune with the larger processes of a natural universe, but also spiritually develops in tune with an enlightened universe.

This view of life in the womb is part of the central theme of *Unity of the Three Wisdoms,* which, as the title implies and its prologue states, is to unify *(itchi)* the three wisdoms *(sanken)* of Buddhism, Shinto, and forms of divination derived from China.[46] The transcendent truth of the three wisdoms is that the body of the universe and the body of each human being are profoundly tied by the same enlightened nature inherent in both. Conception and gestation, initiated through sexual union and the harmonizing of yin and yang, spark the formative experience in which the human being develops a physical body and assumes the same inherency of enlightenment marking the universe's body.[47] Birth becomes the passage into physical life, but also the gateway to realizing the enlightenment one already possesses. As part of this project the text narrates the details of monthly gestation in conjunction with the esoteric Buddhist divinities of death memorial. It conspicuously references the deities' fixed relation with death by identifying each buddha not only with its time referent in the gestation process, but also with its time referent and order in death memorial. The text links Fudō and Shaka, for example, to the first and second months of fetal growth, respectively, while also identifying them by their positions in death memorial's timeline, which is the first seven days (Fudō) and the second seven days (Shaka) after death.[48] This overlay of time frames signals that whether moving toward or away from life, it is all on the same journey of realizing one's inherent enlightenment in an enlightened universe. In Namura's text the explicitness of this overlay has faded. Still, the symbolic outline that *Unity of the Three Wisdoms* describes influenced many later depictions, from Namura's work to latter-period texts.

Original enlightenment thought and *honji suijaku* formed the critical basis of this symbolic outline. Original enlightenment posits the inherent buddhahood of all phenomena: everyone and everything is enlightened as is, as born. This position collapsed tenuous but salient distinctions in Mahayana Buddhism between ultimate and phenomenal by radically valorizing the temporal world and asserting complete identity—a nondual union of enlightenment—between buddhas and all other beings constituting the universal body of buddhahood. Going where no Mahayana development had gone before, original enlightenment became, as Jacqueline Stone notes, a "new paradigm" and "reimagining" of enlightenment in medieval Japan. As Buddhism pushed deeper into Japanese symbolic and ritual life, the imaginative power of original enlightenment began coloring the wider cultural milieu, including literature and art.[49] On this point, "the real engagement with Buddhism" was not through participation in monastic debates, but rather through persistent contact with symbols.[50] In this fashion original enlightenment came to color other, more popular aspects of the culture, such as gestation illustrations. Further, original enlightenment thought was never systematic thought but rather a "mode" meshing "with a number of other discourses, practices, and ideas."[51] The illustrations and their monthly narrative in *Unity of the Three Wisdoms* portray modes of original enlightenment meshing with both the discourse of *honji suijaku* and ideas of pregnancy.

A conspicuous explanatory technique in the text's view of fetal life that signals the interconnecting of *honji suijaku* and original enlightenment is allegoresis, or the intentional fashioning of contemporary meanings onto preexisting texts. The logic of allegoresis—extracting a preconceived interpretation from what one is interpreting—was critical to both reality constructions of combinatory linkage and radical nonduality.[52] Each paradigm was highly intentional in manufacturing reality through disparate parts. *Honji suijaku* related unrelated deities, things, and places, and original enlightenment thought developed undeveloped logical conclusions from received Mahayana tradition. Allegoresis is particularly helpful in this type of intentional manufacturing of the unrelated and undeveloped. At its creative core is the avoidance of clashes between different kinds of symbols, texts, and ideas that history has brought together and the creation of something original by reconciling the new with the old, the foreign with the familiar, and the departure with the tradition.[53]

In original enlightenment the hermeneutical logic of allegoresis is termed *kanjin,* or "interpretation from the standpoint of the contemplation of the mind."[54] Of course, as a form of allegoresis, the interpretation has already been contemplated and assumed true, and thus the real task is to fix that truth onto a text that one is creating or reading. This fashioning of preordained truths can give the logic of allegoresis an illogical character. To observers whose interpretive assumptions fall outside the world-view and sensibility of a text built upon allegoresis, the interpretive exercise smacks of randomness. To those imbued with a sympathetic outlook, however, it opens doors filled with hidden truths that tumble forward to cover the world in meaningfulness. In *Unity of the Three Wisdoms,* whose outlook is imbued with a sensibility of *honji suijaku* and original enlightenment, allegoresis confirms a world covered in divinity that is ordered, linked, and immanent.

Toward this confirmation the author employs a type of etymological allegoresis built on the notion that ideograms possess meanings beyond those conventionally ascribed to them. One may access the true meanings they hide (i.e., fashion meanings onto them) by isolating the characters or breaking them down into smaller radicals for hermeneutical examination. The writer interprets the characters that make up the name of each monthly deity in this manner to create correspondence between the divine name and some component or principle of life. For example, the four ideograms forming the name of Fudō Myōō (the first month of gestation) break down into a number of separate characters and radicals. The author uses the two characters constituting "Myōō" to create correspondence, respectively, between "man and woman" *(myō)* and "father, mother, and child" *(ō),* both of which are strongly suggestive of yin and yang associations. The ideogram representing *myō* combines the characters of sun and moon, and thus according to the text it means man and woman. *Ō,* which conventionally means "ruler" (it is made up of three horizontal lines representing heaven, earth, and humanity, tied together by a vertical line representing ruler), actually stands for "father, mother, and child," according to the author's interpretation of the three horizontal lines.[55] Like sun and moon, this suggests yin and yang associations of heaven–man and earth–woman, who in their unity have sovereignty over the humanity–child they create. "Fudō" separates into *fu,* which typically means "negation," but here combines the two meanings of "single" and "small" based on its character composition. The writer separates *dō* into two independent ideograms, one denoting heaviness and the other power or strength.[56]

Through the deity's full name, the text lays out the essential figures and actions of pregnancy: a man and woman come together to become father and mother to a child by creating a single life that may indeed be small in its first month of existence but is ever gaining mass and strength. Another example of this style of interpretation comes from analysis of the name of Amida, the buddha of the tenth month. The text ties the three ideograms that make up Amida's name to the full trajectory of human existence: birth, length of life, and death. Indeed, through the holy name, the writer asserts, one may understand that "Amida is namely one's own body."[57] Through this type of allegoresis, *Unity of the Three Wisdoms* creates combinatory links between buddhas and the fetus to put forward that the constituents of life itself, from its actors (men and women, fathers and mothers, and fetuses) to its biological processes (gestation, birth, life, and death), share in the same enlightened nature of the buddhas.

In this manner of interpretation, gestation is not only associated with anatomical developments, but also with the child's increasing sentiency and inherency of buddhahood. The fetus physically develops head and ears in the third month of Monju and develops arms and legs in the fourth month of Fugen. In the fifth month of Jizō, however, it gains the six senses of awareness; in the eighth month of Kannon it begins to hear the wisdom of the world, and by the ninth month of Seishi its hands come together in *mudrā* and its mouth forms the holy sound *a-um*. At this point "the living body [of the fetus] is that of a buddha."[58] In the tenth month the body turns its head downward to emerge from the womb and into the world or, as the text describes it, 84,000 hells. This downward, plunging birth out of the womb is a complex event. It is both a "fall" from a paradisiacal environment in which enlightenment comes to inhere in the nature of human life and an entrance into a world that provides the opportunity to realize that nature.[59] Given the text's intentional overlay of death and birth, emergence from the womb is both the pathway to death as well as the necessary existential condition to realize *(satoru)* what one already is: a buddha in this very body *(jishin zebutsu)*.[60] Birth, life, and death—the three constituents of Amida's name—form a continuum of phenomenal reality imbued with primordial enlightenment. The text, punctuating this with a picture of a human figure suspended upside down with hands clasped, states that this kind of birth is the origin of all buddhas *(shobutsu shusshin kore nari)*.[61]

In Namura's text explicit reference to this legacy has disappeared. What remains, though, is not insignificant: the illustrations. They were rooted in a discourse of fetal buddhahood straight from *Unity of the Three Wisdoms* and emerged as a distinct visual genre from popular versions of the Kumano story before authors like Namura incorporated them into lifestyle guides as the primary manner of visualizing the fetus in the seventeenth and early eighteenth centuries. The illustrations in *A Record of Treasures for Women* line up months, fetal development, and Buddhist divinities in a manner largely similar to its predecessors (table 1). In the first four months of gestation the fetus is pictured as ritual paraphernalia: a staff *(shakujō)* and three different types of *vajra (sho* or *kongō),* which are handheld, pronged instruments used in esoteric Buddhist rituals.[62] From the second to fourth months the *vajra* are one, three, and five pronged. Below each *vajra* appears a small face. It is the only intimation of potential human form. In the fifth month the fetus finally takes human form under the reign of Jizō. In the last month the fetus turns upside down, as originally described in *Unity of the Three Wisdoms,* to emerge into the world. The illustrations are divided, with buddhas on top and the fetus on the bottom. This visually captured the links to the *honji suijaku* and original enlightenment paradigms, but it also allowed Namura to describe the bifurcation as showing two views of the womb. One view represents medical writings *(isho)* and the other Buddhist writings *(bussho).*[63] He juxtaposes similes to distinguish these views. "Like a drop of dew" is the medical phrasing to describe the fetus in the first month, and "like the shape of a staff that receives Fudō" represents Buddhist writings. "Like a peach blossom" and "like a one-pronged *vajra* that receives Shaka" are the respective medical and Buddhist views of the sec-

TABLE 1 Monthly Fetal Development and Correspondence with Buddhist Divinities

Month	Fetus	Divinity
First	staff	Fudō
Second	*vajra*	Shaka
Third	*vajra*	Monju
Fourth	*vajra*	Fugen
Fifth	fetus	Jizō
Sixth	fetus	Miroku
Seventh	fetus	Yakushi
Eighth	fetus	Kannon
Ninth	fetus	Seishi
Tenth	fetus	Amida

ond month.[64] In marking these differences Namura holds no bias against Buddhism. The bifurcation is not one of conflict between medicine and Buddhism, which was an epistemological stance that had yet to emerge in the seventeenth century, but one of complement. As he does earlier in the pregnancy chapter when noting the effects of a degenerate age on conception, Namura also puts forward here the importance of faith as part of the experiential totality of pregnancy. He assures pregnant women that if they put faith in each monthly buddha, their children will be wise and free of bodily defects.[65]

TAKAI'S 1847 TEXT

Namura's acceptance of Buddhism as a soothing faith and a complementary view of gestation represents a very different attitude than that of Takai's 1847 edition. Takai redacts an epistemological break between medicine and Buddhism by venting his disbelief about the ontological reality of the original illustrations. Their evocative power likely made them, as Namura originally suggested, objects of devotional activities for some women hoping to secure a safe pregnancy and a healthy child. However, Takai inserted into the text a strong caution against notions of wombs cluttered with ritual objects, of the human form developing from sacramental objects, and of physical bodies receiving buddhas. Along with his intellectual discomfort with buddhas in the womb, Takai also found discomfort in the foreignness of the buddhas. Foreign gods in a Japanese womb, in a Japanese body, was a problematic microcosm of the existence of foreignness—in other words, Buddhism—in the political and social body of Japan. Takai's redactions in the birth chapter are exemplars of the nationalistic, anti-Buddhist critiques that were frothing in certain intellectual circles in the latter half of the Tokugawa.[66] After acknowledging that the belief of protective womb buddhas among women is an old and still popularly entrenched custom, Takai beseeches his female audience, in a critical and nationalistic spirit, to think twice about this faith.

> When you understand the reason for why things are, you will know that being pregnant with ritual objects and having humans developing from *vajra* and such defies reason. Again, since we are the descendants of a land of gods, it cannot be said that we receive the protection of Indian buddhas for ten months straight. No one knows how many tens of thousands of births there are in just a single day, so it goes against reason that so few buddhas, even with their supernatural powers, could be with so many people.

Moreover, if such guardian buddhas exist, then among all the Japanese there would be not one without a deep debt of gratitude. It would mean that the body of Nikkō-sama (Tokugawa Ieyasu) as well as the bodies of your husband and parents would even possess these deities. Birth in divine Japan makes the guardianship of foreign buddhas unnecessary.[67]

Takai does not present this critique with words only. He also includes a second set of womb illustrations to counter the Buddhist version of the original text, although he keeps in place the older illustrations. His preferred set is devoid of divinity. The fetus is alone and develops slowly from a simple cellular-like orb in the first month to a recognizable human form in the fifth month. Looking similar in shape to a gingerbread man at this point, where Jizō used to guide the fetus into human form, it takes on more precise detail with each passing month until, by the tenth month, it actually resembles a mature toddler more than a newborn.[68] Pulling from Namura's original term "medical writings," Takai recommends that his readers put away the view of buddhas in the womb and understand their bodies solely from the perspective of contemporary medical writings.

Takai's old and new views of the womb are evidence that the "obstetrical gaze" of the seventeenth century was multiplying in number and variety as the period went on. Further, the views moved toward greater physiological realism in the latter eighteenth century. This move was part of a larger discourse in anatomy and medical procedures that came under the purview of physicians familiar with Western modes of knowledge, typically called Dutch studies *(rangaku)*.[69] Anatomical realism in the portrayal of fetal bodies and the womb also became linked to political and economic concerns that sought to limit infanticide and abortion.[70] Some interpreters have argued that this link between the science and the politics of reproduction produced in Japan initial sightings of the modern body: a distinct and corporeal entity that finally pulled away from an ancient cosmological camouflage of deities, a morally resonant universe, and the porous borders of this world and the other world.[71] At the center of this shift was the Kagawa School of Obstetrics founded by Kagawa Genetsu (1700–1777). His disciples produced in 1775 a revised edition of Genetsu's work on obstetrics, *A Discourse on Birth (Sanron)*, first published 1765.[72] The revision included realistically detailed illustrations depicting the fetus in the womb and emerging out of the mother's body. The "realism" lies not only in what it portrays, but also in what it does not portray: religious beings. Realism here is as secular as it is anatomical. This sort of realism, which Takai's new pictures represented, "began to supplant," according to one interpreter, "the vague and mysterious image of a fetus symbolized by Buddhist altar fittings."[73]

How fully such images of fetal and divine dimensions were supplanted, and thus how clearly the modern body came into view, is murky. An 1812 text, *Models of Various Lessons for Women (Onna zassho kyōkun kagami)*, is notable for its ten-month view of the fetus. It removes both the child and the deities from the womb and places them in a celestial realm of clouds. In the clouds an individual *kami* joins each monthly buddha, and as a pair the deities guard the fetus as it physically develops. In the tenth month Amida is joined not by an anthropomorphic *kami*, as are the previous nine buddhas, but by a Shinto purifying wand labeled *ujigami*, which is the *kami* that traditionally functions as one's local tutelary god and the birth god.[74] This set of illustrations uses seventeenth-century visual formulations of a child's relation with a divine dimension to express nineteenth-century issues such as an assertive, independent Shinto and the objectively anti-abortion position that the *kami*, particularly the *ujigami*, have as much claim on a fetus as its human community and on any decision that community might make. In this way, if divinized illustrations of monthly fetal development were supplanted to some degree, then to another degree they were retooled to respond to late-Tokugawa political discourses. Ancient cosmologies could still be counted on to camouflage the body in modern discourses of religious and reproductive nationalism.[75]

Even latter-period forms of the obstetrical gaze that were free of divinity still shared a sight line of continuity with the older gaze. Takai's buddha-less illustrations represent this. The most obvious example of this kind of continuity is Takai's inclusion of the traditional illustrations in the reprinted text, if only as fodder for his criticism. Also, the fifth month is still critical in marking the human resemblance of the form despite the erasure of Jizō. Another example of this continuity with the older obstetric gaze comes from the Kagawa School, which depended on a deep cultural association between the placenta and the lotus in its visual depiction of the placenta in the shape of a lotus flower. The ninth-month illustration that is representative of Namura's original text is emblematic of this association, where there emerges from the fetus' navel an umbilical cord-lotus stem. The stem reaches up above the child's head, where a blooming flower droops downward, topping the head like a wide-brimmed hat. Returning briefly to *Unity of the Three Wisdoms*, the ninth month marks the stage when the fetus reaches a high moment of buddhahood.

Seishi, the bodhisattva of wisdom, is the reigning divinity. The lotus capping the fetus's head—the sign of enlightenment—is powerful in its evocation, particularly given the project of original enlightenment thought to put forward the enlightenment of all phenomena. Further, the emphasis in original enlightenment on collapsing the phenomenal and ultimate signifies the lotus as marking both spiritual wisdom and biological life. The uterine lotus also alludes to the mother's life-sustaining placenta. In Tokugawa conceptualizations of in-utero life, the placenta is routinely portrayed as a lotus blossom in a variety of depictions. A disturbing example comes from Saikaku's novel, *The Life of an Amorous Woman*. His aging anti-heroine sees a horrific vision of ninety-five small figures parading outside her window. Each figure, "stained with blood from the waist down," wears "a hat in the form of a lotus leaf."[76] The lotuses worn on the heads of these walking wounded are placentas, and the tiny figures are the fetuses the old woman has aborted during her sexual romp though life. Saikaku does not use the term "placenta" to describe the strange hats, but rather, as the translation above denotes, "lotus hats" *(hasu no ha gasa)*.[77] Saikaku trusted his readers to make the connection. So deep was this connection of the placenta-lotus that a century later the Kagawa School's 1775 sketches, so famed for their realism, still depicted the placenta in the unmistakable shape of a lotus flower.[78]

All of these obstetrical gazes, from Namura's late seventeenth-century view to Takai's nineteenth-century one, focused on the womb and thus, obliquely, on the mother's body. In its gaze each assumed, if differently portrayed, the depiction of two lives shared as one: the fetus and the mother. Pregnancy's symbolization in Namura's text portrayed the womb as the center point of all bodies: buddhas, fetus, and mother. As the fetus is protected and nourished in body and soul by both the water and blood of the womb and a pantheon of buddhas, the carrier of those bodies—the mother's body—also attains special identity. Her body— and her behavior toward her body—becomes the prime initiator of her and her fetus' health. Takai recognized this as well, for when he supplanted the older illustrations with the new set, he left Namura's writings on the centrality of the body and behavior untouched. Similarly, the Tokugawa period produced a rush of varied depictions of the womb and gestation, particularly in the latter half, that flowed from emerging political and medical discourses, but throughout the period there was common recognition of the critical role a pregnant woman's behavior played in the destiny of her body and the fetal body. Namura indicates this recognition when he uses the term *mimochi* in referring to pregnancy.

The word literally means "to have or hold a body." In pregnancy, mother and child each has an additional body other than her own acting and depending on it. *Mimochi* has another meaning as well, which spells out the context of Namura's use. It means "conduct" and denotes practices that a pregnant woman should follow for the benefit of both bodies. For the bulk of his pregnancy chapter, to which I turn next, Namura stresses the beneficial practices of womb teachings *(taikyō)* based on the behavioral link between the bodies of mother and fetus.

The Practice of Pregnancy

Namura's practices of *taikyō* sought to ensure the health of an expectant mother and the child she carried. They belong to a practice and philosophy of health maintenance *(yōjō)*, which stressed forms of right living in one's conduct, customary practices, and diet in order to maintain one's health. Here the emphasis was on not becoming ill more than on overcoming illness. Further, these practices of health maintenance were dependent throughout the Tokugawa period on a worldview positing that the bodily health of pregnant women was dependent on and responded to their ethical and conscientious behaviors that resonated with a moral and ordered universe.[79] We have already seen this broad logic of the physical body responding appropriately to ethical and unethical actions in the nocturnal rite of Kōshin devotees. In the remaining pages I expand on this logic of bodily health and actions by focusing on Namura's recommendations of *taikyō,* in particular the belly wrap, categories of food, and matters at birth, as a type of ordering experience that attempted to produce during pregnancy an ideal environment so as best to bring about an uneventful birth and maintain the health of the mother.

One task of religion is to envisage a world free of phenomena that cannot be explained or incorporated. Fundamental to this is ritual action, which produces a "controlled environment where the variables (i.e., accidents) of ordinary life have been displaced precisely because they are felt to be so overwhelmingly present and powerful."[80] Ritual action is creative because it *makes* its own ideal environment, where actions and outcomes are predetermined, nothing simply happens without cause or purpose, and bad luck and failure are defined not to exist in and of themselves. In this manner, practices of *taikyō* act as ritual in idealizing the environment of pregnancy, and especially the most critical environment of all: that of the linked bodies of mother and fetus. Discerning and maximizing positive influences on the mother's body, and thus on the fetal body, while minimizing negative ones was the essential move in creating an ideal environment for pregnancy. These influences included all sorts of phenomena ranging from spoken and written words to movements of the body and the intake of food. Informing this ordering of the environment was the interplay between *hare* (those forces and states powerfully beneficial to life) and *kegare* (those forces and states powerfully threatening to life). To protect a woman who, by the very fact of being pregnant, was in the midst of a powerful state that entailed mortal risks to herself and her fetus, it was necessary to know which actions exacerbated her situation and which ameliorated it. A woman and those caring for her could put her pregnancy at risk if they were not attentive to the safeguards and dangers that existed in everyday life. Things perceived as mundane and innocuous outside of pregnancy became the powerful property of either *kegare* and aided and abetted the threats of pregnancy or of *hare* and blunted or reduced those threats. Classifying pregnancy in relation to favorable and unfavorable practices and things signified it as a moment of intense concern for a woman and her group. Examples of this concern abound in Namura's text. Virtually all of its pages devoted to pregnancy center around setting things apart and classifying their worth as either beneficial or baneful to the bodies of mother and fetus. The most obvious example of this setting apart is the woman herself, through the wearing of a special obi or belly wrap *(hara obi)* typically at the five-month midpoint of pregnancy, when the fetal body takes form.[81]

THE BELLY WRAP

Namura confines his discussion of the belly wrap's significance to matters of presenting the obi to the woman, its material, and the wearing of it from the fifth month of pregnancy. Takai's version, however, additionally links the wrap's origins to Japanese imperial mythology as part of his nationalist project.

> In our nation the obi's beginnings go back to when the empress Jingū wore one while conquering the Korean Kingdoms of Paekche, Silla, and Koguryō. Fearing the royal child inside her would be frightened, she wore an obi wrapped around her belly, and that is why she could offer a peaceful

birth to the baby Ōjin. It is from this ancient example there developed in Japan, even down to people of little cultivation, the practice of tying an obi around the belly before giving birth.[82]

He cites the Kagawa School for this source of the Jingū-obi link. The school may have developed this legend from the various records that groups of *katsurame* created, which linked their occupation to imperial practices. His redaction of the legend indicates the same nationalistic urge that discharged his critique of Buddhism as a symbolic and faith-centered mediator of pregnancy. More important for our purposes, the legend also indicates the plain truth that wrapping a pregnant woman's belly was an act of great import itself, if made even more so by insisting on a founding in imperial antiquity.

Each text's perception of the significance of the belly wrap signals that its employment as ritual action has multiple meanings, but perhaps at the most basic level of meaning is simply the significance of wrapping itself. The ubiquitous action in Japanese culture of wrapping things, a practice spanning from the preparation of the smallest gift and money transactions to the emperor himself at a critical stage in enthronement rites, is a deeply meaningful activity in and of itself. The significance is in the action of wrapping and less in what is being wrapped. Wrapping produces a new sense of qualitative difference; it communicates ideas of politeness, presentation, and power—power that may be *hare* or *kegare*. It transforms something from being simply an object to being a meaning-filled object. Wrapping, a human action, imparts human values and concern; it gives "spiritual value" to things. In tossing away the wrapping paper in order to get to what is wrapped, observers of Japanese religion and culture risk falling into an interpretive empty box: in looking for meaning in the thing itself they may overlook powerful levels of meaning that human actions have given to the thing.[83]

Modern readers of *A Record of Treasures for Women* get an immediate sense of the significance of wrapping when they turn to the text's final pages, where there is a review of wrapping methods credited to the Ogasawara tradition. A "how to wrap" section is in line with Namura's goal of guiding women toward a lifestyle of cultural literacy, including sophisticated customs. Rather than using written instructions, the text relies on illustrations of specific items and how they ought to appear when properly wrapped. The objects depicted are highly varied in kind, ranging from the practical to the ceremonial, and a few items directly reflect the list's origins in samurai culture.[84] The point of these illustrations is not, as the absence of explanatory words makes obvious, to explain the importance or function of each of these various items; what matters instead—indeed, the only thing that matters in these pages—is wrapping.

A pregnant woman wearing an obi strikes the same cultural chord of significance. A woman wrapping her belly around the fifth month of gestation at once *made* her pregnancy a significant event of concern. Although her body and what was inside her had been changing over the months, it was only the action of wrapping that signified a real change in her status and that of the fetus. She was no longer simply a pregnant woman, but a woman wrapped. Her biological pregnancy became a cultural event demanding attention and decisions from her collective. Again, whether pregnancy culminated in rearing, giving away, or destroying the infant, the choice and the reasons behind it often lay with the immediate needs of the group. The obi's meaning of group acknowledgment and concern may also be seen from the reverse angle of the pleasure quarters. One *senryū* suggests a woman would not wear an obi, at least if the bordello deemed the pregnancy unwanted. "Without tying the obi, [a baby] is born and sent off [in adoption] to Edo" *(Hara obi o sezuni undewa Edo e dashi).*[85] The practice of courtesans not wearing belly wraps, particularly if the child were to be given up for adoption, shows the other side of the obi's meanings: the institutional refusal to recognize pregnancy. A swollen, unwrapped belly powerfully symbolized, as much as a wrapped one, the social reality of pregnancy and a community's attitude toward it. The absence of an obi did not deny the biological fact of pregnancy, but instead denied the collectivity's ties to the product of pregnancy.

Many large shrine complexes also recognized pregnancy only after the wrapping of the belly in the fifth month, in light of their own institutional concerns that pregnant women not pollute the shrines' bounded spaces of purity. The mourning and pollution regulations *(bukki ryō)* of shrines understood pollution *(kegare)* to be a general category of human experience within which existed several types, from killings and family bereavement to menstruation and pregnancy. Each required its own penance of shrine avoidance for a fixed period of time to expiate the stain of death and blood. Several shrine regulations determined pollution tied to pregnancy as commencing from the fifth month until thirty days or more after birth, at which point the parents would take the child and visit the local shrine to present the infant officially to the tutelary deity. Accordingly, before the fifth month, pregnant women could enter shrine grounds to worship. Although pregnant, they had not yet entered into a powerful polluted state. Nagoya's Atsuta Shrine's regulations, for example, state that a woman may visit until the fifth month, when she first ties her obi about her. This policy conflates the fifth month with the wearing of the wrap; it assumes the time and event as a singular phenomenon signaling the start of a woman's polluted state and her exclusion from the shrine.[86]

Wrapping the body in the fifth month, on the day of the dog, as Namura advises, acts to settle the spirit of the fetus while also anticipating easy birth.[87] This links the fifth month of gestation to, as the ten-month illustrations in his text show, the short but critical uterine reign of Jizō, when the fetus develops its human form. Jizō steps in at the midpoint to mediate fetal status as the child balances between what it was and what it is to be, between formlessness and form. This balancing act is true of gender, too, which was as unsettled as the rest of the body, forming over time with the physicality of the child. With the establishment of gender occurring not at conception but later, sometimes the fifth month and sometimes the third month, depending on sources, there were beliefs that early pregnancy offered a woman a window of opportunity to change, or at least increase the chance of influencing, her fetus's gender. These beliefs assumed that the gender change would be from female to male. One such practice called for a woman to drape her body in her husband's clothes and circumambulate a well. She should then peer at her reflection in the well water two times and concentrate on her wish for a boy. Another recommended placing the string of a bow under the belly wrap to assure a male birth.[88]

The links between time (particularly the fifth month), belief (substantiality of human form), and ritual (wrapping the belly) more importantly signaled, from the immediate perspective of the mother, that the risks of miscarriage and spontaneous abortion were considered largely over as the fetus emerged from formlessness into form, passing the state where sudden disintegration and discharge was always at hand. On this point, fetal conceptualization among Tokugawa peasants in northeastern Japan, for example, never applied the term for "dead body" (shitai) to a fetus when a miscarriage occurred before the fifth month of pregnancy.[89] The other side of the fifth month also signaled a critical timeline for abortion specialists. They and their amateur imitators often aborted a pregnancy by spearing the fetal body. They could not accomplish this with any real precision until the fetus had reached a certain size and mass.

A *senryū* making this professional point also touches upon the visual logic of womb pictures like those in Namura's text, suggesting once again the wide referential range of the illustrations. "While [for the first four months a fetus is in the form of] Buddhist ritual items even abortion specialists cannot break [it] up" *(Chūjō mo butsugu no uchi wa kowasarezu)*.[90] If pregnancy was an ambivalent embrace of possibilities, of straddling perspectival boundaries of spiritual purity and pollution, life and death, spontaneous and surgical abortion, male and female, and institutional acceptance and rejection, then its fifth month, signified by a woman wrapping her belly with an obi, enclosed all its complex character. As ritual action, wrapping began moving her and her fetus toward definite sides of these boundaries.

Namura states that the obi should be made of silk cloth. Of course, silk was not necessary; material varied by custom, locality, and availability.[91] Its mention here reflects the elite ritual traditions that *A Record of Treasures for Women* made available for common adaptation. As an object exclusively associated with pregnancy, the belly obi belonged to a realm of generalized female experiences. Similarly, as a manufactured piece of silk it further exemplified this signification in several ways. Women have historically been active in the cultivation of silk in Japan. In the Tokugawa period, labor in serial culture, either as a part-time cottage industry or in textile mills, provided cash for women and their families.[92] This close tie between women and silk may be gleaned from mythology as well. In the stories, silkworms are not associated with women in an abstract way, but instead emerge from the dying bodies of goddesses. In one such story, Izanami lies dying after giving birth to the fire god. In her last act of creation she gives birth to the goddesses of earth and water. The fire god takes the earth goddess as his wife, and they produce a child, Wakamusubi. From the top of her head emerge silkworms and the mulberry tree, which marks the origination of silkworm production.[93] The productive labor of women cultivating silkworms is also tied to their reproductive labor through myth. In one story the emperor Yūryaku (r. 456–479) decides to have his wife and concubines plant mulberry trees to inspire greater silk production in the country. He entrusts an adviser to gather as many silkworms as he can throughout the realm. The adviser fails to fulfill Yūryaku's request due to miscommunication. Instead of collecting the requested silkworms—*kaiko*—he collects babies to bring back to the palace.[94] *Kaiko* is also a compound word combining *ko* (child) with *kai*, from the verb *kau* (to raise or nurture). Thus the "confusion" between raising silkworms and raising babies actually clarifies the centrality of women as cultivators of both, the creative agents of silk production and human production.

Wrapping a woman in the silk folds of an obi intensely brought together the elements of female labor and reproduction. As a celebratory gift the belly obi was typically presented in a woman-to-woman transaction.[95] Even before the exchange from one woman's hands to those of another, the obi was most likely manufactured at every stage by women's hands, from the cultivation of worms and spooling of silken thread to the necessary weaving and needlework to form a belly wrap meant to protect and bring forth life in the midst of an experience that could, as the fatal experiences of goddesses reveals, bring forth death as well.

CATEGORIES OF FOOD

Namura and his readers believed that food consumption during pregnancy also played a significant role in bringing forth a new life that was healthy, strong, and free of disease and deformity. Namura lists four categories of food's significance: combinations of foods that risk the child's health and that of the mother or impair the child's body; foods to be eaten while pregnant and those to be avoided; foods to consume after pregnancy and those to be shunned entirely; and foods that ameliorate low production of breast milk. The section on food combinations *(kuiawase)* is particularly interesting. Namura takes care to spell out specific consequences of consuming specific combinations. This specificity exhibits some of the health concerns of the period as well as the religious contours of belief and practice concerning pregnancy. As the ten-month gestation illustrations and the wearing of an obi indicate, the locus of pregnancy's concern is the womb as the meeting place of two bodies interacting and depending on each other during their time of shared liminality. In the ambivalent spirit of pregnancy, this interaction may lead to either beneficial or detrimental situations. A telling example is the belief that diseases of the skin—from something as innocuous as eczema to as serious as smallpox—infect the child while in the womb. Even if the disease does not reveal itself for months or years after delivery, it is assumed to have entered the child at some point in the womb. In late-period diaries of mothers the term *taidoku* often appears when referring to childhood diseases, especially those of the skin.[96] Combining the characters for "womb" and "poison," *taidoku* denotes the transmission of a pollutant from the mother's body or blood to that of her fetal child.

The mother's consumption of food combinations takes on great importance in controlling the threat of *taidoku*. Namura's text reveals the same concern and understanding of childhood illness as the mothers' diaries. Although he does not use the term *taidoku,* he still understands that a woman's consumption of certain food combinations marks a critical intersection of behavioral choices and time on her unborn child's future health and even sociosexual behavior. This notion of *taidoku* and its relation to food suggests a similar point of food and consumption rules guiding the Hua of New Guinea. Bodily health and social behavior for the Hua are not considered innate to an individual—a product of accidents of birth and personality—but rather develop through a "process of contagion" occurring in the "flow between humans, other organisms, and objects, moving along the lines established by the web of their interconnections."[97] For the Japanese to whom Namura writes, food is also caught up in the web of interconnections. The following exemplify Namura's belief in interconnections built on the consumption of specific foods and their immediate or long-term consequences on mother and child. Eating chicken with glutinous rice during pregnancy risks the development of a tapeworm or other parasite in a newborn. A pregnant woman drinking rice wine with sparrow increases the chances that the child born to her will eventually to fall shamelessly into lascivious ways. Sparrow meat eaten with miso paste may cause discoloration of the face, physically and perhaps socially scarring the child for life. In the same list of combined foodstuffs, there are also singular items that hold potential dangers to the life and health of mother and fetus. Eating crab, for example, leads to the life-threatening experience of lateral birth.[98]

This list reveals much about concerns with health and pregnancy. There is a strong emphasis on mindfulness as the most effective form of preventive medicine. To avoid health risks that may complicate pregnancy, Namura recommends both the consumption and eschewal of certain foods. Some of these preventive measures, especially highlighted by a few of the singular food items, assert a type of thought that understands causes and their effects through a principle of causative similarity—or that like produces like. The careful choosing of foods in anticipation of certain outcomes gives eating a sensibility of magic, in that the eating "works."[99] It has an effect in the perception of the ritual practitioner of either producing or avoiding a particular, preconceived outcome. The fear that consumption of crab, with its sideways stride, might produce a lateral and thus dangerous delivery leads one not to eat it; the fear that chewing on the knobby roots of ginger may cause a child to have deformed hands gives pause to a woman before eating.[100] When neither condition is experienced, it is then attributable to the conscientious eschewal of eating crab or ginger. The ritual sensibility of magic is often rooted in anxiety.[101] Anxiety drove much of the mood of the *taikyō* practices that linked a mother's consumption choices to the immediate and long-term influences on the fetus as she tried to bring a sense of control to the largely uncontrollable.

At the end of his food section, Namura presents a list that further explicates the link between a woman and fetus while shedding light on the motivation behind food classification and consumption. This last list is a seemingly awkward insertion that advises women to avoid copulation and conception in certain environments. Similar to the preceding list of dangerous edible combinations, however, this advisory is highly specific. It lists circumstances for abstaining from intercourse and the consequences a woman might expect if she does not. In addition, like the avoidance of certain food mixtures, the avoidance of certain times and places for sex draws attention to the profound connection between the actions of and influences on a woman's body and that of her fetus, even at the moment of conception. Intercourse is to be put off in times of strong winds and rain that typhoons annually bring to Japan as they race up the archipelago. Onslaughts of thunder and lightning or a sudden earthquake ought to bring an immediate end to sex. Also, a woman is to avoid having intercourse before religious altars or in the presence of any holy statue or image. In ignoring these taboos a woman might risk a difficult pregnancy, dangerous delivery, and even shortening her child's life.[102]

These taboos recall the nightly vigil of Kōshin devotionalism. Propounding similar cautions about intercourse in specific places and at certain times, Namura's advice and the taboos of Kōshin faith both functioned (the former explicitly and the latter implicitly) as a type of *pre*-prenatal care where conception became as critical a player as gestation and rearing. Stressing mindfulness of one's behaviors at specific times and places with regard to possible consequences or benefits, Namura's text shares the same future-oriented motivational sense that encourages women to participate in all-night devotions to Kōshin. The dietary recommendations, which at first glance appear awkwardly to share the same section with intercourse taboos, exemplify the same motivational logic and ultimate concern.[103] Encouraging and discouraging the consumption of particular foods due to their prolonged influence on the child and mother imbued them with the same future-oriented motivational hue of concern that sexual taboos carried.

MATTERS OF BIRTH

For Namura, the greatest variable that demanded a sense of control in creating an ideal environment from the practice of pregnancy was also pregnancy's grim reaper: difficult delivery *(nanzan)*. Facing one's mortality, as all premodern Japanese women did in the pregnancy experience, is often a time of intense ritual activity. For midwives in particular, this ritual activity sought control of a woman's pregnancy. Toward this control, the conscientious practices of pregnancy that Namura advocated acted to create an ideal and predictable order out of the unpredictability of the pregnancy experience. In effect, he imagines through his text an environment replete with explanatory power and the ability to incorporate or define away troublesome facts of life. In this sense, pregnancy as practice acts fully as ritual in that such actions create an environment where all variables, even the most dangerous, come under at least explanatory control. A dangerous birth did not prove that the various practices of pregnancy were largely ineffective; it proved only that a woman and those caring for her failed to carry out the practices faithfully. Namura locates the general cause of dangerous delivery in the poor practices of pregnancy *(mimochi ashiku)*.[104] Similar to the logic of many sacred orderings of reality, the appearance of a threatening variable—here *nanzan*—actually serves to maintain rather than question the order's idealization. In sacred orders typically the only questions asked upon threats of failure and disconnects between hopes and outcomes are those directed—usually self-directed—to the participants of the order and never to the logic and promised claims of the order itself.

With his reason for the stubborn existence of difficult deliveries at hand, Namura moves on to describe several types of dangerous births and a number of practices a woman and her caregivers may employ in order to alleviate fear and bodily threat. Many of these difficult births deal with the various positions of the baby, other than headfirst. He advises those observing these and any other complications to remain calm so as not to alarm the mother. Here he specifically mentions the figure of the midwife *(toriage baba)*. He ranks her professional talents with those of physicians when the task at hand is childbirth.[105] Equating the two professions suggests Namura's intellectual milieu as well as his personal opinion. In the late eighteenth century Kagawa physicians, in rhetorical maneuvers designed to privilege their authority over matters of birth, began to lump together midwifery with other practices it considered superstitious and thus antithetical to its claims of advanced, lifesaving obstetrics. Midwives were seen as rank amateurs, gaining money and success on an undeserved reputation and attending to life-threatening matters about which they knew medically little.[106] This criticism of a centuries-old profession was not representative of the times. Kagawa physicians suffered denigration as well. Their invasive techniques, with hoops and hooks for delivering babies, were more life-threatening than lifesaving, according to some, and their enthusiasm to replace the female midwife with the male physician in the birth space—one traditionally categorized as feminine—only caused anxiety in the minds of already anxious women enduring and praying to survive childbirth.[107] Namura's only concern, however, was that the midwife be skilled. Her authority over matters of birth may be gleaned from both the 1692 and the 1847 editions of *A Record of Treasures for Women,* which show a midwife directing the burial of her charge's placenta (figs. 11 and 12). Not only did Takai insert an updated illustration of the midwife, but he also chose not to add commentary concerning midwives to this chapter. Midwives were likely below his ideological radar, crowded as it was with anti-Buddhist and nationalistic rhetoric. Still, the inclusion of a contemporary portrayal of an authoritative midwife in a nineteenth-century update of a seventeenth-century classic is a reminder that despite the posturing criticism of the Kagawa School, much of the population still recognized the authority of reputable women to oversee birth.[108]

The presence of a midwife, who was knowledgeable and skilled in a variety of techniques, was necessary when pregnancy posed a danger to the mother or child, or both. The simplest techniques involved the use of seahorses and cowrie shells. Namura provides illustrations. He advises his readers to observe the pictures well in advance of obtaining the actual objects, since they may mistake other sea creatures and shells for the real things. Squillas, for example, are easily mistaken for seahorses, but their effect, so goes the logic of Namura's advisory, is not. If the woman grasps a seahorse in her hand as she gives birth, it works to ward off any difficulties. Cowrie shells possess the power of a parturition stimulant. Using it as a petite dispensing cup for administering medicine, a midwife pours in a liquid called "quick medicine" *(hayamegusuri)*—which

FIGURE 11 A midwife oversees the burial of her charge's placenta. From the 1692 edition of *A Record of Treasures for Women*. Courtesy of Tōyoko Gakuen Joshi Tanki Daigaku Josei Bunka Kenkyūjo, Tokyo.

FIGURE 12 Updated depiction of a midwife overseeing the burial of a placenta. From the 1847 edition of *A Record of Treasures for Women*. Courtesy of Ōzorasha, Tokyo.

Namura notes induces quick birth—and administers it orally to the mother.[109]

Another technique that Namura recommends as part of a healing professional's repertoire is a spell *(majinai)*. It calls for writing the two ideograms for "I-Se" on a piece of paper. These are the same two characters that form the name of the Ise Daijingū (the Grand Shrines of Ise), which are dedicated to Amaterasu and other *kami*. The shrine complex during the Tokugawa period was enormously popular as a pilgrimage site, and an amulet obtained during pilgrimage was considered potent and efficacious for safe delivery. Not only did the two characters spell the name of a holy site, but they also possessed power within their own structures as ideograms composed of smaller, independent radicals. Similar to the word logic of *Unity of the Three Wisdoms,* Namura suggests that by breaking down the two characters of "I-Se" into five radicals and writing them in the correct order, one creates a five-character phrase to be read as "The person now being born is of full strength" *(Hito kore mumaru wa maru ga chikara).*[110] This safe-birth spell was just one of several uses derived from the analysis of "I-Se" through allegoresis in Japanese cultural history. Poet-monks in their medieval commentary on the *Tales of Ise (Ise monogatari)* broke down the characters in a different manner to give a reading peculiar to their doctrinal and intellectual interests.[111] Peculiar to Namura's interest, however, is the use of allegoresis to deliver a woman from the threat of a dangerous birth. After the midwife writes the ideograms on paper, she has the mother swallow it with some water. In addition, the midwife reads the five-character phrase invoking its divine power *(jinriki)* to bring about the safe birth of the child.[112]

In spite of a midwife's experience and the techniques of divine invocation, pregnancy could still result in death as well as life. Fetal death in the womb brought about one of the most dangerous "deliveries" a midwife could ever encounter. She had to bring out the fetal corpse "safely" so that the mother would not become infected with rotting tissue, suffer pain, and risk death. The fetus was dead in the womb, so the need for a safe and easy delivery *(heizan)* was more critical than ever. For this reason Namura understood death in the womb as a type of difficult birth. Prominent signs of fetal death were darkening of the mother's tongue and severe abdominal discomfort similar to labor pains.[113] Diagnosing the source of pain as either that of a dying fetus or one alive and kicking was critical. Once a midwife had made a correct diagnosis of in-utero death, she could respond with certain procedures. Some had parallels to elective abortion. In his mid-Meiji study of traditional medicine, *A Consideration of Japanese and Chinese Medicine (Wakan yaku kō)*, Koizumi Eitarō finds that one type of medicinal formula used to discharge a dead fetus from the body was also purported to be effective as an insecticide, an antidote to poison, and as an abortifacient.[114] Namura offers a similar formula but recommends it for flushing out the fetus in the event of in-utero death. He calls for using the dried sex gland of a male musk deer. A midwife crushes a small amount of the gland with a larger measure of cassia bark to produce a powder, which she then gives to her patient along with sake. Another formula recommends charred and crushed deer antler.[115] In the case of in-utero death, these concoctions induce expulsion of the fetus or, as Namura euphemistically puts it, result in the dead child being "born as is" *(sonomama mumaru)*.[116]

"Born as is" captures well not only the culmination of a dangerous delivery, but also the full ambivalence of the event of pregnancy itself. The child was born "as is," dead or alive, through birth that was safe or difficult, whether welcomed by a community or not; born "as is" from the instruments and symbols of ritual that some believed in and others denied; born "as is" by the hands of a seventeenth-century midwife or the hoops and hooks of a nineteenth-century male physician; and born "as is" in the household or in Minowa. The "as-is-ness" of giving life and risking death, of confronting life's two starkest choices with no other alternatives, which a woman had to face when pregnant, placed her within an experience both unique to her gender and common to her culture in terms of ambivalence, symbols, and practices. By placing herself in the personal and ritual experience of pregnancy, a woman also placed herself out of two sharply different sets of values, neither one of which could exclusively place what she was undergoing within its borders.

FIVE

EXIT

ENTERING INTO THE LIFE of a wife or courtesan also implied an exit from the life of a daughter. Fertility values idealized this exit as properly permanent. Pleasure took a different approach. Since it put forward the concupiscent need for young women, it institutionalized this ideal with a system of retirement that called for a woman's contract to expire at some point during the twenty-seventh year of her life. For these exits, fertility practiced rites of betrothal and bridal exit from the natal home, whereas pleasure instituted rituals of retirement, either at the age of twenty-seven or earlier if a patron bought out the woman's contract. These were communal celebrations publicly marking movement into new roles and social identities. Still, women could employ ritual forms outside of these celebratory occasions to effect different exits that broke with the values of each model. Unauthorized practices—female-initiated divorce from the marriage household and escape from the pleasure quarters—dramatically signaled resistance against the values of each model. Practices of divorce and escape were highly varied, but they shared aspects of being marginal, intentional, strategic activities set unequivocally against the respective values of fertility and pleasure. In this chapter I first examine exits of communal celebration and then move on to exits of individual resistance.

Exiting the Natal Household and Quarters

Marriage was divided into two sets of rites. One set, discussed in chapter 3, took place at the groom's household. Another set, comprising betrothal and departure, occurred at the bride's residence. This second set prepared a young woman for entrance into her new life, but it also indicated symbolic ambivalence toward the notion of moving a daughter's identification away from her own household. Central to betrothal was the presentation of gifts sent from the groom's family to the bride's household that marked the two as betrothed. Departure followed at a later date, at which time a bride and her procession stepped out on the road toward the groom's residence and the concluding ceremony. Rites at the bride's home served, in the paradoxical manner of ritual, to affirm her current identity while initiating the transformation of this identity by moving her from one side of the daughter and daughter-in-law per-specitval boundary to the other. This ritual paradox expressed the ambivalence inherent in the fertility model. The symbolic action suggested that in crossing the boundary she journeyed to her husband's house in body but not always in spirit.

Exit rites from the quarters exhibited no such ambivalence. While a courtesan's exit may have anticipated marriage, particularly if her contract was bought out, thus shortening her stay in the quarter, her departure was less about a definite sense of the future and more about a definite break with the past. Nevertheless, through common tales and literature of courtesans leaving their profession as lovers of the wealthy, the handsome, the powerful, or the just, the quarters provided their own myths of exit tinged with hopes of marriage and love. Saikaku's fictionalized account of the marriage between the historical Yoshino and his novel's protagonist is such an example. These stories valorized both the life of courtesans and life after prostitution. Without blurring the distinction between sexual values before and after exiting the quarters, such stories speak in the same paradoxical tone of ritual, namely affirmation and transformation. Rites of exit similarly served this process of affirming a woman as a courtesan while also anticipating her transformation into a woman whose life now lay beyond the walls of her pleasure quarter.

BETROTHAL

The conspicuous mark of betrothal was a gift presentation to the bride's family by the groom's household. Gifts were not, however, the only mark. Before betrothal, important steps were taken tying the couple and families together. Successful investigation into each family's history, religious affiliation, and financial background was common, as was divining lucky days for the betrothal, procession, and marriage.[1] In this way, families affirmed the match on both worldly and spiritual planes. Because of its contractual-spiritual nature binding individuals and families, betrothal was as important as the wedding ceremony that followed, which may be understood as ritually carrying through a promise between families. So important was betrothal in establishing the reality of a woman's role as wife that broken engagements were functionally equivalent to divorce in some circumstances. Divorce temples, which were nunneries that the shogunate sanctioned to mediate divorce for women who entered their gates, reveal the importance of betrothal as marking ties already bound. The nunneries of Tōkeiji and Mantokuji both accepted women seeking sanctuary as a means to break off engagements once betrothal gifts had been exchanged.[2]

Engagement presents served notice that the daughter and son were not only matched, but that a transaction had occurred that ideally made the match immutable. In this transaction, betrothal and the wedding ceremony proper worked in tandem. Betrothal signified a down payment, as it were, on the daughter's nascent identity as daughter-in-law; the wedding ceremony symbolically worked to dye her in the ways of her new household and establish her fertility to serve it as a wife. What kind of transaction was involved in betrothal? Arima Sumiko and Nishigaki Yoshiko give one answer by putting forward three types of marriage consciousness *(ishiki)* that have been active in Japanese history.[3] The first type is pillage marriage *(ryakudatsukon)*. The term intentionally evokes the image of a woman being carried off against her will; coerced transport from home and family is the operative metaphor. It highlights the processional element of *yometori* marriage where the bride is taken to the groom's house. Ritualized and celebratory transportation signals an accrual of ceremonialism *(gishikika)* hiding an ancient attitude toward women under the gloss of ritual veneer. This attitude holds that anyone or group such as parents and the household authority may uproot a woman even if it is against her wishes.[4] The second type of consciousness comes under various names such as donation marriage *(zōyokon)*, transaction marriage *(baibaikon)*, and exchange marriage *(kōkan-kon)*. As the names suggest, this arrangement is largely an economic transaction. The seller is the daughter's family, the buyer is the groom's household, and the product is the daughter and her sexuality. Gift giving in betrothal is the ritual expression of this purchase. As evidence of this consciousness, Arima and Nishigaki point to the word *urenokori*, which means both "unsold goods" and "old maid," as a linguistic survival of this marriage consciousness.[5] The final type of consciousness is that of contemporary Japan, where a woman and man come together largely of their own accord.[6] Casting aside this final form of consciousness as a recent phenomenon with little precedent before postwar Japan, Arima and Nishigaki summarize Tokugawa marriage as largely void of any sensibility of female authority.[7] As scholars whose methodology is representative of the kind I discussed in chapter 1—that is, one focusing on social structures and ideologies of inequality—they stress that this sense of marriage reflects the period's patriarchy and its social and economic disenfranchisement of women. Thus the typological Tokugawa *yometori* marriage pattern incorporated a sense of the woman spirited away through gilded ceremony, which, if the gold foil were peeled away, would reveal the cold, hard fact that a daughter betrothed was a daughter sold.

This view of betrothal and marriage as a transaction reflecting patriarchal ideology and social structure draws equivalency between betrothal, transaction, and the devaluing of female authority. The equation is sound in terms of Arima and Nishigaki's interest in drawing a direct relationship between Tokugawa notions of female value and the period's poverty of female authority. Still, at another level of social and familial reality was the fact that most families loved their daughters and wanted the best for them, and for many such families betrothing their daughters and seeing them off in wedding rites signaled the hope that a good portion of that "best" had been achieved. When we pay attention to betrothal ritual as not simply a social expression of a patriarchal ideology, but also as a symbolic expression of love and hope for a daughter, then we gain a fuller meaning of betrothal as transaction: recognition that as a transaction betrothal was a shared sense by both parties that the item of concern—the bride—possessed value. Through ritual and symbol, betrothal gave a daughter and her family an important means to demonstrate what they held in their hearts as family—that she held value as a member of the household. It was due to the paucity of public realms of female value and authority that betrothal became an important avenue for a family to state symbolically the value of its daughter in the absence or narrowing of other avenues, such as household head, inheritance, and property ownership. Betrothal may have reflected the dominant social structure and ideology, but it also deflected power into the hands of a bride's family to be exercised through symbol and ritual. Betrothal gifts, typically called *yuinō,* acted as a sign of transaction, but in the end which party maintained emotional possession of a daughter upon completion of the transaction remained ambiguous. In his text, Namura states that the gifts act as a request for marriage *(tanomi o tsukawasu).*[8] As touched upon above, mutual investigation into each household's social and financial background, which constituted an important step in premarriage consultation between families, shows that for economically rising commoners with an *ie*-consciousness and family pride, sending a daughter into marriage was not a step taken lightly. For a daughter's family, betrothal gifts signified not only the financial worth of the fiancé's household, but also showed the emotional worth she held in the eyes of both his family and her family. If betrothal, as Arima and Nishigaki argue, was the face of patriarchy through its function to craft women into items of exchange, it also acted through gift giving in the face of patriarchy to establish for a family and its daughter ritual affirmation of her value as a member of a family.

The recommendations that lifestyle guides made for betrothal presents were grounded in older, elite forms. As with the marriage ceremony at the groom's house, these guides provided details for formal ritual styles. The details, however, acted less as fixed forms to be replicated whole and more as idealized guidelines meant for each home to adapt as necessary to its own customs, needs, and income. Namura recommends that the gift package include two kimono (or the material for making kimono), one of which would be white both inside and out, and the other a shade of red.[9] (Ideally a bride would wear these kimono during the nuptial rites at the groom's house, and the change from white kimono to one dyed with color marked the *ironaoshi* stage of the ceremony.) The colors are obvious symbols of the way wedding ceremonies balanced the themes of death/life and purity/fertility on the fulcrum of female sexuality. Other gifts could express the same symbolic language of white and red, as well as contemporary female customs. Sashida Fujiakira (1795–1871), a Shinto priest and teacher in a village called Nakatō (now an area of western Tokyo), noted in his diary an example of betrothal gifts that had been prepared on an August day in 1851. Although lacking white and red kimono, it included wrapped gifts of white twine, as well as wrapped bundles of white facial powder and safflower *(benibara)* to be used for lip rouge.[10] Application of makeup had long been a sign of marriage status among warrior women, and its inclusion among betrothal gifts in a Tokugawa village is evidence of the spread of this formerly elite custom to rural commoner women from economically comfortable families.[11] A century and a half before, Namura's text helped initiate this infusion of elite beauty and gift customs into the commoner population by, among other things, describing to his readers how, how much, and where to apply makeup.[12]

Whether expressed through kimono or white facial powder and lip rouge, the interplay of white and red in gifts was ubiquitous. The white kimono a daughter might have worn to her new home covered not only her body, but also a set of meanings about her body. As with corpses dressed in white for funerals, the bridal kimono suggested both a woman's death and separation from her household and a new life in the role of daughter-in-law. White symbolizes purity. With her assumed chastity, she brought sexual purity, and thus untapped fertile potential, to the groom's house. That potential to produce life was symbolized in the red color of her second kimono, which covered her body during the *iro-naoshi* stage of the wedding. Red signaled celebratory change from chaste daughter now dead to one household to fertile daughter-in-law now alive to another home, its way, and its desire for an heir. Her body was the same, but the meanings associated with it changed with the robes. Thinking of the white and red kimono as types of wrapping, as enclosures of her physical person that signify different meanings about the same body, the discussion of wrapping in chapter 4 comes again to the forefront. Treating something in a prescribed fashion—wrapping it in an obi or special paper—imparts meaning to it. Meaning may be apprehended to inhere in a thing, but this takes place only after human activity such as ritual practice has imparted that meaning. It is not that human activity and human apprehension are opposing views on sacred reality, but that human action predicates—and thus defines, orders, and articulates—human apprehension of sacrality. As further evidence of this dynamic of ritual activity, the practice of wrapping was extended to the preparation of kimono and other betrothal gifts. As Sashida's account informs us, the white facial powder and rouge were wrapped in bundles. Likewise, Namura's guide states the importance of wrapping the kimono and other gifts. Each roll is wrapped in two layers of special paper called *sugihara,* which was often used for objects for ceremonial occasions, and then each is wrapped again around the middle with a thin ribbon called *mizuhiki*[13] In the text's spirit of being a complete guide to female lifestyle, its last chapter's final section, detailing Ogasawara wrapping techniques, gives examples of how to wrap some of these betrothal gifts.[14] Wrapping these gifts, especially the rolls of kimono, which in turn the bride uses to wrap her body, was an activity that went beyond simply reflecting notions of aesthetics. It was an activity central to creating an articulation of fertility's linked concerns: bringing a stranger into one's household, making her identify with her new role, and placing hopes of generational continuity upon her body.

Rice wine and harvests from the ocean were also included among betrothal presents. Namura lists two grades of wine and fish offerings: five barrels of sake and five types of sea produce or, as an alternative, three barrels of drink and three items from the sea.[15] This grading of styles and matching of wine and sea products is evidence of earlier warrior ceremonial forms, which were sensitive to internal hierarchy within the samurai class, and it also reflected contemporary Tokugawa sensibilities of hierarchy and other indices of social order among commoners. As Sashida noted in his diary, the betrothal gifts leaving his village included two barrels of sake and two fish.[16] Sea products in Namura's version of the minimal three offerings include kelp, cuttlefish, and bream.[17] He further recommends abalone and dried bonito as additions for those families of grooms who choose to offer a higher grade of *yuinō*.[18]

Some of these items have a prominent place in the history of Japanese ceremonialism regarding prosperity and success of various kinds. Abalone has a particularly strong historical association with luck and long life. Dried and cut into long strips, it is called *noshi awabi*. Signifying the hope of a successful and long life, *noshi awabi* was a celebratory food of the aristocracy in the Nara and Heian periods.[19] Likely under the influence of the aristocracy and eager to emulate royal ways, the rising samurai incorporated the use of *noshi awabi* in various ceremonies.[20] Typifying meals that celebrated the attainment of a long life *(juga)*, its consumption became ubiquitous in ceremonies centering around hopes of the production and maintenance of life.[21] With these felicitous meanings, *noshi awabi* also served as an accompanying and decorative flourish to gift-giving occasions, and most particularly for betrothal, where concerns of success and long life for two households were symbolically on intense display. On a related symbolic note, the gifts that Sashida describes included, in addition to two kinds of fish, barracuda *(kamasu)*, which in his diary he uniquely spelled by applying three characters connoting the meaning of "gaining a full and long life."[22] As a traditional symbol signifying the same wish for success and longevity, *noshi awabi* became, by the middle of the Tokugawa period, a customary gift to be sent on occasions such as betrothals to celebrate hopes for prosperity and long life.[23] As a mark of its prominence in the presentation of gifts, it is the first example of wrapping given in the final section of *A Record of Treasures for Women* that reviews styles of wrapping. The dried abalone and the other food items and sake formed a ritual meal to be shared by representatives of both families.[24] Consumption of the groom's family's offerings signified not only acceptance of the gifts, but, as a meal symbolically tying two families together in a shared decision, it also held unique long-term consequences for each household measured against the respective loss or gain of a member.

In this way the contractual nature of betrothal gained a large measure of its power from ritual and its components, such as sake, food, wrapping, and communal eating, rather than juridical authority. The head of the Ise House, Sadatake, as we saw earlier, argued that all such celebrations are ways of worshiping *kami*. In ritual the act of displaying items "wrapped in double folds, with presentations of fish and fowl, sake ewers, and the like in one's parlor are offerings made to the *kami*."[25] Sadatake was concerned that people were practicing rites without proper consciousness of the deities at whom the rites ultimately were directed. As a means of edification, he specifies different celebratory occasions and links them to their proper deities. Among these links, he aligns marriage with the creator gods Izanagi and Izanami.[26] In this linkage Sadatake advocates a view that ritual actions ultimately refer to a divine realm, which through the power of ritual is made contiguous with the human world. However, by suggesting that while events and *kami* change accordingly, and the act of displaying food, drink, and wrapped items remains the same whatever the occasion or deity, he obliquely emphasizes the primacy of core ritual actions and symbolic items as the constant feature of celebratory worship. The root ritual actions of displaying and consuming gift foods and drink between families signaled not only that a groom and bride were a match made in heaven and in the image of Izanagi and Izanami, but that they were also a match made between and for two families. Betrothal symbolically made the two families one in their agreement concerning one woman's destiny. Still, this agreement acted as an evocative avenue for a daughter's family to declare her value as a natal member in spite of her inevitable departure. This ambivalence became more apparent with departure rites.

DEPARTURE

Departure rites prepared a woman for her processional journey into liminality, where her sexuality and social role were held suspended between the former chaste daughter and the as-yet fertile daughter-in-law. Rites at the groom's household pulled her out of this suspended state to serve her new family with obedient and energetic harmony and the hope of productive fertility. Symbolically, the practice of pre-procession was to make the young woman a blank slate upon which her new family could begin writing its hopes. While departure literally accomplished the task of sending a daughter away, symbolically it subverted its task of wiping clean her and her family's slate of identity and loyalty to each other. In this way, pre-procession both prepared an exit for a daughter to take her leave while also allowing a family to extend its hold on her and, as eventually happened in some cases, even anticipate her return.

Departure rites received their ambivalence from the interplay of death and fertility motifs. The dead and virgin daughter gradually gave way to the living and fertile daughter-in-law as she was carried in her palanquin and later participated in the rites conducted at the groom's home, which, as we saw in chapter 3, were rich with metaphors of sexuality and new life. This was the symbolic trajectory of her wedding day. In his description of bridal departure, which is the front half of this trajectory, Namura concentrates on death symbolism. As becomes clear later in this section, death symbolism and departure for some like Namura were essential in promoting fertility values. This identity was controversial among some advocates of the fertility model and, further, expressed ambivalence toward, as much as promotion of, the model's values.

Namura's guide represents well this power of departure to evoke metaphors of funeral rites and the dead. In the opening section on wedding ritual, Namura reminds his readers that they are not to make their parents' homes their own, but rather need to make their place inside their husbands' homes.[27] He then turns to the theme of one's moral duty and notes that with marriage comes a new understanding of the home to which one returns. Marriage signaled the duty of going home to one's husband and forsaking the practice of returning home to one's parents. Namura stresses that a woman must not regard her parents' home as her own, and that marriage for a woman meant she would not return to her natal home. This act of not returning was what made the bride like the dead. "As it is that the dead never return to their homes, people compare marriage to death in that a daughter never returns again to the home of her mother and father."[28] He follows this logic of resemblance with practices of resemblance, most notably the use of ceremonial fires or torches *(kadobi),* which were lit at the gates of houses during funerals and bridal departures as a means of sending off the dead as well as daughters.[29] Like a daughter leaving on her journey to another household, a corpse, too, would pass by lit torches when carried out of the household on its journey to the other world. Other period texts describe similar practices and employ shared terminology for funeral and departure fires, such as "on the day of the wedding, when the bride passes through the gate, sending-away fires *(okuribi)* are lit."[30] In addition to the funerary symbol of fire, Namura also calls for the use of salt and ash at departure for purification.[31] He does not give any specific instructions about these items, but this is probably because his audience was ritually knowledgeable concerning their use in funerals.

As ritual, the actions and symbols constituting departure were open to interpretation, and thus open to controversy in the fertility model. Namura is unequivocal in his interpretation. After noting the symbols of death (burning torches at the gate and employing salt and ash) appropriate for use in seeing off a daughter, Namura explicates these meanings by metaphorically referring them to the custom of cursing the dead. One cursed the dead to establish a taboo that kept them from returning too often to the living. Likewise, frequent returning of a daughter to her natal home was a matter best avoided, a taboo best respected, as it took her away from her new home and responsibilities.[32] He links not returning home to a woman's cultivation of *tashinami*—the idealized behavior of an obedient wife. "In that she does not return home she shows herself to be prudent, modest, and selfless."[33] Dead to her parents and to the home of her birth, she should turn to a new life in serving her parents-in-law and their—and also now her—household. In this way, Namura effectively sees the symbols of death and the rite of departure as supporting the fundamental concern of fertility that a bride live not simply in but *for* another household. Symbolic death, or at least its logic, freed her to offer her loyalty, skills, and sexuality to the authority of a new household.

Although Namura claims that the employment of funerary symbols is popular among all classes of people, the practice of mixing death ritual in wedding rites was not without its contemporary criticism.[34] Sadatake strongly opposed death symbolism in marriage, although he, too, acknowledges in his work the popularity of the ritual trend. Further, he is familiar with the type of symbolic argument that Namura uses in advocating funerary symbols amidst marriage as supportive of fertility values, but he completely rejects it as grossly mistaken *(hanahada ayamari nari)*.[35] Rather than depend on death symbols and taboo for encouraging values in a daughter, Sadatake argues instead that parents need to teach their daughter before her wedding the importance of filial piety and obedience. As he notes, all the death symbolism in the world will not keep a household from divorcing and sending back a bride whose behavior has brought her husband or her in-laws unhappiness and regret.[36] He argues further that reliance on symbols and rituals resembling the dead and funerals forgets that the purpose of a wedding is to celebrate the hope of household prosperity and children. When people mix symbols of death and mourning in a rite of fertility and life, they tempt fate and the power of resemblance. They invite on themselves childlessness and risk the extinction of their households. "The dead do not give birth to children . . . and thus if you resemble the dead, you, too, will not bear any children."[37]

As fertility moralists Sadatake and Namura concurred on the importance of marriage in the lives of women, but as ritualists they parted ways on differences concerning the appropriateness and meaning of death symbolism in marriage ritual. Multiplicity of meanings and the power of evocation can give to ritual a sense of ambivalence even when it is linked to a unified clarity of value advocacy. The ambivalence of departure ritual, specifically its allusions to death, clouded the values that fertility moralists tried to associate with it. The use of ash and torches allowed parents to show love for their departed daughter through the symbols of grief and loss. Building upon betrothal, death symbolism and ritual resemblance may have acted more to affirm identity with and loyalty to one's daughter and less, as Namura wants to argue, to cut her from family bonds. Treating the bride as dead was symbolically problematic, as Sadatake realized. However, the reasons for his objection—bad form, a poor substitution for moral education, and a foolish toying with fate— miss the larger problem that Namura sensed and attempted to answer through death symbolism: the danger of bridal return.

There were customary occasions for a young wife to return to her family for brief visitation. Although not cited in Namura's text, the last step in virilocal wedding traditions called for *satogaeri*, or when a bride returned to her family and hometown for a number of days after her nuptials to present her parents with gifts and present herself as a new wife.[38] However, outside of fixed times and events such as *satogaeri*, and in some cases birth, a wife who returned home repeatedly was cause for unease in the promoters of fertility values. Namura thought a wife's frequent returns ought to be forbidden *(yokuyoku kaeru koto o imu)*, and he found death symbolism appropriate for creating a sense of taboo, of respecting borders of time and place.[39] Cursing the dead at funerals acted to create borders between the living and the nonliving so that spirits of the departed would not return outside the restraints and order of fixed ritual time. When the dead transgress boundaries of time and ritual custom they bring disorder to the world of the living. Namura sought through death symbolism to create a parallel between brides and the dead and the need to limit the return home of each to fixed times and formal occasions. Nevertheless, this similarity between the bride and the dead on the issue of returning home was symbolically problematic. The most notable fixed time for ritual interaction between the living and the dead in Japan was and continues to be the annual Buddhist festival of the dead, or *o-bon*. In high summer, spirits of deceased family members return to commune with the their living descendants after being guided by the light of fires set outside homes; at the conclusion of the festival they are sent away by fire. Burning fires and torches with the departure of a daughter in marriage signals farewell to her, as Namura insists. However, fire as a symbol of both a welcome and a send-off for the dead also signals a strong theme: family bonds of identity holding fast despite time's passing.

The evocative power and multivocality of death symbolism suggesting permanent loss as well as anticipated return opens, rather than resolves, the issue of a daughter's identity. Departure allowed a daughter's family to give her away to another while still making emotional claims to her family membership. Betrothal and departure produced a symbolic tug-of-war over claims to a daughter/bride. In spite of the ubiquitous advocacy of fertility values in Tokugawa society, the rituals of marriage proved at times inharmonious with this advocacy. The tug-of-war that rituals exposed and values shunned was sometimes resolved only through marriage failure and divorce, which is another form of exit to which we will return shortly.

RETIREMENT FROM THE QUARTERS

Retirement for a courtesan presented no such conflict of claims as existed in betrothal and departure. Her exit was not a move between families but a move out of a role and value system. Retirement rites suggested an ordering of sexual role and place that proposed what was good for a woman inside her quarter was ill fitting once she returned to the outside. As departure put a woman on the journey from chaste daughter to fertile daughter-in-law, retirement put a woman outside the gate of pleasure on a journey from the role and values of prostitution toward a sometimes uncertain future.

Departing the world of pleasure was built into the model as part of its own ideals about female sexuality. The few extant bordello contracts remaining make clear that the bordello's legal possession of a woman was temporary. In 1862 a woman named Watō sold her younger sister,

Yasu, to a Yoshiwara bordello. The contract states the day Yasu had to start employment and the day it would end, which, according to the contract, made her term of service three years and four months.[40] The contract does not give any reason for this precise time frame. It may have been a point of negotiation on which Watō and the bordello agreed, but the date may also have been configured in line with Yasu's age to meet the quarters' official retirement age of twenty-seven.[41] Several *senryū* refer to the age of twenty-eight not only as the first full year of a woman's life back in regular society, but also as a time of specific actions, which were small but socially powerful changes a woman made to her body that publicly altered her social identity from courtesan to ordinary person *(heimin)*. One *senryū* puts it thus: "When a courtesan turns twenty-eight, she can wear socks—at last!" *(Keisei wa nijūhachi ni yatto tabi).*[42] Reflecting their low status in the official Tokugawa social order, courtesans did not wear split-toed socks *(tabi)* with their sandals, as did townswomen. In the earliest days of the Yoshiwara, courtesans went completely barefoot. Footwear eventually became a stylish accessory, but they were still worn without *tabi*.[43] The uncovered foot was a common marker of social hierarchy and not exclusive to courtesans. Other contractual employees laboring low on the social ladder, such as servants in households, both female and male, also did not wear socks.[44] Retirement, however, allowed a woman to slip socks back on and publicly identify herself as possessing normal status. Another *senryū* observes, "At twenty-eight, both your world and your forehead widen" *(Shaba mo hitai mo hirō naru nijūhachi).*[45] The widening of the forehead refers to the practice of shaving the eyebrows upon retirement, thus giving the appearance of a larger forehead. Since courtesans were typically not allowed to leave the quarter during employment, retirement not only led to a "wide" shaved forehead, but also to the wide world outside the walls.

Shaving the eyebrows was a sign of female social maturation and status. Another was blackening the teeth *(haguro)* upon engagement or marriage. Kitagawa Utamaro captured the contrast well in a print simply titled *Mother and Daughter (Haha to musume)* portraying a daughter with full brows looking upon her mother's hairless face as the older woman applies blackening to her teeth.[46] In the absence of brows, wives used brow blackening, especially after applying formal makeup. Among the long list of items Namura catalogs for a woman to take into marriage are implements for blackening teeth, ink and brush for drawing on brows, and a razor for shaving brows and fine hair on the forehead.[47] With these tools a woman constructed a social body that acknowledged her status and sexuality as that of a wife. In sharp contrast, not unlike the young daughter of Utamaro's print, courtesans were conspicuous with their white teeth and unshaved eyebrows. Light trimming of the brows was acceptable, but courtesans were encouraged to follow a "less is more" principle of beauty. Fujimoto Kizan (1626–1704), author of *The Great Mirror of the Erotic Way (Shikidō ōkagami)*, a 1678 dandy's guide and etiquette book on the pleasure quarters, cautions that too much plucking of brows and use of blackening leaves a woman unattractive to her clients.[48] This emphasis on beauty is based on *not* looking like shaved, ink-smeared townswomen *(machi no onna)*.[49] Leaving the brow's unshaved created a different social body that embraced a markedly different role and set of sexual values. In this way, both fertility and pleasure moralists were sensitive to the body as an expression of particular morals via particular constructions of external beauty.[50] Fujimoto notes such awareness in the contemporary custom of Shimabara's courtesans of shaving their eyebrows the night before departure.[51]

This concern with women's eyebrows prompts us to look upon them as a type of hair symbolism. Deliberate cutting of hair is a ubiquitous, pan-cultural act marking transition in social status and identity.[52] In Japanese religious history the most conspicuous example is the shaved pate of a tonsured Buddhist monk or nun. Symbolism, however, does not depend on quantity for its evocative power. Historically, Japanese women have had preliminary, and even temporary, options available to them on the nun's path—whether or not they chose to walk toward ordination and tonsure—that required them simply to cut short, rather than shave off, their hair.[53] Bobbed rather than bald, such women still stood apart from ordinary women both visually and in the sexual values they and their distinct hair reflected—celibacy and distance from men. Similarly, the removal or nonremoval of even small lines of hair growth above the eyes resonated inside the chamber of Tokugawa sexual values. Hair symbolism is diverse. To make a categorical statement about it is to assure that a categorical refutation, via a single contrary example, is near at hand. Still, risking one's own warning, longer or unadorned hair tends to reflect to some degree being outside the norms of society, and adorning and styling, pulling up, cutting, or removing hair tends to signify either initiation into/reentering the norms of society or living under a particularly strict and disciplined subset of rules in society.[54] This characterization of hair symbolism is relevant in gaining perspective on why models of fertility and pleasure, in their constructions of social bodies, paid so much attention to so little hair. Eyebrows may be small wisps of hair, but their symbolism can be comparatively large. Women's eyebrows took in the disparate meanings of multiple sexual values in Tokugawa culture and magnified them again in the ritualized activity of women either conspicuously beautifying them or shaving them off completely. The presence of hair above a courtesan's eyes amplified, more than any sex act possibly could, her status from the norms and women outside the quarter. Like a wife, her sexual activity was a private act, even if publicly sanctioned and purchased, but her eyebrows were a public symbol of her status and role. Her eyebrows expressed the private act, the public role, and the valuation of both. Reentering ordinary society and its orientation toward a different set of values encouraged a retiring courtesan, at some point, to remove her carefully crafted eyebrows. As public symbol, the loss of hair above the eyes stated her separation from her outsider status as play lover to many men. A hairless forehead also symbolized her cultural preparedness, like that of many women her age, to limit her sexuality to one man and one household.

The preparation of clothes prior to departing her quarter also spoke of reorientation from pleasure and reentering wider society. Bordello custom and a woman's rank determined the dispensing of clothes and bedding acquired during a courtesan's career. A lower-ranking woman retiring with few kimono and accessories might take them with her upon retirement if she so chose, but a woman of higher status and reputation possessed not only many items, but also was involved in many layers of human relations within the quarter, such as with the teahouse staff, her bordello family, and her own entourage of teens and young girls. In the rounds of gift giving that were required upon a ranking courtesan's retirement, donating her clothes and other items to staff members, her entourage, and friends was one way of meeting her farewell obligations.[55] The clothes and bedding a woman had purchased and received throughout her professional years reflected, like her eyebrows, the status and the valuation of her sexuality in the model of pleasure. The ritual language of customarily giving away one's acquired finery upon retirement was acknowledgment that they had no place outside a courtesan's life. This language was also echoed in the round of gift giving marking a woman's departure when she, upon giving away her old clothes, received one or more new kimono depending on the wishes of her employer or redeemer. According to *The Great Mirror of the Erotic Way,* these new clothes should come from her bordello owner, her clients, or, if her contract was being redeemed, from the paying patron.[56] The latter was under obligation to outfit her appropriately for an ordinary life with him outside the quarter. Appropriate to this exit into ordinariness, Fujimoto notes that the new clothing should reflect weaving patterns governing the rules of ordinary life *(heizei hatto)* rather than those of the floating world. He suggests the popular striped pattern called *kanoko,* which, with her shaved brows, would transform the former courtesan's appearance into the very model of a commoner woman.[57] On her last night in the Shimabara, she would visit her old teahouse of assignation to say farewell to the owner and staff. Shaved and cloaked in commoner clothing, and in so doing having moved from one side of her perspectival boundary to another, she would stand before her colleagues not as a courtesan but as an ordinary woman.

Retirement practices of shaving the eyebrows and changing clothes could take on additional meaning when a patron paid off a woman's contract. This purchase usually totaled the remaining debt on the woman's term of service plus any additional costs. The redemption price went up proportionately with the woman's rank, popularity, and her owner's inclination to pad her price. The contract Watō signed in selling Yasu states that if an interested party wished to take Yasu as a wife, concubine, or adopted daughter, then her contract could be bought out and her employment terminated.[58] Yasu's consent, significantly, had to be obtained for the sale of her contract. The document includes the phrase "upon the woman's satisfaction" *(joshi mo tokushin no ue)* as a condition to purchasing her contract.[59] With the backing of legal contracts—minus any coercion from their owners angling for a better deal—courtesans held some measure of control over a portion of their fates. They possessed legal authority to decline offers from clients either in hopes of better choices in the future or in determination to finish their terms of service and leave on their own terms. In this manner, a daughter toiling away in erotic labor legally had more authority over her destiny than a daughter (or son) in the household, who had no legal authority concerning decisions about her life. A woman accepting an offer of contractual redemption may have received, in addition to a new set of clothes appropriate for life on the outside of pleasure, a headdress called *watabōshi,* according to the rules of courtesy in *The Great Mirror of the Erotic Way.*[60] This headdress had different colors and functions. Many brides wore a white *watabōshi* on their wedding day, but women also sported them in public as conventional headwear, and these came in a variety of colors such as red, purple, light blue, and saffron.[61] Whether white bridal wear or colorful daily wear, it was meant to be worn outside of the quarter as a statement of a woman's new identity. Torii Kiyonaga (1752–1815) depicts such a woman leaving her palanquin and entering the house of her new husband in a 1786 work (fig. 13). She is conspicuous in her commonness. She dons a *watabōshi,* and, unlike her porters, whose bare feet signal their lowly status as laborers, she walks toward her new home wearing *tabi* like any ordinary woman.

Other parallels signifying the transformative change of the exit experiences of brides and courtesans existed. A Yoshiwara courtesan likely washed her feet at the quarter's well, located near the Inari tutelary shrine, prior to her departure.[62] Such a practice was in line with a wider number of actions and symbols focusing on the feet and soil as measures of one's place and role. Since place and role were malleable markers for women at critical points in the life cycle, it is not surprising that this reservoir of ritual and symbol involving aspects of the feet—and the dirt one's feet pick up as one moves from one place to another—often centered on women in the process of change. This is particularly true of brides. Interpreting the "feet and dirt" of brides helps us understand the ritual context of a courtesan's foot washing. Placing one's feet on the new ground of a husband's household demanded ritual attention to keep intact the distinction between the place and role of daughter and daughter-in-law. The idea that where one puts her feet grounds who she is

FIGURE 13 A now former courtesan is dropped off at her new home. From an original reproduction of Torii Kiyonaga's illustration by Mitani Kazuma. Courtesy of Rippū Shobō, Tokyo.

finds various expression in marriage rituals. Among the betrothal gifts Sashida lists in his diary are two pairs of *tabi* and two pairs of straw sandals.[63] Similarly, Namura lists footwear among many things a bride might bring with her in marriage.[64] The literal idea expressed in the gift of new footwear is not to mix the dust on one's old sandals with the ground of a new husband's household. The phrase "pollution from the bottom" (*shita kara no kegare*) captures this idea well,[65] and it reveals more than an aversion to dirty feet or footwear. It suggests an aversion to dirt's carriers—shoes and thus the people who wear them—being out of place, crossing boundaries, and threatening the social order. Dirt is simply another name for something out of place and thus a threat to the social order and the way it systematizes things based on cultural notions of purity and pollution or, in the Japanese context, *hare* and *kegare*.[66] Making a symbolic line of association between the need to distinguish one set of ground, sandals, and role from another set in marriage customs acts on the same source of unease as death symbolism in weddings: the anxiety of bridal return. Certainly many women stayed close to their families throughout their marriages by making frequent visits to their natal homes, but the symbolism suggests a cultural anxiety that perceived both a bounded order separating natal and marriage homes and a potentially unbounded bride. She posed the risk of encroaching boundaries with an ease and recurrence that could contribute to strains and disorder between her and her marriage household. Although new sandals suggest a hope for order and household harmony, they also intimate a fear of becoming worn and dirty from a wife never staying in place because she crosses, with too much frequency and informality, the boundary between natal and marriage homes and between daughter and daughter-in-law.

The symbolic association linking feet and footwear, the crossing of boundaries, and the change of role and identity may be seen in Tokugawa divorce temples as well. The *bakufu* granted only two convents—Tōkeiji and Mantokuji—the authority to mediate female-initiated divorce as long as the woman's claim was just and she agreed to live the austere life of a nun until her suit was concluded. Each temple claimed historical ties to shogunal power and prestige, which made them powerful institutions straddling the border of both religious and governmental authority. A wife seeking sanctuary from her husband in either convent was entitled to protection from him as long as her sandals or any article of clothing or accessory attached to her body could be tossed ahead of her inside the temple's gate.[67] Whether or not a woman actually threw her sandals ahead of her to escape the clutches of a pursuing

husband, such an action was grounded in the ritual logic that symbolically spoke to the real political authority of divorce temples. This is captured in a painting of Mantokuji that has become iconographic. It shows
a wife attempting to rush into the open gate of the temple, throwing her
sandals ahead of her into the convent's grounds just as her pursuing husband's hands are about to grasp her hair.[68] Footwear was not simply a
covering for one's feet or a sign of one's role, but was also an extension
of the social body that, depending on the situation and needs of a
woman, held the promise (of a bride) or the threat (of a woman seeking divorce) of changing loyalties, ties, and places.

Washing of the feet was also employed in some localities as a ritual
for welcoming brides, and it functioned in the same symbolic manner as
the removal of old sandals. Certain customs called for washing the bride's
feet on her wedding day as a way of removing "pollution from the bottom" by placing her feet in a water basin upon her entrance into the husband's house.[69] A courtesan washing her feet on the occasion of departing the quarter exhibited the same symbolic effect of status change as did
a bride changing her footwear or washing her feet upon entering a
household. In the case of a courtesan, the ritual practice of washing the
feet *(ashi arai)* was tied to *upward* status change: she moved upward from
an "outcast" class back into normal society. I enclose "outcast" in quotes
because even though courtesans officially existed below the four classes
of Tokugawa society—warrior, farmer, artisan, and merchant—which by
definition made them *hinin* (non-persons) and therefore outcasts from
the rest of society, their actual status was much more ambiguous. They
labored under contracts with a set retirement deadline, which thus made
them legally equal to laborers in ordinary society who toiled under the
demanding strictures but ultimate promise of their contracts. The *hinin*
were made up of a variety of people and occupations. Some of these
occupations, most notably those of the *eta*—people who effectively constituted a caste of laboring families whose work was deemed polluting—
were inherited. Other people, however, such as courtesans and those
given *hinin* status as a form of legal punishment, were recognized as constituting a temporary, nonhereditary *hinin* class with various options
available for moving back into the world of ordinary people *(heimin).*[70]
It is this sort of upward move—not simply one of status, but also one of
social cleanliness—to which *ashi arai* as a term and as a practice generally
refers. The practice of Yoshiwara courtesans washing the quarter's dirt
from their feet upon retirement and moving out from the actual ground
and social role of prostitution reflected the same ritual and symbolic logic

of bridal footwear and foot washing. The simple gesture of pouring water on the feet evoked an order of social classifications and boundaries of persons in Tokugawa society. Though the Yoshiwara could be a muddy place due to its marshy location, the "mud" a woman washed from her feet was less the literal mud of a marsh than the social mud of a role and its values. By washing it away, a retiring courtesan washed away a role and value system that was no longer a part of her life. Keeping the mud in its own place, she moved out and headed for a new one.

Escape from the Household and Quarter

Although betrothal and departure accomplished the task of placing a daughter in the home of another family that she would ideally serve throughout her life, they also suggested ambivalence about such a one-sided move. These cracks of uncertainty had the potential to split when wives chose to turn away from their husbands and in-laws and return home. The successful exit from a husband's home and resolution of conflict could be accomplished through time, patience, bullying, or, as I examine here, the strategic use of available institutions, rituals, and symbols. Women in the quarters, like some wives in their husbands' homes, also took advantage of rituals and symbols when they found their situation intolerable and contemplated flight. Unapproved departures from both household and quarter fell outside the ritual mechanics of fertility and pleasure models. Fertility idealized a wife's role as permanent, and, with the exception of customary, ritually timed excursions, such as returning home after her nuptials, the model revealed a sense of anxiety toward a wife exiting on her own initiative and inclinations. Likewise, pleasure had a ritual structure for approved and timely exits only upon retirement or contractual buyout. Neither model possessed any sanctioned practice of a woman initiating premature departure. This absence turns our attention toward institutions, subversive symbols, ritual practices, and juridical processes scattered throughout the social and cultural landscape in which women attempted to escape roles and places they did not wish to occupy.

With the exception of the severely limited institution of divorce temples, of which there were only two, other forms of symbolic and strategic behavior are less easy to grasp historically. Much of this is due to their being in a different and shadowy category than the more public ritual and documented practices we have seen thus far in marriage, first meeting, pregnancy, betrothal, and retirement. Contrary to these practices, hopes of escape and the ritual activity and symbols tied to them were often either intensely individual or strategically conspiratorial and involving another person or group, such as a love interest or one's family. The two sanctioned divorce temples, whose fame for mediation in terminating marriages was known far outside their immediate locales, however, stand in contrast to this historical enshroudment.[71] Their presence in society represents in some ways the institutional and juridical, and thus controlled, legitimization of broader and murkier forms of female strategies and practices. All functionally acted, however, to initiate desired change in a woman's life that, depending on the practice, either rode roughshod over (divorce) or slipped quietly past (escaping the quarters) the values of fertility and pleasure. Further, as a group, these practices are distinguished by "ritualizing." Ritualizing is a deliberate and self-initiated practice falling outside the boundary and legitimacy of mainstream institutions and actions. It is ritual practiced "in the margins, on the thresholds" of society in the face of real and immediate needs.[72] Whether practiced in the confines of a convent, at the base of a tree, or at a small shrine in the corner of a quarter, plots to escape were always, both by definition and by the social and legal makeup of Tokugawa Japan, peripheral activities. Ritualizing entails a variety of purposeful, strategic activities in which women could engage to effect departures that were as much individually desired as they were, in some cases, illegal, and in others officially sanctioned but never officially recommended.

These ritualizing practices make up a broad complex that centered on cutting social relations between individuals or between an individual and her group. In Japanese this complex is known as *enkiri shinkō* (cutting-ties faith). *Shinkō* (faith) may include notions of explicit religious belief and confession, but typically it involves reliance on ritual, addressing situational and concrete concerns, and an experimental, trial-and-error approach to see what works to address real and pressing needs.[73] In this sense it is better to think of *shinkō* as a "working faith." The faith aspect suggests the hope of the participant in realizing the goal of her aspirations; the working aspect directs attention to ritual activities and symbolic behavior in which the person engaged as a response to her faith in attaining a goal. *Shinkō* is activity that faithfully seeks definite results for the betterment of one's life, usually understood to mean measurable improvement in this present life by gaining worldly benefits. The varied practices examined in the previous chapter dealing with safe birth may be thought of as *anzan shinkō* (safe-birth faith), with the benefit being uneventful birth and the mother's full recovery.

In the case of wives and courtesans who hoped to make an unapproved departure from the household and quarter through various actions of *shinkō,* the benefits they sought were divorce and successful escape. The actions and results of *enkiri shinkō* sat stubbornly opposite those of the rites of marriage and debut or first meeting, which were forms of another working faith called *enmusubi shinkō* (creating-ties faith). The latter were formal, public rituals of celebration that tied not only a woman and man in a fixed relation, but also individuals to a larger collectivity such as a household or bordello. *Enkiri* is the antipode of *enmusubi,* the private conspiracy against public celebration. It represents symbols and actions, ranging from the juridical and magical to the divine and deceptive, that take place at the margins of society, on the underside of values, and in the face of celebratory rituals. This takes place at the margins of society when wives leave the center of their official identity—their husbands' households—to effect divorce, and when courtesans pray in small, unlucky corners of the quarter to help them in their schemes to flee. It happens on the underside of values because these practices openly reject the values of fertility and pleasure. It takes place in the face of celebratory ritual because the actions of individual wives and courtesans attempt to tear asunder what *enmusubi* rites have brought together.

ESCAPE FROM THE HOUSEHOLD

Among commoners the power of unilateral divorce possessed by the husband's household was one form of discipline that the man and his family could employ to threaten a woman whose behavior was not in line with that of the household. Among the warrior class divorce required consent from both families, negotiated settlement, and notification of the shogunate before finalization.[74] Thus it is in the world of commoners that the right of divorce resting with the husband—which has long been viewed as one the clearest indicators of the dearth of female authority in the Tokugawa—was legally salient and practiced. This lack of female authority did not, however, leave women without options or prerogatives to reverse the power husbands and their households possessed. Actually, for many women the problem of legal prerogative in the hands of their husbands was less in the right to divorce than in the right *not* to divorce. A woman unhappy with her marriage and wanting out could try to make her husband and in-laws miserable with her behavior and thus hasten a divorce decree. In this way the fertility model's seven classic reasons for divorce may also be seen as a conspiratorial blueprint for a woman to use in making her household wretched enough to divorce her. Divorce decrees are good sources for understanding the diverse human dramas produced by divorce among commoners in the Tokugawa period. Popularly called *mikudarihan* (three and a half lines), writs of divorce were often no longer than this, simply stated a reason for the divorce, and were signed by both the husband and wife. Many made clear through phrases such as "selfish" *(wagamama)* "ill suited" *(fusō)* and "misconduct" *(fugyōseki)* that a wife's bad behavior, whether strategically planned or not, had a direct impact on her loss of marital status.[75] Although an unwanted divorce could be costly for a woman in terms of lost status and possible humiliation for her family, many women still desired it. Indeed, as divorce temples and their housing costs indicate, women were willing to pay for divorce through their own and natal families' finances.[76] Thus one dilemma that a woman had to overcome was not when a husband divorced her, but when he chose not to do so. Husbands and their households not only possessed the right of *enkiri,* but also by logical extension the right to keep the marriage ties, the right to maintain *enmusubi.* All the options available to women— juridical and institutional and devotional and magical—attempted to shift some of the power of *enkiri* to a woman's corner. With this she could try to counteract her husband's prerogative of *enmusubi.*

The most conspicuous options were the divorce temples of Tōkeiji and Mantokuji. Tōkeiji was founded in 1285 as a Zen nunnery in Kamakura.[77] Mantokuji's origins are less clear. A warrior descended from the shogunal Minamoto line, Nitta Yoshisue (d. 1246), purportedly founded it in the province of Kōzuke. Beside their common function in mediating divorce, Mantokuji and Tōkeiji also both were closely associated with the ruling Tokugawa family, from which much of their institutional authority derived. This is particularly true of Mantokuji. Many of its abbesses, as well as financial donations, came from the women's quarters *(ōoku)* of the shogunate.[78] Futher, Ieyasu claimed it as his ancestral temple in 1591 as a political bid to tie his family name to that of the temple's founder, Yoshisue, and, through him, Minamoto Yoritomo, the founder of the country's first shogunate, the Kamakura *bakufu.*[79] Ieyasu's funerary tablets were installed in Mantokuji's main hall. They stood, until the passing of the shogunate, as a powerful symbol of the small temple's political clout.[80]

In their capacity to mediate divorce, the convents were known as "cutting-ties temples" *(enkiridera)*. Upon entering one of the convents a wife initiated a divorce suit against her husband, with temple authorities acting as mediator between her family and her husband. If efforts to get a husband to sign a writ of divorce through the office of the temple failed, Tōkeiji initially required a woman to reside there for three years, after which she would be considered divorced and could leave to renew her life, but in the 1740s it reduced this period of service effectively to twenty-four months.[81] Mantokuji required twenty-five months.[82] However, apart from being nunneries, their function of mediating female-initiated divorce was not unique in Tokugawa society. Other institutions were available for a woman to house herself and pursue a claim against her husband. Such institutions were imbued with localized or extraterritorial power and included homes of *daimyō* retainers, offices and personal residences of magistrates, the homes of village heads, and even priest-run temples.[83] Further, within each convent the legal process of divorce was handled by male secular authorities and largely separate from the daily devotional activities of the nunnery and its women, both tonsured nuns and wives seeking divorce.[84]

Rather than examining divorce temples as a Buddhist phenomenon, one may view them as reflecting a larger complex of similarly functioning institutions and practices of female-initiated *enkiri*. This wider view clarifies the dynamics of power and practice of divorce in a society where the values of fertility, particularly that of wifely obedience, were heavily idealized. Whether through a divorce temple, a magistrate's house, the brute intervention of one's family, or the practice of ritual magic, the quantifiable goal of a wife's *enkiri* was to obtain a writ of divorce from her husband. These various methods available to a woman with hopes of gaining a divorce from her husband suggest a dynamic of power in which the execution of power by a group or individual lies in "guiding the possibility of conduct and putting in order the possible outcome."[85] Because the authority to write a divorce notice and have the wife co-sign it lay with the husband, a woman who wanted a divorce from an uncooperative spouse needed to take action to force or direct the power of her husband to write out a notice. This dynamic of a wife forcing her husband to wield his authority was at the heart of female-initiated *enkiri*.

With each temple's connection to shogunal authority, a woman rushing into either Mantokuji or Tōkeiji was entering into one of many satellites branching off from the center of power in Edo. Herman Ooms identifies the period phrase "go to Edo" as one invested with great meaning.[86] It implied a desire to seek justice as well as the knowledge of how to make justice work by traveling to Edo and engaging the sources of power for righting assumed wrongs. It was, as Ooms argues in his embrace of Bourdieu, a rhetorical and practical use of the "habitus"—a feel for and know-how of the rules of the social game—of the Tokugawa juridical field.[87] To "go to Edo" so as to rectify one's situation may be understood also in the context of divorce temples, especially given their close association with *bakufu* power. A woman rushing into either Mantokuji or Tōkeiji was rushing into an extended power center of Edo. She did not need to go to the city of Edo to rectify a claim against her husband because "Edo"—in this sense the opportunity to petition authority and gain for herself a sense of justice served—existed within the grounds of the nunneries. Other ad-hoc institutions of sanctuary and divorce, such as the homes of retainers, magistrates, and village headmen, also represented localized extensions of national, provincial, and village power.[88] Despite the presence of institutions literally within sight of Mantokuji that also served as a refuge and offered divorce mediation, women who could afford it preferred the temple, presumably because of its known connection to Tokugawa power sources.[89] This preference indicates the knowledge and sense—the habitus—that individuals possessed and employed in the hopes of making the juridical system work in their favor. Entrance into a divorce temple or another place of refuge did not itself guarantee a divorce.[90] Nevertheless, it changed power relations almost immediately. Upon entering a place of recognized power, a woman was in the position to bargain in a manner that was not available to her outside such a power center. As indicated by the symbols of the constancy of family ties in betrothal, divorce brought a woman's family actively to the forefront to represent her. Although the wife initiated proceedings with her decision to seek refuge, it was her family that acted on her behalf as it negotiated with her husband and his family through the office of the temple or other place of refuge. In this way, divorce was the reverse of betrothal: families came together not to negotiate *enmusubi,* but rather *enkiri.* Still, a daughter's decision, which was evidence of her sense of how the juridical system worked, moved a private conflict (between her and her husband and in-laws) into the public sphere—indeed, into the very heart of local political power—and created a broader conflict that now involved her family. Fertility's behavioral ideals of *tashinami* immediately fell into inconsequence, and restoration of order took precedence. Order was the paramount concern of local authorities, who, as representatives of provincial and national power, were responsible for adjudicating claims of conflict and contradiction between spouses and households.[91]

The public, conflicting, and contradictory nature of divorce is captured in a late-Tokugawa case, which is valuable in itself because some of the documents were written by the female petitioner herself, a very unhappy wife named Kane who sought sanctuary in Tōkeiji in the autumn of 1850. Her writings, when read in the light of fertility values and their idealization of the nobility of patience, stand in sharp contrast to the letter that Uesugi wrote to his granddaughter urging patience, introspection, and unfailing faith in her new husband. Kane made public her hatred of her husband, Kanjirō, and his behavior, which, assuming that her words are true, was horrendous. He was physically abusive, tried to force her into private prostitution, harangued her to get money from her family, and pawned parts of her dowry. On the other hand, Kanjirō strongly defended himself against these charges by asserting that Kane was hardly the victim she claimed to be. He filed a countersuit with the local magistrate two months later accusing her, among other things, of having an affair with a village neighbor. Because so many documents of divorce temples have been lost, the case of Kane and Kanjirō unfortunately ends with his countersuit.[92] We can assume Kane, if she were ultimately successful in her claim, resided in the convent for Tōkeiji's required duration of service given Kanjirō's adamant refusal to back down.

This conflict, or its potential, was not isolated to the realm of jurisprudence and the need to assert social order, just as it was not isolated only to divorce temples. It was played out as well through the context of household needs, ritual practice, and engagement with symbols. The issues involving household and marriage, pregnancy and children, and patterns of symbolic activity discussed throughout this study come to the forefront in many divorce notices. Examples of actual divorces serve to highlight how some of these issues lie scattered on the field of broken marriages.

The burdensome privilege of maintaining the household sometimes played a role in divorce. In 1842 the natal family of a woman named Oiyo acted to help her divorce her husband. As his writ of divorce states, she and her family desired that she return home. Her brother had died and left no heir, and thus it was incumbent upon her to return to her natal home and assist in some manner with maintaining the household.[93] As mentioned in chapter 3, temporary female headship was one means of maintaining a household. Perhaps headship was Oiyo's destiny, or her return home may have been made in anticipation of securing an adopted son-in-law for her to marry and who would then become official head.[94] In another 1842 divorce notice we can glean a strange but telling twist on the centrality of household and marriage. A young man named Toragorō sought sanctuary at a local official's house in the vicinity of Mantokuji and demanded a divorce from his new wife, Tomi. Although as husband he officially possessed unilateral authority to divorce her, he chose instead to follow a female pattern and sue for divorce from a position of sanctuary. No evidence in the writ is given, but it is likely that while he may have been unhappy with his new wife, his parents were happy with her dowry and did not want to lose it through divorce.[95] A dowry was a woman's own. While it contributed to the overall material wealth of a husband's household, it remained legally hers and would be taken with her in divorce. In this capacity, though, a wife and her family might use some of her dowry to pay off a husband and his family in order to get a quick letter of divorce.[96] This indicates that a husband and his family, once put in a corner, also were familiar with the juridical game and could play it to get something out of potentially nothing.

Children and pregnancy sometimes played roles in the drama of divorce. Among commoners, the right of custody was generally the province of husbands, although in practice many different arrangements were made.[97] This may be seen through divorce as well. An 1839 *mikudarihan* from Mino Province shows that a man named Sadasuke divorced his pregnant wife, Hii. In the notice he added an amendment stating that when Hii gave birth he would take custody of the child.[98] Another case involved a pregnant petitioner at Mantokuji named Taki. She was one of only three women who sought refuge there known to have been the mothers of young children. She received a divorce through the temple in 1853. In the divorce agreement she gave up custody of her daughters to her husband, Ichiemon, and in return he agreed that Taki could keep the child she was carrying.[99] Since Ichiemon was an adopted son-in-law, he moved out of Taki's family home and took the daughters back to his father's house. A wife living in her own natal home with an adopted son-in-law as husband, as was the case with Taki, had to seek refuge in order to initiate a divorce against him if he was not willing to write a notice of separation and sign it. The situation must have been terribly awkward for everyone involved, but an adopted son-in-law had his and his own natal family's claim to represent in case of divorce, especially when a child—considered a precious commodity—was involved. Possibly due to his desire to keep his daughters, Ichiemon did not write out a divorce form immediately. Such a delay would have forced Taki to leave her own home and seek refuge in order to get him to act on her wishes. In this way, a wife taking refuge could work in the husband's favor to produce a situation where he could then negotiate for something, such as children, in return for the divorce notice the woman so eagerly sought.

Divorce also produced many types of symbolic practices both within its juridical expression and in more obvious forms of ritual expression. Cutting was a salient action in many such practices. Returning to Sadasuke's divorce of Hii, either he, his wife, or someone involved in the process made a cut between their two names on the divorce notice.[100] Cutting *(kiri)* was the root metaphor of several symbolic practices tied to divorce—the cutting of ties, or *enkiri*. Hair is again an important example. Although women seeking divorce through convents lived the lifestyle of nuns, they did not receive tonsure. As with other preliminary and temporary stages on the nun's path, nuns in divorce temples cut their hair short.[101] Short hair symbolized their liminal status. They were not quite wives, and yet they were not nuns; they were through with their marriage, and yet they were not in possession of a letter of divorce. Cutting hair, however, was not only a sign of unclear status, but could also, conversely, be a sign of clear intention. Kane, for example, urged Kanjirō many times to write out a divorce notice before she finally sought refuge in Tōkeiji. Prior to this final move she had left him to return to her own home and forwarded him a letter again requesting a divorce in which she placed hairpins and strands of hair she had cut.[102] She hoped, although in the end to no avail, that the act of cutting off locks of her hair would be a powerful statement that her commitment to be rid of him was stronger than his commitment to remain with her. Similarly, in 1762 a woman named Miyo became ill and wanted to seclude herself by receiving a divorce and returning home. She shaved her head and left on her own. After this action, her husband quickly agreed to write her a divorce notice. He later discovered from an associate familiar with his ex-wife's hometown that she had indeed taken vows and become a tonsured nun.[103]

Another cluster of practices marking clear intention and sharing in the metaphor of cutting also existed. We know little about them because, unlike cutting hair and seeking sanctuary in institutions of vested authority, they were shadowy and secretive. Still, they were strategic actions that sought to alter a husband's power to maintain *enmusubi* and effect *enkiri*. A passage relating the 1749 bridal procession of a princess, Isonomiya, on her way to wed into the Tokugawa family in Edo states that when the party passed by a particular tree at Itabashi on the Nakasendō highway, two people familiar with the area advised the procession to detour and not pass in front of the tree. As the writer records, this tree was known by many names, but its reputation was the same: women and men passing by it in wedding processions would suffer very brief marriage ties.[104] In 1804 another princess and her procession party also decided to bypass this tree on her way to Edo to wed.[105] This problematic tree was a nettle or hackberry *(enoki)*. The tree and others of its species offered a powerful symbol of cutting ties. Unlike the princesses, who decided to avoid the tree, women who hoped for divorce embraced the symbol of the nettle tree because of its of ruinous reputation.[106] A *senryū* describes this reputation as follows: "One goes to Itabashi to give thanks for the divorce letter" *(Itabashi e mikudarihan no reimari).*[107] This poem uses the term *reimairi* to indicate visiting the nettle tree, which typically refers to visiting a shrine or temple to give thanks to the deity for prayers answered. Equating the tree with a temple or shrine visit suggests that reputable nettle trees operated in a manner common to a class of sacred places in Japan, such as trees, stones, and other natural phenomena, that are recognized and visited for their power to bring about beneficial results in people's lives. They become a kind of "ecographic" space: natural settings assumed to have significance that people engage through ritual actions, both simple and complex.[108] Often these natural objects in Japan are spatially segregated through the use of ropes and festoons of paper called *shimenawa*. By the Meiji period the nettle tree came to be represented on *ema* (wooden votive tablets upon which one writes her prayer or request) as surrounded by sacred rope and praying women attempting to effect *enkiri*.[109]

While the presence of votive tablets depicting nettle trees suggests a degree of institutionalization of divorce devotionalism by at least the Meiji period, various Tokugawa-period *senryū* also show evidence of devotional and ritual activity centered around nettle trees. One gives a specific idea on how some women used the tree to effect divorce: "When you pray to rend your tie, strip the bark from the nettle tree" *(Namaki saku gan wa enoki no kawa o muki).*[110] The symbolic act of separating bark from tree suggests the desired effect of separating a wife from her husband's household. Another interpretation also intimates a practice of magical efficacy. After peeling bark from the tree and taking it home with her, a woman would then grind it into a powder and slip it into the food she had prepared for her husband. Ingesting the bark of a tree noted

for its power of shortening relationships would prove efficacious in altering a husband's desire to stay in the relationship.[111] Although dependence
on prayer and magical properties are qualitatively different actions than
that of seeking sanctuary in a convent, they all speak of the same working faith *(shinkō)* in achieving separation. In this common spirit of *shinkō,*
several *senryū* compare the nettle tree and Tōkeiji, often through a play
on the word "pine" *(matsu)* as a metaphor for Tōkeiji. In literature, the
convent is referred to as Matsugaoka, which is the name of the hilly,
pine-covered area surrounding the temple. This use of pine is especially
effective not only in linking the convent to the *enoki* tree, but also in
showing that while the practice of faith is varied, the substance of faith
—the hope of divorce—is not. One poem states, "First the nettle tree—
if this won't cut, then try the pine" *(Mazu enoki sore de ikanu to matsu de
kiri).*[112] Another poem, implying that devotion to the divorce tree is a
readily convenient and cheaper option, creates a parallel between the
convent and the tree by playing on the notion of rushing into a nunnery to seek sanctuary. "Rather than the far away pine, try rushing to
the nettle tree" *(Tooi matsu yori enoki e kakete miru).*[113]

   This last *senryū* suggests the impracticality of divorce temples for most
women seeking to cut marriage ties. Not only were the convents few
and far between, but they were also costly. A stay of a few weeks, let
alone two or three years, required a substantial financial commitment
from a woman and her family. Nettle-tree ritual, while presumably
largely ineffective compared to divorce temples, was widely available and
free. Still, nettle worship and other forms of ritualizing, such as cutting
hair, as we saw with Kane and Miyo, were not driven simply by con-
venience and economics, but rather as one part of an array of practices
that a woman might attempt in her life. In the end, cutting hair, cutting
strips of bark, and cutting losses and running to a convent were practiced on the same working faith that sought to gain the benefit of better days ahead.

ESCAPE FROM PLEASURE

Some women in the quarters also sought to secure the benefit of a better future through symbols and practices available to them within the
walls of pleasure. Although the Yoshiwara, along with the Shimabara
and Shinmachi, was typically considered a glittering island of style and
panache in the dreary, gray seas of Confucian social order, the attention
to symbols and practices that it shared with the wider society obscured

the shoreline between island and sea. At the same time, the fact that religious symbols coexisted at both the periphery and in the center is evidence of the ability of Japanese religion to make graphic the heterogeneity of society and the multiplicity of values. Further, with respect to the quarters, its religious symbols could sometimes promote both the corporate concerns of bordellos for profit through paid sex and the individual concerns of courtesans to cut ties and escape. In the Yoshiwara, no symbol embraced this kind of heterogeneity more than Kurosuke Inari, the quarter's tutelary deity *(chinju)*.

As one manifestation of the popular cult of the deity Inari, Kurosuke's history and symbology is tied to that deity. Inari worship originally spread throughout the country from its western base at Kyoto's Fushimi Shrine. It became particularly popular in eastern Japan and in the city of Edo when the western daimyo, under the system of *sankin kōtai* that required all daimyo to set up second residences in Edo, brought Inari worship to the city by establishing secondary shrines within the spacious precincts of their new homes. Peripatetic ritual specialists and healers also helped spread Inari throughout the country.[114] This diffusion fit the urbanization of the early modern period, which Edo emphatically epitomized. In the cities a tutelary deity did not encompass an entire population, as it might in a village, but instead represented an urban subdivision and functioned as the religious and social center for that particular population.[115] Inari found a home as a tutelary deity in a number of Edo's burgeoning subdivisions, including the Yoshiwara.

Mythology in the Yoshiwara traced a different history. Its founding myth of Kurosuke reaches back to the year 711, when a farmer named Chiba Kurosuke began to worship Inari in his rice field.[116] The year is significant to the official mythology of Inari as constructed by the Fushimi Grand Shrine. On the first day of the horse in the second month of 711, the god is said to have alighted on Inari Mountain, where its worship and name first originated.[117] This day, called *hatsu-uma,* became the fete day of Inari at all Fushimi-sponsored shrines throughout Japan, including Kurosuke's shrine. Kurosuke's myth states that on Chiba's rice paddies a black fox and white fox descended from heaven as Inari's messengers.[118] The black fox landed on the footpaths between the paddies, and the farmer recognized the animal as highly auspicious. He established a small shrine on the footpath and began making offerings. Soon the god gained a reputation for answering all pleas made to it. Nine centuries later, when the Yoshiwara was built on the same spot where tradition claimed that Chiba Kurosuke first worshiped Inari, the quarter erected a small shrine to the *kami* making it its tutelary deity. When a conflagration consumed Edo in 1657, the Yoshiwara moved from its original location to a more remote area to keep it separate from the rebuilding of a still expanding city. Pleasure's proprietors also brought Kurosuke into this new location.[119]

Edo eventually enveloped this new locale as well, but by this stage of development the Yoshiwara and its surroundings, including the great Buddhist temple of Sensōji, had become an integral component of commoner culture and of profitable and popular festivals and entertainments. As a sign of the deity's popularity and the Yoshiwara's widening influence on the cultural life of the city, with its famed festivals, Kurosuke Inari and its shrine received the honorary sobriquet of first-rank revered deity *(Shōichii Kurosuke Inari daimyōjin)*, which is a designation typical of Inari shrines. The history behind Kurosuke gaining this title is not clear. One period source, *For Your Amusement and Pleasure (Kiyū shōran)*, states that the title was granted in 1734 as part of the careful planning of Yoshiwara's leaders to build up Kurosuke's fete days as major festivals. In their orchestrations of festival creation, the leaders took careful note of famous festivals in Kyoto such as Gion and those of the Shimabara pleasure quarter.[120] With this title and the god's reputation as a popular draw with both the quarter's residents and people outside the Yoshiwara, a new and larger shrine was erected to replace the deity's smaller abode.[121]

Kurosuke was not the only sacred symbol in the Yoshiwara given in service to the quarter's need to promote the communal benefits of profits and sex. Another one was the *kayou kami* (travel god). According to the *Yoshiwara Compendium,* courtesans customarily wrote on the seal of obligatory "love letters" to their clients the term *kayou kami,* which was the Yoshiwara's name for the more commonly designated *dōsojin* (traveler's deity).[122] Through its root meaning of "travel," *dōsojin* broadly incorporates meanings of boundary crossings and liminal spaces and experiences. Stone statues on the roadside, variously depicting an embracing couple, Jizō, a phallus, and other motifs, ubiquitously stand as representatives of *dōsojin*.[123] Their multiple representations may suggest any number of meanings, though a prominent one is sexual energy and creativity— symbolically the crossing of male and female borders—as shown explicitly by the loving couple and phallus motifs. In the Yoshiwara, a courtesan's handwriting on her letter's seal, rather than on stone statuary, represented, simply and elegantly, *kayou kami,* and it expressed several meanings common to the symbol of *dōsojin,* such as traveler's god, border guardian, and sexual energy. As the verb *kayou* denotes intentional and regular travel, the seal of *kayou kami* served to protect a courtesan's client the next time he was traveling to rendezvous with her, which required crossing a border between ordinary society and the world of pleasure. With her letter in hand, the client also had *dōsojin* in hand, not as a fixed, stone statuary, but rather as written seal—intensely personal, portable, and ready for his next journey and crossing from one world to the next.[124]

Kurosuke Inari, compared to *kayou kami,* was far more complex. In addition to its capacity to incorporate meanings of sexuality and corporate prosperity like *kayou kami,* it also evoked resistance to these meanings, such as those lying at the heart of a courtesan's desire to cut her ties. This symbolic complexity tied both *enmusubi shinkō* and *enkiri shinkō* to Kurosuke. The capacity to incorporate "shared semantics and private persuasions" typifies Inari worship and its symbolism.[125] Inari is at once broadly communal and intensely individual, supportive of harmony and group identity as well as dangerously suggestive of the breaking of social norms and acting on one's own; it is boisterous and public as well as silent and personal. As a manifestation of Inari, then, Kurosuke was symbolically well suited for both tasks of tutelary deity and private god, of *enmusubi* and *enkiri,* despite the high contrariety. Typical of Inari legends, the Yoshiwara's origin myth associating Kurosuke with foxes and rice fields, and its suggestion of rice cultivation and production is at the root of the deity's multivalent symbolism.[126] Growth, strength, health, prosperity, sexuality, and change are just a few of the meanings Inari has generated through its core signification in fecundity and rice cultivation. In addition, Inari's strong association with foxes creates additional levels of evocation that we have already noted in metaphors tied to courtesans. Inari's multiplicity of meanings could be evoked by a number of needs and concerns, both corporate and individual. In the remaining pages I examine three of these meanings—prosperity, sexuality, and change— that were critical to Kurosuke's symbolic feat of expressing the heterogeneous needs of the god's community and the god's individual petitioners.

In each of the four corners of the Yoshiwara stood a shrine to a particular Inari deity, but Kurosuke was the center of cultic life.[127] The *kami* was also famed outside the quarter. A contemporary writer and observer of the times, Saitō Gesshin (1804–1878), made special note of Kurosuke as one of the city's most popular Inari deities during the Hatsu-uma Festival.[128] Since it was a nationwide celebration, the Yoshiwara's festival competed with those of other Inari shrines to attract the public. Kurosuke's shrine rivaled other major Inari sites in Edo for hosting some the most popular and crowded festivals in the city.[129] As purveyors of good times, the Yoshiwara's bordello and teahouse owners were skilled at using religious festivals to increase visitor traffic inside the quarter in order to increase profits. Bright lanterns were hung from each of the quarter's four shrines during the festival. This sight, especially at night, became a hugely popular draw, bringing in throngs of people from the outside to view them, according to Saitō.[130] Although he does not detail other activities, it is easy to imagine such visitors in the "culture of prayer and play" making offerings at Kurosuke's shrine and then spending more of their money in the quarter's teahouses, restaurants, and bordellos.[131] Such was the marketing strategy of the quarter's leaders as seekers of gain in worldly benefits as business. The intertwining of religious and economic activities, while not unique to Japan, is readily observable in Japanese cultural history. Whether derivative, as in the building of markets outside temple gates and on the roadside of pilgrimage routes, or central, like the purchasing of ritual and devotional items such as amulets, votive tablets, and belly wraps, economics and religion have easily mixed together in the Japanese experience. Some interpreters of the Yoshiwara criticize its easy fusion. To paraphrase one such critic, Kurosuke's festivals burned only with a passion for money and thus there was no true spiritual fire in the hearts of the people.[132] This criticism, steeped as it is in a conceptualization of religion as something measurably true and, at its best, unconcerned with worldly matters, ignores the context of community and seeking of worldly benefits in Japanese religion. When focus is placed on the wealth-creation meaning of Inari, there emerges in Kurosuke's festival a symmetry between symbol and practice, between prosperity and purpose, and between sacred and profane.

Much of the Yoshiwara's prosperity was tied to sexuality. The two were inseparable, and they became linked most intensely in the summer festival dedicated to Kurosuke. Unlike the Hatsu-uma Festival, which was a celebration of all Inari throughout the country, the summer festival was Kurosuke's own as the tutelary deity of the Yoshiwara. It was held on the first day of the eighth month, which placed it in the middle of a month's worth of festivities in the quarter. It was one of several events that the Yoshiwara's proprietors created throughout the early decades of the eighteenth century.[133] In addition to Kurosuke's fete days, the cherry blossom festival, held in the third month, and the seventh-month lantern festival, which grew out of an o-bon memorial for a popular tayū named Tamagiku (1702–1726), made up the quarter's largest yearly celebrations.[134] The Yoshiwara began to combine Kurosuke's fete day, as it did with other celebratory days of the calendar, with additional forms of entertainment such as public exhibitions of dancing and singing. These originally ad-hoc forms of merriment developed over the years into a major festival in celebration of Kurosuke, which was famed throughout the city for its parades of floats and musicians. These were not traditions of antiquity, but rather of contemporary manufacture.[135] Nevertheless, through its innovations and fabrications of festivals, the quarter acted in the same manner as many Tokugawa communities, even the most "traditional" of all: the rural village. Despite the perception of village life as fixed and antiquated in its festivals and religious observances, many rural communities in the Tokugawa period frequently improvised on tradition and even created new festivals to attract more people and acquire more renown and prosperity for the village.[136] The proprietors of the Yoshiwara constructed their elaborate events for the same reasons of increased patronage, fame, and wealth.

The elaborateness of Kurosuke's fete day was impressive. Large floats moved through the five boulevards of the quarter and stopped at each teahouse, where a courtesan and her teen and child attendants danced atop the vehicles.[137] Courtesans dressed in white kimono paraded with musicians down the streets, singing, drumming, and dancing.[138] It was surely a sight not to be missed. For many courtesans, however, this day also meant fulfilling their responsibility to secure as many of their regular clients as possible. On this day clients paid double for sexual services, thus doubling the coffers of the women's bordellos. This practice of double-price days *(monbi, monobi)* often fell on festival days when the quarter was brimming with customers, and Kurosuke's celebration, with its parade and floats, was perennially one of the Yoshiwara's biggest times for visitors and sightseers.[139] Courtesans likely dreaded such days, for if they failed to secure enough reservations from their clientele, they were forced to offset the shortfall of their bordellos' books with their own money.[140] Still, from the standpoint of the collective's success and continuity, double-price days well typified how economic activity and sexual activity were pursued as one, and intensely so within the energetic celebrations taking place on the festival day of the community's deity. As tutelary deity, Kurosuke symbolized the community united in common purpose and identity in the pursuit of economic gain through sexual play.

As Inari, Kurosuke was not limited to collective concerns; it also evoked meanings of individual concerns. Along with prosperity and sexuality, the notion of "change" is another meaning clustered around the symbolism of Inari, as captured in the growth and change that rice plants undergo from seedlings to mature, sprouting stalks. Unlike prosperity and sexuality, which in the context of the Yoshiwara were linked to communal identity and success, change was often linked to the individual identity of a courtesan. Inari's close association with foxes directly touches on this notion of change and courtesans. Foxes in Japanese folk religion have long been characterized as tricksters and changelings. The underlying religio-sexual logic of many fox legends is that it is a yin creature always on the prowl for yang, which it needs in order to ascend into celestial realms. This logic produces the mythic theme of foxes taking advantage of unsuspecting men by changing into the form of a desirable woman, engaging in sexual relations, and, for a time, marrying them. Through this sexual trickery they gain possession of the men's yang by receiving semen through intercourse.[141] Such themes were easily linked to courtesans. A skillful courtesan's role required her not only to make a man expend his semen, but also to make him spend his money, all under the playful illusion of a sincere and loving relationship. Slang and comic poetry often reveal this association. "White-faced foxes," for example, was common jargon for courtesans, referring both to an incarnation of Inari as a white fox and the white powder the women wore on their faces when meeting clients.[142] A *senryū* links the Yoshiwara's tutelary god to the quarter's women through the common denominator of the fox: "Kurosuke's parishioners are, of course, foxes!" *(Kurosuke ga ujiko yappari kitsune nari)*[143]

The association between change, courtesans, and foxes, however, is not restricted to the image of the skilled woman plying her trade of *iki*. Many courtesans indeed sought change through the divine mediation of Kurosuke the fox deity. The change they hoped for, however, was one in role, in venue, in life. Unlike with a tutelary deity of a village or city ward, Kurosuke's charges were not part of an organic community; they were from ordinary society, its villages and towns, lying beyond the god's walls. Further, by definition, their contractual presence in the community was temporary. Most women were content to wait for either retirement or a lucky match with a client to exit the quarter's gate. Others hoped to escape back into the outside world as soon as they were able. To reduce the chances of women taking flight, the Yoshiwara had a full-time watchman guarding the quarter's sole gate. That the potential for escape was an acknowledged reality is seen not only in the presence of a watchman, but also in the language of a courtesan's contract. To return again to Yasu's contract, it threatens that if she escapes or elopes, her sister and relatives will be responsible for compensating the bordello in her absence and for finding her and returning her to her duties.[144] If change were desired, as a quarter's own contractual language recognized that it might, then it could not be obtained in such a simple manner as walking out of the gate.

Female-initiated change—unapproved departure before retirement or the buyout of a contract—required strategy. A woman had many options. If she desired to flee Kurosuke's domain and change her identity, she might approach the shrine surreptitiously and pray to the *kami* for divine assistance. The artist Utagawa Kuninao depicts such a moment in an 1841 illustration for a book of love stories. Utagawa's courtesan stands alone at night, praying fervently in front of Kurosuke's shrine (fig. 14). Several *senryū* capture the peculiar moment of making an entreaty to Kurosuke for successful escape from the deity's own community. One poem puts it, "The only entreaty to Kurosuke is to forsake him" *(Kurosuke o mikagiru yō na gan bakari)*.[145] Another similarly states, "The only plea offered to Kurosuke is to change and leave" *(Kurosuke e bakete detai no gan bakari)*.[146] This last *senryū* holds a double meaning in its use of the

FIGURE 14 A courtesan at night petitioning Kurosuke Inari at his shrine in the Yoshiwara. From an original reproduction of Utagawa Kuninao's illustration by Mitani Kazuma. Courtesy of Rippū Shobō, Tokyo.

verb "change" *(bakeru)*. It not only implies the desire to alter one's identity to that of an ordinary woman, but also suggests using trickery to achieve it.

Successful escape for a courtesan often required one last act of trickery. Like foxes changing forms, some courtesans tried to escape by changing their appearance. One way was to "change" one's gender by dressing in male attire in order to pass under the watchman's gaze as just another departing visitor. Another *senryū* points to this strategy. "At Kurosuke's side one changes into a man" *(Kurosuke no waki de otoko ni bakete iru)*.[147] Such trickery was at times successful, thus forcing gatemen to be extra vigilant.[148] A woman donning men's attire was a practice aimed at reaching a specific result, but it had links to broader forms of practice. As mentioned earlier, a pregnant woman donned men's clothing as a homeopathic element in a magical rite meant to secure the male gender for her fetus. Also, one the most popular religious confraternities in the second half of the Tokugawa period, the millennial Fuji-kō, stressed radical equality between men and women. Male and female members changed clothes as a sign of their equality and faith in anticipation of the new world that would be ushered in with the coming of the new Buddha, Miroku.[149] While it was obviously strategic behavior meant to aid her own escape, the intentional changing of clothes was also linked to similar actions designed to encourage and effect change: change of fetal gender, of a world age, or, in the case of a courtesan, of one's social identity and place. "Changing" one's state of health was another deceptive technique that a woman might use to escape the quarter. Outside of retirement and the buyout of her contract, a courtesan's only other approved reason for departure was serious illness. Yasu's contract states that if she were to contract a long-term and grave illness she would be let go and returned home.[150] Feigning sickness was sometimes a successful ploy for Yoshiwara women hoping for an early exit.[151] A seriously ill woman was of no use to her bordello. Since she could no longer perform her erotic labor, and since her illness was a chronic drain on her employer, her contract was cancelled. A final strategy of change was the use of votive tablets to petition Kurosuke for various benefits. According to one interpretation of an intriguing *senryū,* a courtesan might have a ghostwriter *(daisaku)* pen a verse, likely cryptic, on a votive tablet and offer it at Kurosuke's shrine for her if her request was one that needed to be guarded along with her identity.[152] The poem suggests that the prayer placards directed toward the *kami* were full of ghost verses *(daiku):*

"Offer to Kurosuke votive tablets covered in ghost verses" *(Kurosuke e daiku darake no ema o age).*[153]

Along with ghost verses, Kursosuke was covered in meanings and evocations that both worked toward and against the heterogeneous needs of its community as a single collective and a collection of individual women. As much the spiritual locus of an isolated community as it was the focus of popular festivals drawing visitors from the outside, as much a tutelary deity as a god of personal petition, and as much a symbol of community identity as the hope of an individual to escape from that community, Kurosuke's multivalency represents well the Tokugawa ritual and symbolic landscape of female exits and their ambivalence practiced amidst heavily idealized values. Betrothal, bridal departure, and retirement from the quarters were formal and celebratory occasions of exits, but they were fraught with evocative symbols that acted on the potential unease about a woman's real loyalties and sense of place embedded in the models of fertility and pleasure. This underlying ambivalence could erupt in other exits—private, strategic, and antipodal to formal celebratory ritual. Such exits were peripheral, intentional, and pointedly set against the values of fertility and pleasure. Each exit is evidence that the fates of Tokugawa women were not so easily sealed by powerful discourses obsessed with sexuality and ideals of behavior. If these discourses cast a shadow over women's lives so as to produce the so-called dark age for women, then ritual and symbol offered a light that could shine through sexual ideologies and their idealized values and shine on unraveled bonds of natal identity, hopes for a better tomorrow, and even secret, unapproved pathways toward that tomorrow.

SIX

CONCLUSION

HENRIETTA MOORE NOTES that "competing, potentially contradictory" discourses on gender and sexuality" mark many societies. Given this multiplicity, she puts forward as an important inquiry of social research the question dealing with how people "take up a position in one discourse" among many.[1] Utamaro's portrait of a courtesan dreaming of her wedding, which opened this volume, provides an outline of one answer that Tokugawa Japan gave to this question: ritual practice. Ritual mediated a daughter's entrance into the sociosexual role of either a wife or courtesan. A woman could also employ ritual to exit either role through a variety of forms, ranging from celebrations of transfer to disruptive acts of cutting ties between her and people and institutions. At the same time, a host of practices associated with pregnancy tied women to specific experiences of gender that cut across lines of class, status, and institutional values. This multiplicity of practices indicates heavy "ritual density."[2] In other words, as exemplified even by the narrow range of practices discussed here, Tokugawa society represents a complex grouping of "competing, potentially contradictory" collectives and individual members dependent on forms of ritual to produce a degree of ordering, and at times disordering, in their institutional and personal lives. The task of these final pages is to consider this density in broader reflections of Tokugawa society and in consideration of religion in light of women taking advantage of this density.

The purpose of female sexuality was contested, as the models of fertility and pleasure exemplify. Pierre Bourdieu's mapping of social and ideological conflict is helpful in initially charting these contested meanings as part of Tokugawa society. He posits two types of "universe" through which forces of social conservation and change are in constant, tense relation. One is the "universe of the undiscussed," or the given, undisputed assumptions of a society. This is *doxa*. Embedded in the wider *doxa* is the narrower "universe of discourse," which is the realm of disputation and conflict. This universe concentrates on the poles of orthodoxy and heterodoxy; it is indicative of conflicting social discourse.[3] Tokugawa *doxa* placed much female social value within the confines of sexuality. Masuho Zankō epitomized this, though he distinctly posited the same confines for a man and charged male-female coupling with divine energy. His critique of relations in models other than his own also indicates the narrower existence of disputation concerning the purpose of female sexuality that lay within the wider *doxa*. For Bourdieu such disputation marks the poles of orthodoxy and heterodoxy. Heterodoxy has a strong interest in contracting the undiscussed borders of *doxa* in order to expose and discuss the arbitrariness of social reality as construed by orthodoxy. The driving force behind orthodoxy is its insistence that the arbitrary is real, that given assumptions of social reality must be unquestioned, and that the universe of the undiscussed remain as vast as possible. However, the contested sexual values in Tokugawa society, including alternatives outside of fertility and pleasure, such as monastic celibacy and forms of village sexual associations, were co-sanctioned by the various powers that were. This co-sanctioning produces a problematic portrait of orthodoxy and heterodoxy in the Tokugawa. Fertility and pleasure, as well as other models, coexisted on a social plane drawn on institutional, behavioral, and sexually purposeful lines of center and periphery. All of those lines, however, possessed legal and social legitimacy. In a society crisscrossed with multiple and co-sanctioned values, the question of which were orthodox and heterodox is not so obvious.

Attention to ritual practice goes around this question by reconfiguring Bourdieu's notion of contested discourse. If *doxa* represents a universe of the undisputed, which in the Tokugawa period was the notion that sexuality defined much of a woman's social significance, then there is another universe that also needs to be considered and that offers a different view: the universe of praxis. By reconfiguring Bourdieu's mapping of *doxa,* orthodoxy, and heterodoxy into praxis, orthopraxy, and heteropraxy, we can better handle the problematic social ground of multiple co-sanctioned values and their models. This reconfiguration is able to diagram, like Bourdieu's orthodoxies and heterodoxies, conflict *between* models, but it also draws our attention to conflict *within* each model.

The Tokugawa universe of praxis consisted of ritual forms and symbols constituting much cultural and religious activity. In this manner it differed from the universe of *doxa* because it was not something to be validated or invalidated amidst conflicting claims of orthodoxy and heterodoxy. Praxis was open for the construction of both ortho- and hetero- rituals; orthopraxy and heteropraxy both pulled from the universe of praxis. Orthopraxy was ritual practice that was not definitive of any group in possession of power over groups lacking such power, as Bourdieu's orthodoxy denotes. Instead, in the context of sexual values, orthopraxy gave expression to an institution's values and mediated a woman's transformation of role identity as a member of a specific community. Orthopraxy was collective centered in this respect. Both the center and periphery engaged in orthopraxy as institutionalized collectives. Heteropraxy pulled from the same universe, but it operated antagonistically toward the dominant values of a woman's primary community. Such antagonism toward a community could even lead to violence. In the latter half of the period, violence sometimes erupted in villages between long established youth groups, called *wakamonogumi* or *wakamonorenchū*, and individual households over which collective—the youth group or the household—held authority to regulate a daughter's social and sexual development. Expansion of the *ie*-consciousness among some successful villagers contributed to decisions to remove their daughters from the control of traditional communal organizations so that they could directly educate the girls in the household and prepare them for marriage into another *ie,* free of influence from the outside. The loss of institutional influence in regulating behavior, development, and the sexual decisions of village females at times led some members of youth groups to respond violently against the girls and their families.[4] Here, household fertility values acted as new and intrusive heteropraxy that called into question the orthopraxy of the traditional sexual values of the village. Typically, heteropraxy is often initiated as individual activity employed as a strategy of resistance toward collective values. Any group —household, bordello, and youth organization—could experience, often to its collective dismay, individual women or, as in the above case, individual household heads employing heteropraxy against its interests and its orthopraxy.

Further, similar experiences could act as either orthopraxy or heteropraxy depending on the social identity of the practitioner, her situation, and her institution. Pregnancy was one such experience. In a home in need of or desiring a child, pregnancy acted as a form of orthopraxy. It tied a woman's role as wife and new mother to her husband's household and its desire to establish posterity. In the quarters, bringing a pregnancy to term not only set a woman apart from the values of sexual play, but also placed her literally outside of her role as she gave birth and recuperated in an isolated dormitory, such as the one in Minowa. Even if a woman's bordello allowed the pregnancy to culminate in birth for the purpose of adopting the infant or putting it up for adoption, pregnancy was imbued with a mood of heteropraxis given its contrast to the values of the quarter and the lifestyle of a courtesan. Abortion and infanticide further reveal the situational character of orthopraxy and heteropraxy in pregnancy. Terminating new life within either the household or the bordello was an institutionally orthopraxic act in that it was decided upon and performed for the needs of the collective, and not the individual woman, to better maintain its own sense of order and viability.

The orthopraxy and heteropraxy in which women engaged also generated an intensification of perspectival boundaries marking Tokugawa society. Ritual activity, notably orthopraxic weddings and celebratory rites of sexual relations in the quarters, strengthened the border of daughter affirmation and wife or courtesan transformation. Heteropraxy brought to light other, sometimes inverse, perspectival boundaries as well. A courtesan, in taking her private petition to Kurosuke, affirmed her status as a member of the quarter vis-à-vis her engagement with her community's tutelary deity while also anticipating transformation to an identity away from her role as courtesan and devotee to Kurosuke. In this way, a woman's use of ritual practice, from public and formal orthopraxy to largely individual acts of heteropraxy, both magnified on which side of the border she either wanted or had to be at a particular juncture in her life, and placed her there as well.

The dynamic of women enacting rituals, crossing borders, and taking up positions in, and sometimes outside of, value-based institutions and idealized discourses encourages us to consider how the ritual lives of Tokugawa women contribute to the sketching of a more accurate cartography of religion so that we may better track the various human routes of religious practice. Maps are necessary for comprehending the world around us, which also includes the cartography of humanity and its religious life. No single map can adequately chart the full historical and anthropological breadth of religion. There are problems, however, with mapping religion through often tried but ultimately unsatisfactory categories, such as traditions of world religions or the assumed holistic nature of primitive and folk expressions. The former leaves large numbers of people off the map, and the latter, while attempting to find cartographic space for those displaced from the map of traditions, may inadvertently advance notions of simple men and women unreflectively but contentedly snared in a folk system of taboo, spirits, myth, and ritual.[5] Each map fails to place humans in the active center, where they not only "do" religion but also "make" religion. A map overemphasizing the traditions places humans as passive participants within a preexisting institutional, doctrinal, and ritual history that comes to them ready-made, with no assembly required. A map of holistic religion places people in an environment free of choices, independent thought, and self-conscious—even self-serving—actions. In the end, cartography of religion, to borrow the terminology of Peter Berger, too often draws on "objectivation," that is, seeing religion as an "objective reality" lying outside of its human construction, rather than seeing it as "externalization," or the active attempt to create meaning in the world.[6]

The rituals that some Tokugawa women practiced amidst conflicting values exemplify the importance of being attentive to the human centricity in any religious map. Despite the assertion of difference concerning the valuations of female sexuality that the ideals of fertility and pleasure exhibited, the fullness of the Tokugawa symbolic universe and its offering of ritual, symbols, mythological elements, sacred sites, and figures was open to all communities and individuals vis-à-vis the situations and needs they determined as ultimate at a critical moment in their institutional and personal lives. Religion acted not as a group of discrete traditions or as an organic, totalistic system. It was, rather, *acted upon* as an array of evocative, potentially meaningful ritual practices, symbolic elements, and concepts that could be variously construed and appropriated to express and attempt to meet collective or individual needs. When collective and individual needs meshed, orthopraxy was enjoined; when they did not mesh, an individual might turn to employing a form of heteropraxy. Women's practice of ritual to map out places of meaning, of safety, and of hope in their lives amidst the cross-currents of sexual values, multiple roles, predicaments of the life course, and collective and individual concerns shows the human-centered transparency of their religious actions. It draws the curtain and reveals those actions, and indeed all religion, as a product constantly shaped by and for the hands of human need. In this light, the dream of Utamaro's courtesan—enacting ritual to transform her identity and place herself within a new and hopefully more meaningful life—is truly a religious vision.

Guides to Trousseau and Behavior in the Household

The following is an abbreviated list of items from *A Record of Treasures for Women* that a bride might take with her into marriage.

shell box
storage cabinets
clothes rack
folding screen
bedroom curtains
storage chest
kimono and clothing chest
wicker chest
carrying pole and pail for transporting
    items
inkstone case
brush and ink
writing-brush holder
letter box
comb box
box for placing strands of hair pulled out
    by combing
artificial hair
hairbrush
toilet case
vanity
mirror stand
makeup and comb box
small washbasin
larger washbasin
vinegar-based liquid containing a piece
    of iron used for blackening teeth

box for holding powder used to blacken
    teeth
bowl for mixing blackening ingredients
    for the teeth
container for heating the mixture of
    blackening ingredients
shallow container for face powder and
    rouge
container holding oil to be combed into
    one's hair
eyebrow brush
hairpins
tweezers
scissors
nail cutter
razor for shaving the forehead and
    eyebrows
lacquered boxes
lacquered sandals
straw sandals
sewing box
pincushion
spools of thread
ruler
cloth cutter
container for spooled hemp
rack for holding spun threads

spinning wheel
threading loop
crescent-shaped bow used for pounding
    cotton to clean and soften it
weaving loom with warp and woof
cup for gargling
birthing chair
placenta bucket used in burying
    afterbirth
crescent-shaped rod for stretching
    washed and dyed clothes
fulling block
dolls, used as toys and amulets
sake ewers
tin sake flask
ceremonial serving trays
games

koto
lute
samisen
books
bamboo and silk screen
toothbrush
round fan
folding fan
shuttlecock and paddle
hats
sleeping pillow
ink for drawing eyebrows on the
    forehead
small bags for carrying fragrances to
    guard against body odor
incense, incense box, and censer

The following is a list from *Women's Imagawa* of twenty-two behaviors that a wife must avoid.

1. You slacken off in your resolve and dim the way of womanhood.
2. You do not rectify even small errors and then when faced with failure on account of this you act bitterly toward others.
3. You fail to bear in mind matters of true importance while chatting without any reservation to anyone at all.
4. You forget the deep debt of gratitude you owe your father and mother, and you are negligent in the way of filial piety.
5. You disrespect your husband, assert yourself, and have no fear of Heaven.
6. Even though you act in rebellion to the way, you desire signs of prosperity and success.
7. You look down upon the meek even if they are straight and wise.
8. You play too much, focus on leading men of the stage, and take frivolous pleasure in spectacles and attractions.
9. You are short-tempered and jealous, and yet are unashamed of people snickering at you.
10. You become lost in your own shallow cleverness and criticize others for countless things.
11. You spread rumors among people and then take pleasure in the worries such talk causes them.
12. You are enamored with clothes, furniture, yourself, and beauty, while your house servants go about looking shabby.
13. For things high and low, you have no sense of what is proper and prefer willfulness.
14. You point out the faults of others while thinking you are wise.
15. Even when it is just meeting with a Buddhist priest, you draw very close and act too familiar toward him.

16. You fail to realize your social position, are arrogant, or are discontent.

17. Failing to understand the strong and weak points of those working under you, you do not rightly manage the tasks of servants.

18. You treat your parents-in-law carelessly and earn the ridicule of others.

19. You neglect your stepchild and have no shame when others sneer at you.

20. Speaking of men in general, you act in ways that are too intimate even with your own close relatives.

21. You despise people who protect the way, but love friends who flatter you.

22. When guests come, you allow your bad temper to rise, show your anger, and become unceremonious with your rudeness.

Guides to Trousseau and Behavior in the Pleasure Quarter

The following is a list of items from the *Yoshiwara Compendium* that make up a courtesan's trousseau.

bedding
storage chest
chest of drawers
pot and small brazier for boiling cloves
    to scent a room
game of Go
game of Japanese chess

board game
koto
samisen
bookshelf
various articles included in a simple vanity,
    such as a makeup box and mirror
other suitable items

The following is a list of eighteen ideals from *The Greater Learning for Courtesans* that a courtesan and others should follow.

1. Having a client willing to pay off your contract means you have achieved position in life, and this is a cherished thing.

2. Because of your constant charm men will fall in love with you, which will raise your sense of elegance and polish.

3. The heart of a courtesan, more than her face, must be superior.

4. A courtesan is different from a faithful wife, for she has many husbands and is praised by the number of pillows she piles up.

5. In accordance with piling up [pillows and clients], you make yourself friendly with men, but without good reason do not let go of all reserve [literally, "reveal your skin"]—even with your *najimi* partners.

6. Because there are more women who do not achieve high rank than those who do, you should take note of this by paying attention to your professional conduct.

7. Do not make promises concerning the future to a client who is married and is a father.

8. For self-improvement develop a taste for voice and instruments. Also gain skill in reading and writing, poetry, flower arrangement, tea, incense, and other arts.

9. One's sleeping form is a grave matter for a courtesan.

10. After entering into the parlor, do not adjust your makeup in front of your client.

11. For teahouse entertainers, skillful performance with koto and samisen is essential.

12. For such entertainers, before you start playing your samisen at a party, first get a sense of the parlor's mood and the client's demeanor. Take your seat and be neither a wallflower nor a fuss.

13. Novice entertainers should exert themselves fully in their musical training so as not to become fearful of their superiors.

14. Entertainers need to judge well a client's preferences so as to prepare the mood of the parlor.

15. The patterns of a courtesan's wardrobe are to be devised variously with the seasons. Do not search for what is popular, but rather create something popular. This is the true intention of a courtesan.

16. When it comes time for a courtesan to part ways with a client, a courtesan should do so without causing any discord by using all her skills.

17. When you go out to parade or see a play, consider well your future and by all means expertly play the womanly and attractive role.

18. The master of a bordello must have compassion for his female laborers. Teaching them well the way of the courtesan and her arts is at the root of his prosperity.

1. Introduction

1. *Koma-e* is a smaller visual image within an illustration meant to draw a comparison between the two. Utamaro portrays the tired traveler Rosei, the main character from the one-act Nō drama *Kantan* (ca. 1400s). Rosei stops for a meal at an inn and comes into possession of a mysterious pillow, upon which he rests his head. He falls asleep and dreams of a life filled with fifty years of unparalleled success and political might. When he awakens to the nudges of the innkeeper bringing his supper, he realizes the glory was a phantom arising from his own weary sleep. The story, whose author is unknown, points to the Buddhist notion of impermanence. Utamaro's *koma-e* suggests through visual juxtaposition that a courtesan's dream of a marriage to end her days of prostitution is as ephemeral as Rosei's dream.

2. Donald Keene, trans., *Four Major Plays of Chikamatsu* (New York: Columbia University Press, 1964); and Ivan Morris, ed and trans., *The Life of an Amorous Woman* (New York: New Directions Books, 1969).

3. Emori Ichirō and Koizumi Yoshinaga, "*Ezu daijiten no henshū kōki,*" in *Edo jidai josei seikatsu kenkyū* (Supplement to *Edo jidai josei seikatsu ezu daijiten*), ed. Emori Ichirō (Tokyo: Ōzorasha, 1994), 8–9.

4. For a study of this demarcation, see Jinnai Hidenobu, "The Spatial Structure of Edo," trans. J. Victor Koschmann, in *Tokugawa Japan: The Social and Economic Antecedents of Modern Japan,* ed. Nakane Chie and Ōishi Shinzaburō (Tokyo: University of Tokyo Press, 1990).

5. Marius B. Jansen, *The Making of Modern Japan* (Cambridge, Mass.: The Belknap Press of Harvard University Press, 2000), 147–151.

6. The grid of 360' x 480' x 720' mapped the divisions of Kyoto when it was constructed as the new capital. See Jinnai Hidenobu, *Tokyo: A Spatial Anthropology,* trans. Kimiko Nishimura (Berkeley: University of California Press, 1995), 40.

7. Marcia Yonemoto, *Mapping Early Modern Japan: Space, Place, and Culture in the Tokugawa Period (1603–1868)* (Berkeley: University of California Press, 2003), 2.

8. Donald H. Shively, "*Bakufu* versus *Kabuki,*" in *Studies in the Institutional History of*

Early Modern Japan, ed. John W. Hall and Marius B. Jansen (Princeton, N.J.: Princeton University Press, 1968), 241.

9. Ibid., 242.

10. Sone Hiromi, "Prostitution and Public Authority in Early Modern Japan," trans. Terashima Akiko and Anne Walthall, in *Women and Class in Japanese History,* ed. Hitomi Tonomura, Anne Walthall, and Wakita Haruko (Ann Arbor: Center for Japanese Studies, University of Michigan, 1999), 170.

11. For a discussion of the growth of Edo, see Nakai Nobuhiko and James L. McClain, "Commercial Change and Urban Growth in Early Modern Japan," in *The Cambridge History of Japan,* vol. 4., ed. John Whitney Hall (Cambridge: Cambridge University Press, 1991), 565–568.

12. Gilbert Rozman, *Urban Networks in Ch'ing China and Tokugawa Japan* (Princeton, N.J.: Princeton University Press, 1973), 194–199.

13. Cecilia Segawa Seigle, *Yoshiwara: The Glittering World of the Japanese Courtesan* (Honolulu: University of Hawai'i Press, 1993), 40.

14. Miyamoto Yukiko, "Kuruwa to shukuba," in *Nihon joseishi,* ed. Wakita Haruko, Hayashi Reiko, and Nagahara Kazuko (Tokyo: Yoshikawa Kōbunkan, 1987), 129. For original text, see Shōji Katsutomi, *Ihon dōbō goen* [1720], in *Enseki jisshu,* vol. 5 (Tokyo: Chūō Kōronsha, 1980).

15. Sone, "Prostitution and Public Authority," 181–182.

16. Sone Hiromi, "'Baita' kō," in *Nihon josei seikatsushi: Chūsei,* vol. 3, ed. Miyashita Michiko and Kurachi Katsunao (Tokyo: Tōkyō Daigaku Shuppankai, 1990), 118–121.

17. Gary P. Leupp, *Male Colors: The Construction of Homosexuality in Tokugawa Japan* (Berkeley: University of California Press, 1995), 156.

18. Donald Keene, "A Note on Prostitution in Chikamatsu's Plays," in *Four Major Plays of Chikamatsu* (New York: Columbia University Press, 1964), 210.

19. Charles Bernheimer, *Figures of Ill Repute: Representing Prostitution in Nineteenth-Century France* (Cambridge, Mass.: Harvard University Press, 1989), 7.

20. Seigle, *Yoshiwara,* 40.

21. Wakita Haruko makes this point often in her works on household and gender in medieval and early modern Japan. See Wakita Haruko, "The Medieval Household and Gender Roles within the Imperial Family, Nobility, Merchants, and Commoners," trans. Gary P. Leupp, in *Women and Class in Japanese History,* ed. Hitomi Tonomura, Anne Walthall, and Wakita Haruko (Ann Arbor: Center for Japanese Studies, University of Michigan, 1999), 92–93.

22. For the structural vagaries of medieval relationships, see James C. Dobbins, *Letters of the Nun Eshinni: Images of Pure Land Buddhism in Medieval Japan* (Honolulu: University of Hawai'i Press, 2004), 75–79.

23. Gary P. Leupp, *Servants, Shophands, and Laborers in the Cities of Tokugawa Japan* (Princeton, N.J.: Princeton University Press, 1992), 15. For an example of the use of *hōkō* in legal reference to courtesans, see a sample prostitution contract in Ishii Ryōsuke, *Edo no yūjo* (Tokyo: Akashi Shoten, 1989), 154–157.

24. Wendy Chapkis, *Live Sex Acts: Women Performing Erotic Labour* (London: Cassell, 1997).

25. For titles of such texts, see Yokota Fuyuhiko, "Imagining Working Women in Early Modern Japan," trans. Mariko Asano Tamanoi, in *Women and Class in Japanese His-*

tory, ed. Hitomi Tonomura, Anne Walthall, and Wakita Haruko (Ann Arbor: Center for Japanese Studies, University of Michigan, 1999), 157–160.

26. I am indebted to Yokota's insight for drawing my attention to the social context of this illustration. See ibid., 157.

27. The woman is labeled *kasha.* This term applied to both courtesan managers and bordello wives having reputations as hard taskmasters. *Kasha* (fire vehicle) refers to an afterlife punishment in which one of hell's own taskmasters hauls the fated person's soul around in a cart constantly consumed by flames.

28. One is a nun. The widow nun *(goke ama)* was an option available to older women upon the death of their husbands. For a discussion of nun options, see Dobbins, *Letters of the Nun Eshinni,* 83–85.

29. See the illustration in Namura Jōhaku, *Onna chōhōki* [1692], in *E-iri Onna chōhōki: Honbunhen,* ed. Arima Sumiko, Wakasugi Tetsuo, and Nishigaki Yoshiko (Tokyo: Tōyoko Gakuen Joshi Tanki Daigaku Josei Bunka Kenkyūjo, 1989), 6–7.

30. This discussion of female labor as morally problematic and as raising the concern to teach young women morals and proper behavior comes from Yokota, "Imagining Working Women in Early Modern Japan," 153–167.

31. Ibid., 160–163.

32. For a discussion of this market, see Peter Kornicki, *The Book in Japan: A Cultural History from the Beginnings to the Nineteenth Century* (Honolulu: University of Hawai'i Press, 2001), 136–142.

33. Arima Sumiko and Nishigaki Yoshiko contextualize the genre in the late seventeenth-century growth of Japanese-scripted books over a period of twenty-two years, ending in 1692. Buddhist, scholarly, medical, and Japanese-scripted writings constitute their sample. The last category, unlike the others, which were typically written in Chinese, ranged from fiction to forms of *jokun.* The number of publications in their sampling doubled to over seven thousand titles. As a percentage of total share, however, Buddhist, scholarly, and medical writings fell, while Japanese-scripted books rose to more than one-third of that share. For details and numbers, see Arima Sumiko and Nishigaki Yoshiko, "Edoki josei no seikatsu ni kansuru kenkyū: *Onna chōhōki* ni miru shussan to byōki," *Tōyō gakuen joshi tanki daigaku kiyō* 25 (1990): 5. Kornicki, *The Book in Japan,* 156, also notes that the number of Buddhist titles, which took up substantial space in seventeenth-century catalogs, declined in later catalogs.

34. Donald Shively, "Popular Culture," in *The Cambridge History of Japan,* vol. 4, ed. John Whitney Hall (Cambridge: Cambridge University Press, 1991), 745.

35. Kornicki, *The Book in Japan,* 171.

36. Martha C. Tocco, "Norms and Texts for Women's Education in Tokugawa Japan," in *Women and Confucian Cultures in Premodern China, Korea, and Japan,* ed. Dorothy Ko, JaHyun Kim Haboush, and Joan R. Piggott (Berkeley: University of California Press, 2003), 197.

37. For a discussion on functional pre-Meiji literacy, see Kornicki, *The Book in Japan,* 269–276.

38. Ibid., 273.

39. Anne Walthall, "The Lifecycle of Farm Women in Tokugawa Japan," in *Recreating Japanese Women, 1600–1945,* ed. Gail Lee Bernstein (Berkeley: University of California Press, 1991), 48–49.

40. Walter Edwards, *Modern Japan through Its Weddings* (Stanford, Calif.: Stanford University Press, 1989), 38.

41. Herman Ooms, *Tokugawa Village Practice: Class, Status, Power, Law* (Berkeley: University of California Press, 1996), 340–341.

42. Marius B. Jansen, "The Meiji Restoration," in *The Cambridge History of Japan,* ed. Marius B. Jansen (Cambridge: Cambridge University Press, 1989), 5:320.

43. Susan B. Hanley, "Tokugawa Society: Material Culture, Standard of Living, and Life-styles," in *The Cambridge History of Japan,* ed. John Whitney Hall (Cambridge: Cambridge University Press, 1991), 4:704.

44. The Ogasawara was particularly renowned for its expertise in archery, horsemanship, and the outdoor arts, while the Ise gained fame for its knowledge of activities primarily related to duties executed within the household. See Shimada Isao, "Kaisetsu," in *Teijō zakki,* ed. Shimada Isao. *Tōyō Bunko* 444 (Tokyo: Heibonsha, 1985), 1:314–315.

45. For a discussion of moral and lifestyle texts as textbooks, see Tocco, "Norms and Texts for Women's Education," 193–218.

46. This characterization of the *ie* is derived from several studies. See for example Susan B. Hanley, "Family and Fertility in Four Tokugawa Villages," in *Family and Population in East Asian History,* ed. Susan B. Hanley and Arthur P. Wolf (Stanford, Calif.: Stanford University Press, 1985): 219–223; Nakane Chie, "Tokugawa Society," trans. Susan Murata, in *Tokugawa Japan: The Social and Economic Antecedents of Modern Japan,* ed. Nakane Chie and Ōishi Shinzaburō (Tokyo: University of Tokyo Press, 1990): 217; and Bitō Masahide, "Thought and Religion: 1550–1770," in *The Cambridge History of Japan,* ed. John Whitney Hall (Cambridge: Cambridge University Press, 1991), 4:376–377.

47. Poorer women labored harder than commoner women of better economic means. Further, while childbirth was a common hope, motherhood as a full-time occupation was not the norm. Child care was spread out among family members or given over to maids and nursemaids in wealthy households because of its time-consuming nature. For these and other differences, see Kathleen S. Uno, "Women and Changes in the Household Division of Labor," in *Recreating Japanese Women, 1600–1945,* ed. Gail Lee Bernstein (Berkeley: University of California Press, 1991), 22–34.

48. The juridical and ideological construction of the *ie* in the Meiji period, particularly its codification in the Civil Code, has encouraged certain scholars to assume the patrilineal household as an "invention of tradition" that did not exist among commoners in the Tokugawa period. For a prominent advocate of this view, see Ueno Chizuko, "Modern Patriarchy and the Formation of the Japanese Nation State," in *Multicultural Japan: Paleolithic to Postmodern,* ed. Donald Denoon et al. (Cambridge: Cambridge University Press, 1996), 213–223. However, as some scholars of women's history make clear, such a position is simply untenable. The weight of evidence and consensus among researchers of folk history and women's history *(joseishi)* versus that of women's studies *(joseigaku)*—which is a field that tends to be extremely theoretical and less interested in the hard work of historical data gathering and description—is that the patrilineal *ie* was a growing pattern throughout the Tokugawa period. For this view, which is both a historian's critique of Ueno's assertions concerning the Tokugawa *ie* and a critique of women's studies from the perspective of women's history in Japan, see Sone Hiromi, "Joseishi to fueminizumu—Ueno Chizuko cho *Rekishigaku to fueminizumu* ni yosete," *Joseishigaku* 6 (1996): 73–82.

49. In her work on Okayama domain, for example, Mega Atsuko argues that eco-

nomic stability and an *"ie-*consciousness" grew throughout the period to include middle- and some lower-class commoners by the second half, and she links this expanding consciousness to households taking greater control of their daughters' social and sexual development. See Mega Atsuko, *Hankachō no naka no onnatachi* (Tokyo: Heibonsha, 1995).

50. This was likely the situation from the start of the quarters. Scholars of prostitution suggest that the assumed high social skills of many seventeenth-century courtesans may have been due to the fact that they were daughters from warrior families that ended up on the wrong side of history in the final clashes against the nascent Tokugawa hegemony such as Sekigahara (1600) and the siege of Osaka Castle (1615). High-class prostitution was one of the few doors open to them as women stripped of status, and as women possessed of their cultural knowledge and sense of style. For this view, see Nakayama Tarō, *Baishō sanzennenshi* (Tokyo: Parutosusha, 1984), 302; Takigawa Masajirō, *Yūjo no rekishi* (Tokyo: Shibundō, 1967), 43; and Seigle, *Yoshiwara*, 28–29.

51. Donald Richie, "Forward to the Facsimile Edition," in *The Nightless City, or the History of the Yoshiwara Yūkwaku* (New York: IGM Muse, Inc., 2000), xvi.

52. Thomas C. Smith, "The Japanese Village in the Seventeenth Century," in *Studies in the Institutional History of Early Modern Japan,* ed. John W. Hall and Marius B. Jansen (Princeton, N.J.: Princeton University Press, 1968), 269.

53. For a study of the publication and readership of a specific text, the *Onna shōgaku,* see Unoda Shoya, "Kinsei jokunsho no okeru shomotsu to dokusha—*Onna shōgaku* wo tegakari toshite," *Joseishigaku* 11 (2001): 15–31.

54. Reasons and styles behind the practice of pennames varied. See Kornicki, *The Book in Japan,* 238. Namura created much of his penname by rearranging the radicals of his actual name.

55. For this work on male lifestyle, see Namura Jōhaku, *Nan chōhōki* [1693], in *Onna chōhōki Nan chōhōki, Nihon shigaku kyōiku kenkyūjo chōsa shiryō,* no. 122, ed. Namae Yoshio, Sekishita Toshihide, and Saitō Junkichi (Tokyo: Nihon Shigaku Kyōiku Kenkyūjo, 1985).

56. For a sketch of his meager biography and questions about dates concerning his life and death, see Arima Sumiko, Wakasugi Tetsuo, and Nishigaki Yoshiko, "Kaisetsu," in *E-iri Onna chōhōki: Honbunhen* (Tokyo: Tōyoko Gakuen Joshi Tanki Daigaku Josei Bunka Kenkyūjo, 1989), 176–177.

57. Ibid., 176.

58. John Allen Tucker, *Itō Jinsai's* Gomō Jigi *and the Philosophical Definition of Early Modern Japan* (Leiden: Brill, 1998), 1.

59. Wm. Theodore de Bary, ed., *Sources of Japanese Tradition* (New York: Columbia University Press, 1958), 1:403.

60. To read the commentary of Takai's edition in contrast to the original text, see Yokoyama Manabu, "Joshi kyōyōsho kōka-han *Onna chōhōki* to Takai Razan," in *Edo jidai josei seikatsu kenkyū* (Supplement to *Edo jidai josei seikatsu ezu daijiten*), ed. Emori Ichirō (Tokyo: Ōzorasha, 1994), 100–114.

61. Uno, "Women and Changes in the Household," 20.

62. Joyce Chapman Lebra, "Women in an All-Male Industry: The Case of Sake Brewer Tatsu'uma Kiyo," in *Recreating Japanese Women, 1600–1945,* ed. Gail Lee Bernstein (Berkeley: University of California Press, 1991).

63. Jennifer Robertson, "The Shingaku Woman: Straight from the Heart," in *Recre-*

ating Japanese Women, 1600–1945, ed. Gail Lee Bernstein (Berkeley: University of California Press, 1991).

64. Anne Walthall, *The Weak Body of a Useless Woman: Matsuo Taseko and the Meiji Restoration* (Chicago: University of Chicago Press, 1998), 8.

65. Wakita Haruko, "Marriage and Property in Premodern Japan from the Perspective of Women's History," trans. Suzanne Gay, *Journal of Japanese Studies* 10 (1984): 97.

66. For this perspective on ritual, see Jean Comaroff, *Body of Power, Spirit of Resistance* (Chicago: University of Chicago Press, 1985).

67. Catherine Bell, *Ritual Theory, Ritual Practice* (New York and Oxford: Oxford University Press, 1992), 76.

68. Helen Hardacre, *Shintō and the State, 1868–1988* (Princeton, N.J.: Princeton University Press, 1989), 110–111.

69. Miyata Noboru, *Kankonsōsai* (Tokyo: Iwanami Shoten, 1999), 106.

70. Japanese scholars of folklore studies have used various terms to categorize wedding forms. *Jizen kekkon,* which may broadly refer to pre-Meiji weddings, also gives the sense of a non-religious wedding. In this sense it may also refer to civil ceremonies. For these and other terms and usages of wedding forms in recent scholarship, see Murao Yoshie, "Kekkon girei ni miru 'sahō' no eikyō," *Nihon minzokugaku* 235 (2003): 66–67.

71. For this view, see Edmund Leach, *Culture and Communication: The Logic by which Symbols are Connected* (Cambridge: Cambridge University Press, 1976).

72. Fred W. Clothey, *Rhythm and Intent: Ritual Studies from South Asia* (Madras, India: Blackie and Son Publishers, 1983), 1–7.

73. For this discussion of Japan as a unitized society, see Brian J. McVeigh, *Wearing Ideology: State, Schooling, and Self-Presentation in Japan* (Oxford and New York: Berg, 2000), 23–27.

74. Clothey, *Rhythm and Intent,* 16–17.

75. Ibid., 17–18.

76. These three crises are based on the work of Clifford Geertz, *The Interpretation of Cultures* (New York: Basic Books, 1973), 100.

77. Jonathan Z. Smith, *To Take Place: Toward Theory in Ritual* (Chicago: University of Chicago Press, 1987). Smith's argument is a refutation of classical conceptions of a single sacred center, an *axis mundi,* which the work of Mircea Eliade typifies. See Mircea Eliade, *The Sacred and the Profane: The Nature of Religion,* trans. Willard R. Trask (San Diego: Harcourt Brace Jovanovich, 1959), 20–67.

78. J. Smith, *To Take Place,* 45.

79. Ronald L. Grimes, *Beginnings in Ritual Studies* (Washington, D.C.: University Press of America, 1982), 66–67.

80. Ibid., 66.

81. Victor Turner, *The Forest of Symbols: Aspects of Ndembu Ritual* (Ithaca, N.Y.: Cornell University Press, 1967), 51.

82. For this perspective on symbols, see Dan Sperber, *Rethinking Symbolism* (Cambridge: Cambridge University Press, 1974). Also see Grimes's discussion of Sperber in Ronald L. Grimes, *Reading, Writing, and Ritualizing: Ritual in Fictive, Liturgical, and Public Places* (Washington, D.C.: The Pastoral Press, 1993), 19–22.

83. For this critique of methodologies in religious studies and the importance of functional definitions, see Robert Baird, *Category Formation and the History of Religions,* 2nd ed. (Berlin: Mouton de Gruyter, 1991).

84. Laurel Kendall, *Getting Married in Korea: Of Gender, Morality, and Modernity* (Berkeley: University of California Press, 1996), 10.

85. My use of ultimate concern follows Robert Baird and his employment of it as most methodologically useful as a functional definition of religion to analyze a variety of data.

86. Melford E. Spiro functionally defines religion as being a culturally patterned belief in superhuman beings. He also critiques ultimate concern as too broad, pointing out that politics and sports, which may well garner great concern in many people's lives, must also be considered investigative fodder for the study of religion. See Melford E. Spiro, "Religion: Problems of Definition and Explanation," in *Culture and Human Nature: Theoretical Papers of Melford E. Spiro,* ed. Benjamin Kilborne and L. L. Langness (Chicago: University of Chicago Press, 1987), 187–222.

87. This bifurcation is due to a split in the field between scholars trained in Buddhist doctrine and scholars approaching religion from various methodologies outside doctrinal and sectarian studies. Robert Sharf, "Sanbōkyōdan: Zen and the New Religions," *Japanese Journal of Religious Studies* 22 (1995): 452.

88. Jamie Hubbard, "Premodern, Modern, and Postmodern: Doctrine and the Study of Japanese Religion," *Japanese Journal of Religious Studies* 19 (1992): 3–28; and Neil McMullin, "Which Doctrine? Whose 'Religion'?—A Rejoinder," *Japanese Journal of Religious Studies* 19 (1992): 29–40.

89. Neil McMullin, "Historical and Historiographical Issues in the Study of Pre-Modern Japanese Religions," *Japanese Journal of Religious Studies* 16 (1989): 3–40.

90. Hubbard, "Premodern, Modern, and Postmodern," 19.

91. For important studies of *genze riyaku,* see Ian Reader and George Tanabe, *Practically Religious: Worldly Benefits and the Common Religion of Japan* (Honolulu: University of Hawai'i Press, 1998); and Miyake Hitoshi, *Shugendō: Essays on the Structure of Japanese Folk Religion,* ed. H. Byron Earhart (Ann Arbor: Center for Japanese Studies, University of Michigan, 2001), 199–215.

92. For a critique of metanarratives in the study of Japanese religion, see Jane Marie Law, *Puppets of Nostalgia: The Life, Death, and Rebirth of the Japanese Awaji Ningyō Tradition* (Princeton, N.J.: Princeton University Press, 1997), 13–16. Also see Brian J. McVeigh, "The Vitalistic Conception of Salvation as Expressed in Sūkyō Mahikari," *Japanese Journal of Religious Studies* 19 (1992): 41, for a critical view of scholarship's tendency to rely heavily on worldly benefits to interpret Japan's new religions at the risk of overlooking their varied schemes of cosmology and salvation.

93. Baird, *Category Formation and the History of Religions,* 21.

94. One of Law's concerns with metanarratives in the study of Japanese religion is that they tend to gloss over the actual social heterogeneity that has historically marked Japan. See Law, *Puppets of Nostalgia,* 13.

2. Value Models

1. *Precepts for Women* (Ch. *Nü jie;* Jp. *Jokai*) is a latter Han-period work by Ban Zhao (AD 45–117). Her text became essential reading for elite women in imperial China.

2. Uesugi Yōzan, *Momo no wakaba,* in *Jokun sōsho,* vol. 5, ed. Ōbayashi Tokutarō (Tokyo: Shiritsu Takanawa Shukujo Gakkō, 1912).

3. Hagiwara Tatsuo, "The Tokugawa Shogunate and Religion: Shinto under the

Shogunate," trans. Paul McCarthy and Gaynor Sekimori, in *A History of Japanese Religion*, ed. Kasahara Kazuo (Tokyo: Kosei, 2001), 350–351.

4. Kurachi Katsunao, "Seikatsu shisō ni okeru seiishiki," in *Nihon josei seikatsushi: Kinsei*, ed. Miyashita Michiko and Kurachi Katsunao (Tokyo: Tōkyō Daigaku Shuppankai, 1990), 3:206.

5. Masuho Zankō, *Endō tsugan* [1715], in *Kinsei shikidōron, Nihon shisō taikei*, ed. Noma Kōshin (Tokyo: Iwanami Shoten, 1976), 60:209.

6. Ibid., 210.

7. Ibid., 212.

8. Ibid., 213.

9. Excerpted from Kurachi, "Seikatsu shisō ni okeru seiishiki," 206.

10. Hagiwara, "The Tokugawa Shogunate and Religion," 351.

11. For an analysis of male/compassion and female/sincerity in Masuho's thought, see Kobayashi Junji, "Kinsei Nihon ni okeru koi to jendā: Masuho Zankō *Endō tsugan* ni okeru dansei no imèjī," *Joseishigaku* 8 (1998): 1–13.

12. Quoted in Kurachi, "Seikatsu shisō ni okeru seiishiki," 208.

13. Ibid.

14. Quoted in ibid., 210.

15. For a study of the man in relation to Tokugawa intellectual history, see Peter Nosco, "Masuho Zankō (1655–1742): A Shinto Popularizer between Nativism and National Learning," in *Confucianism and Tokugawa Culture*, ed. Peter Nosco (Princeton, N.J.: Princeton University Press, 1984), 166–187.

16. H. D. Harootunian, *Things Seen and Unseen: Discourse and Ideology in Tokugawa Nativism* (Chicago: University of Chicago Press, 1988), 232–233.

17. Ibid., 220–221.

18. Masuho, *Endō tsugan* [1715], 332.

19. Ibid.

20. Uesugi, *Momo no wakaba*, 7.

21. Yashiro Hirotaka, *Tsuma ni atauru sho*, in *Kinsei joshi kyōiku shisō, Nihon kyōiku shisō taikei*, ed. Umezawa Seiichi (Tokyo: Nihon Tosho Sentā, 1980), 16:1.

22. Ihara Saikaku, *Kōshoku ichidai otoko* [1682], in *Nihon koten bungaku zenshū*, ed. Teruoka Yasutaka and Higashi Akimasa (Tokyo: Shōgakkan, 1971), 38:234. For English, see Kenji Hamada, trans., *The Life of an Amorous Man* (Rutland, Vt.: Charles E. Tuttle Company, 1963), 167.

23. As Shively, "Popular Culture," 747, notes, the "artistic emphasis on the pleasures of social and cultural intercourse made the sex act almost incidental."

24. Seigle, *Yoshiwara*, 96–97.

25. Although authorship is traditionally credited to Kaibara Ekken (1630–1714), scholarly consensus no longer holds this view.

26. *Onna daigaku* (ca. early 1700s), in *Kaibara Ekken Muro Kyūsō, Nihon shisō taikei*, ed. Araki Kengo and Inoue Tadashi (Tokyo: Iwanami Shoten, 1970), 34:203. For another translation, see Basil Hall Chamberlain, *Women and Wisdom of Japan* (London: John Murray, 1905), 38–39.

27. Egawa Tanan [aka Egawa Tarōzaemon], *Shinpu ni atauru sho*, in *Kinsei joshi kyōiku shisō, Nihon kyōiku shisō taikei*, ed. Umezawa Seiichi (Tokyo: Nihon Tosho Sentā, 1980), 16:1.

28. Historically in China these grounds for divorce were trumped by any one of three

"extenuating circumstances": 1) she had experienced the loss of her parents and thus had no natal home to which she could return; 2) she had performed mourning rites for one of her parents-in-law; and 3) her husband had been impoverished at the time of their marriage and subsequently accumulated some wealth and sought a divorce on that basis. See Theresa Kelleher, "Confucianism," in *Women in World Religions,* ed. Arvind Sharma (Albany: State University of New York Press, 1987), 143.

29. *Onna daigaku,* 202. For English, see Chamberlain, *Women and Wisdom of Japan,* 36.

30. For Kuki's original study, see Kuki Shūzō, *Iki no kōzō* (Tokyo: Iwanami Shoten, 1930). For a study of Kuki and his thought, see Nakano Hajimu, "Kuki Shūzō and the Structure of *Iki,*" in *Culture and Identity: Japanese Intellectuals during the Interwar Years,* ed. J. Thomas Rimer (Princeton, N.J.: Princeton University Press, 1990), 261–272.

31. Kuki analyzes *iki* as exhibiting a historically developed aesthetic structure that fully came together during the Tokugawa period. He breaks it down into its constitutive parts of *hari* (strong spirit), *bitai* (allure), and *akanuke* (sophisticated behavior). See Kuki, *Iki no kōzō,* 18–19. Nishiyama Matsunosuke picks up this triadic analysis and examines each item as an independently existing element with its own distinct traits. See Nishiyama Matsunosuke, *Edo Culture: Daily Life and Diversions in Urban Japan, 1600–1868,* trans. and ed. Gerald Groemer (Honolulu: University of Hawai'i Press, 1997), 56. Seigle, *Yoshiwara,* 219, also cites Kuki in her notes, but goes on to a different configuration of *iki.*

32. Ihara, *Kōshoku ichidai otoko,* 243–244. For another translation, see Kenji Hamada, *Life of an Amorous Man,* 167–168.

33. According to Teruoka Yasutaka, dramatic memorializing of Yūgiri began in the same year of her death with the now non-extant play *Yūgiri nagori no shōgatsu* (1678). Chikamatsu produced several puppet plays about her in the decades following her death. His *Yūgiri sanzesō* became the foundation for many other plays about her, including a later drama of his called *Yūgiri awa no naruto,* which concerns Yūgiri and a fictitious lover, Izaemon. As late as 1808 this play was adapted to kabuki under the title *Kuruwa bunshō.* See Teruoka Yasutaka, "Pleasure Quarters and Tokugawa Culture," trans. C. Andrew Gerstle, in *18th Century Japan,* ed. C. Andrew Gerstle (Sydney: Allen and Unwin, 1989), 13–14. For original plays, see Chikamatsu Monzaemon, *Yūgiri sanzesō* [1686], in *Chikamatsu zenshū,* vol. 2, ed. Fujii Otoo (Osaka: Asahi Shimbunsha, 1925); *Yūgiri awa no naruto* [1712], in *Chikamatsu zenshū,* vol. 9, ed. Fujii Otoo (Osaka: Asahi Shimbunsha, 1927); and *Kuruwa bunshō* [1808], in *Meisaku kabuki zenshū,* vol. 7, ed. Toita Yasuji (Tokyo: Tokyo Sōgen Shinsha, 1969).

34. Hashimoto Katsusaburō, *Edo no hyakujo jiten* (Tokyo: Shinshō Sensho, 1997), 68.

35. Kurachi Katsunao, *Sei to karada no kinsei-shi* (Tokyo: Tōkyō Daigaku Shuppankai, 1998), 80.

36. Johan Huizinga, *Homo Luden: A Study of the Play Element in Culture* (Boston: Beacon Press, 1955), 8.

37. Uesugi, *Momo no wakaba,* 6–7. The phrase *kafū ni somaru* expresses this same point. Meaning "to be dyed in the family ways," it captures vividly the goal of acclimating a bride to the routines of a new and unfamiliar family. See Kittredge Cherry, *Womansword: What Japanese Words Say about Women* (Tokyo: Kodansha International, 1987), 60.

38. Punishment varied according to domain, time, and class. Mega's research on the Okayama domain, for example, shows that although warrior women suffered more severe punishments than commoner women for the same sexual crime, commoner

women sometimes faced capital punishment. By the second half of the period, however, punishments noticeably lessened in severity. See Mega, *Hankachō no naka no onnatachi,* 125–181.

39. Ihara, *Kōshoku ichidai otoko,* 229–233.

40. Seigle, *Yoshiwara,* 36.

41. See Buyō's excerpt in Mitani Kazuma, *Edo Yoshiwara zushū* (Tokyo: Rippū Shobō, 1977), 241. Other observations from the events of daily life are found in his work: Buyō Inshi, *Seji kenbunroku* [1816], ed. Hanjō Eijirō (Tokyo: Seiabō, 2001).

42. For his classic and functional definition of religion, see Emile Durkhiem, *The Elementary Forms of Religious Life* [1912], trans. Karen E. Fields (New York: The Free Press, 1995), 44.

43. Joseph M. Kitagawa, *On Understanding Japanese Religion* (Princeton, N.J.: Princeton University Press, 1987), 160.

44. Allan G. Grapard, "The Shinto of Yoshida Kanemoto," *Monumenta Nipponica* 47 (1992): 45.

45. Sawada Kichi, *Onna Imagawa* [1700], in *Edo jidai josei seikatsu ezu daijiten,* ed. Emori Ichirō (Tokyo: Ōzorasha, 1993), 1:209. First published in 1687, this text is a collection of simple teachings and admonishments directed toward girls. It takes its title and writing style from an educational genre widely disseminated throughout Tokugawa society generically called *Imagawa,* which denoted a textbook of morals often structured around maxims and admonitions. The original *Imagawa,* attributed to the warrior-scholar Imagawa Ryōshun (ca. 1326–1414), was directed toward sons of warriors and commoners and centered around matters of just behavior, wise counsel, and introspection and self-correction of flaws. The *Onna imagawa,* which was a popular educational text and was republished many times even into the Meiji period, is an adaptation for girls designed to enhance their moral education. For a study of the original and its educational use, see Carl Steenstrup, "The Imagawa Letter: A Muromachi Warrior's Code of Conduct Which Became a Tokugawa Schoolbook," *Monumenta Nipponica* 28 (1973): 295–316.

46. Quoted from Ernst Cassier, *An Essay on Man* (New Haven, Conn.: Yale University Press, 1944), 25.

47. Ibid., 33–36.

48. J. Smith, *To Take Place,* 109.

49. "Ethical paradox" comes from Geertz's discussion, in *Interpretation of Cultures,* 100, of these root crises.

50. *Yūjo daigaku* [1807], in *Edo jidai josei bunko,* vol. 31, ed. Morita Kōichi (Tokyo: Ōzorasha, 1995).

51. Donald Keene, trans., *Chūshingura: The Treasury of Loyal Retainers* (New York: Columbia University Press, 1971), 87–94.

3. Entrance

1. Hitomi Tonomura, "Re-envisioning Women in the Post-Kamakura Age," in *The Origins of Japan's Medieval World,* ed. Jeffrey P. Mass (Stanford, Calif.: Stanford University Press, 1997), 152.

2. See Peter Nickerson, "The Meaning of Matrilocality: Kinship, Property, and Politics in Mid-Heian," *Monumenta Nipponica* 48 (1993): 429–467. An earlier study of Heian

marriage, to which Nickerson makes several references, is that of William H. McCullough, "Japanese Marriage Institutions in the Heian Period," *Harvard Journal of Asiatic Studies* 27 (1967): 103–167.

3. Mass aptly describes the perspective. "Women were daughters and sisters before they were wives, mothers, and widows." See Jeffrey P. Mass, *Lordship and Inheritance in Early Medieval Japan* (Stanford, Calif.: Stanford University Press, 1989), 17.

4. For these perspectives, see Dobbins, *Letters of the Nun Eshinni,* 76–77; and Tabata Yasuko, *Nihon chūsei no josei* (Tokyo: Yoshikawa Kōbunkan, 1987), 6–8.

5. For an overview and analysis of female inheritance in the Kamakura period, see Hitomi Tonomura, "Women and Inheritance in Japan's Early Warrior Society," *Comparative Studies in Society and History* 32 (1990): 592–623.

6. Tonomura, "Re-envisioning Woman in the Post-Kamakura Age," 153.

7. Nagano Hiroko, "Bakuhansei kokka to shomin josei," in *Nihon joseishi,* ed. Wakita Haruko, Hayashi Reiko, and Nagahara Kazuko (Tokyo: Yoshikawa Kōbunkan, 1987), 119.

8. Namura, *Onna chōhōki,* 38.

9. Shikitei Sanba and Ryūtei Rijō, *Ukiyodoko* [1813–1823], in *Edo no fūzoku shiryō,* vol. 5, ed. Ono Takeo (Tokyo: Tenbōsha, 1974), 57.

10. Much of this research is in response to the pioneering work of Takamure Itsue (1894–1964), whose thesis, in short, put forward a historical decline of female political and economic authority, reaching its nadir in the Tokugawa, tied to changes in marriage patterns that shifted from original duolocality to matrilocality and finally to virilocality. See Takamure Itsue, *Nihon kon'in shi,* in *Takamure Itsue zenshū,* vol. 6, ed. Takamure Itsue and Hashimoto Kenzō (Tokyo: Rironsha, 1966). For a discussion in English of Takamure's thesis in reference to fourteenth-century marriage, see Tonomura, "Re-envisioning Women in the Post-Kamakura Age," 147–153.

11. *Tsumadoi* is considered an ancient pattern, which, given its vagueness of visiting, easily fit the practices of polygamy and endogamy considered normative in ancient Japan. Mikiso Hane, *Premodern Japan: A Historical Survey* (Boulder, Colo: Westview Press, 1991), 20.

12. For this outline of divers and marriage, see Anne Bouchy, "The Chisel of the Women Divers and the Bow of the Feudal Lords of the Sea: The Dual Structure of Labor and Village Organization in Women Divers' Society—A Case Study of the Town of Ijika," trans. John Davis, in *Gender and Japanese History,* ed. Wakita Haruko, Anne Bouchy, and Ueno Chizuko (Osaka: Osaka University Press, 1999), 2:380–382; and Arne Kalland, *Fishing Villages in Tokugawa Japan* (Honolulu: University of Hawai'i Press, 1995), 175.

13. Nagano, "Bakuhansei kokka to shomin josei, " 122–124.

14. Ibid., 124.

15. For an analysis of Tokugawa female headship and inheritance in a village in the province of Musashi (present-day Tokyo and Saitama Prefecture), which indicates the relatively low incidence and temporary character of the practice, see Ōguchi Yūjirō, "Kinsei nōson ni okeru josei sōzokunin," in *Ie-Shinzoku no seikatsu bunka, Nihon rekishi minzoku ronshū,* ed. Fukuta Ajio and Tsukamoto Manabu (Tokyo: Yoshikawa Kōbunkan, 1997), 3:119–151.

16. Noriko Sugano, "State Indoctrination of Filial Piety in Tokugawa Japan: Sons and Daughters in the *Official Records of Filial Piety,*" in *Women and Confucian Cultures in*

Premodern China, Korea, and Japan, ed. Dorothy Ko, JaHyun Kim Haboush, and Joan R. Piggot (Berkeley: University of California Press, 2003), 179–188.

17. Laurel Louise Cornell, "Peasant Family and Inheritance in a Japanese Community: 1671–1980." Ph.D. dissertation, The Johns Hopkins University, 1981, 111.

18. Ibid., 112.

19. Arakida Moritake (1473–1549) penned this poem as part of a collection titled *A Thousand Verses Composed by One Man (Dokugin senku)*. See Donald Keene, *World Within Walls* (New York: Holt, Rinehart, and Winston, 1976), 14.

20. Wendy Holloway, "Gender Difference and the Production of Subjectivity," In *Changing the Subject: Psychology, Social Regulation and Subjectivity,* ed. Julian Henriques et al. (London: Methuen, 1984), 238.

21. For a critique of Holloway's notion of investment on this point of individual choice, see Henrietta L. Moore, *A Passion for Difference: Essays in Anthropology and Gender* (Bloomington: Indiana University Press, 1994), 64–66.

22. Winston Davis, *Japanese Religion and Society: Paradigms of Structure and Change* (Albany: State University of New York Press, 1992), 17.

23. For a detailed study of the development and practice of Kōshin faith in Japan, see Kubo Noritada, *Kōshin shinkō kenkyū* (Tokyo: Daiichi Shobō, 1996), 2:63–204.

24. Katsuki Gyūzan, *Fujin kotobuki gusa* [1692], in *Nihon sanka sōsho,* ed. Kure Shūzō and Fujikawa Yū (Tokyo: Shibunkaku, 1971), 70–71.

25. Miyata Noboru, *Edo saijiki* (Tokyo: Yoshikawa Kōbunkan, 1981), 15.

26. See English version in C. Andrew Gerstle, ed. and trans., *Chikamatsu: 5 Late Plays* (New York: Columbia University Press, 2001). For original language, see Chikamatsu Monzaemon, *Shinjū yoi kōshin machi,* in *Chikamatsu Monzaemon zenshū, Nihon koten bungaku zenshū,* vol. 44, ed. Torigoe Bunzō (Tokyo: Shōgakkan, 1975).

27. Davis, *Japanese Religion and Society,* 17–18.

28. Sawada, *Onna Imagawa,* 207.

29. Uesugi, *Momo no wakaba,* 8–9.

30. Namura, *Onna chōhōki,* 57.

31. Ibid., 8.

32. Ibid.

33. *Onna daigaku,* 205.

34. Suzanne K. Langer, *Philosophy in a New Key: A Study in the Symbolism of Reason, Rite, and Art* (Cambridge, Mass.: Harvard University Press, 1942), 145.

35. For this discussion on symbols (what I call metaphors) as empty signifiers and their role in the production, interpretation, and consumption of myth, see Roland Barthes, *Mythologies,* trans. Annette Lavers (New York: Hill and Wang, 1972), 128–131.

36. H. Paul Varley, *A Chronicle of Gods and Sovereigns:* Jinnō shōtōki *of Kitabatake Chikafusa* (New York: Columbia University Press, 1980), 13–15.

37. Ise Shinto (also Watarai Shinto) sought through myth to privilege the priesthood and primary divinity (Toyouke) of the complex's outer shrine *(gekū)* over that of the inner shrine *(naikū)* and Amaterasu. Kitabatake used the narrative preferences of Ise Shinto to put forward his own linked ideas, during a time of a weakened and divided imperial line (1332–1392), of Japan as a divine country ruled by an emperor and of the importance of proper imperial succession.

38. Namura, *Onna chōhōki,* 5. Different from Namura's myth, the classical mythologies of *Nihongi* and *Kojiki* state that divine pairs of male and female deities existed prior

to Izanagi and Izanami. The two *kami*, however, were the first to use their gendered difference in creative copulation to produce the land of Japan and its myriad *kami*. See W. G. Aston, ed. and trans., *Nihongi* (London: George Allen & Unwin, Ltd., 1956), 1–15; and Donald L. Philippi, ed. and trans., *Kojiki* (Tokyo: University of Tokyo Press, 1968), 47–51.

39. Namura, *Onna chōhōki*, 5.

40. *Nihon shoki*, in *Nihon koten bungaku taikei*, ed. Sakamoto Tarō et al. (Tokyo: Iwanami Shoten, 1967), 67:80–81. The *Kojiki* employs a string of seven characters, each matching one of the seven syllables of *mitonomaguwai*. See *Kojiki*, in *Nihon shisō taikei*, ed. Aoki Kazuo et al. (Tokyo: Iwanami Shoten, 1982), 1:22–23.

41. Namura, *Onna chōhōki*, 5.

42. Ibid.

43. Ibid.

44. Ibid. Namura encloses the passage in quotes, which suggests its status as a popular trope for writers and readers alike. It is virtually identical to one found in an earlier lifestyle guide for women, with which he was surely familiar. For this, see Okuda Shohakkan, *Joyō kunmō zui* [1687], in *Kaseigaku bunken shūsei zokuhen Edoki*, ed. Tanaka Chitako and Tanaka Hatsuo (Tokyo: Watanabe Shoten, 1970), 8:283.

45. Virginia Woolf, "Professions for Women," in *The Death of the Moth and Other Essays* (New York: Harcourt, Brace, and Company, 1942), 237.

46. Modern bridal headwear, called *tsuno kakushi*, which came into use in the twentieth century, continues the legacy of these conflicting metaphors. Literally meaning "hiding of horns," the white head covering signifies both the potential threat of the incoming bride and her promise to put the threat to rest and become an obedient wife living in harmony with her new family.

47. Namura, *Onna chōhōki*, 8.

48. Ibid.

49. Arima Sumiko, Wakasugi Tetsuo, and Nishigaki Yoshiko, *Onna chōhōki: Chūkaihen* (Tokyo: Tōyoko Gakuen Joshi Tanki Daigaku Josei Bunka Kenkyūjo, 1989), 5. Also see chap. 1, n. 27, of this volume.

50. Mitani Kazuma, *Edo Yoshiwara zushū* (Tokyo: Tachikaze Shobō, 1977), 258.

51. Davis, *Japanese Religion and Society*, 175–178. The following example of Meiji Buddhism is part of Davis's analysis of passive enablement.

52. The *tayū* rank disappeared in the 1760s, but a ranking system and the image of top courtesan remained part of the serious play of the Yoshiwara throughout the period. See Seigle, *Yoshiwara*, 229–232.

53. Ihara Saikaku, *Kōshoku nidai otoko* [1684], in *Shin Nihon koten bungaku taikei*, ed. Fuji Akio, Inoue Toshiyuki, and Satake Akihiro (Tokyo: Iwanami Shoten, 1991), 76: 258–259.

54. Saeki Junko, *Yūjo no bunkashi* (Tokyo: Chūkō Kōronsha, 1990), 93.

55. See illustration and description in Yamaguchi Keizaburō and Asano Shūgō, eds., *Genshoku ukiyoe daihyakka jiten* (Tokyo: Taishūkan Shoten, 1982), 6:103, fig. 241. Also see Richard Lane, *Images from the Floating World: The Japanese Print* (New York: Konecky and Konecky, 1978), 226, fig. 58.

56. Seigle, *Yoshiwara*, 125–128.

57. For an examination of double identity, see Barbara E. Thornbury, *Sukeroku's Double Identity: The Dramatic Structure of Edo Kabuki* (Ann Arbor: Center for Japanese Stud-

ies, University of Michigan, 1982). For the play, see *Sukeroku: Flower of Edo*, in James R. Brandon, *Kabuki: Five Classic Plays* (Honolulu: University of Hawai'i Press, 1992).

58. See this episode in Ihara, *Kōshoku ichidai otoko*, 212–214. For translations, see Kenji Hamada, *Life of an Amorous Man*, 212–214; and Seigle, *Yoshiwara*, 38–39.

59. Karen A. Smyers, *The Fox and the Jewel: Shared and Private Meanings in Contemporary Japanese Inari Worship* (Honolulu: University of Hawai'i Press, 1999), 135.

60. Takigawa Masajirō, *Yoshiwara no shiki* (Tokyo: Seiabō, 1971), 266–267.

61. Asai Ryōi, *Tōkaidō meishoki* [1662], vols. 1 and 2, ed. Asakura Haruhiko, *Tōyō Bunko* 346 and 361 (Tokyo: Heibonsha, 1979).

62. Sexual encounters with prostitutes were common on major roads. Highways were dotted with small brothels, restaurants, and inns seeking to take advantage of the flow of travelers. During times of pilgrimage, securing prostitutes (both female and male)—usually on the return journey, when purification was no longer of import—was a common practice.

63. Carl Steenstrup, *A History of Law in Japan until 1868* (Leiden: E. J. Brill, 1996), 129.

64. "Liminality" cannot be fully separated from Victor Turner's influential studies. Although one may apply an explicitly Turnerian analysis to processions, I am not interested in the task. In using "liminality" I simply mean, to paraphrase Tamar Frankiel, a common characteristic possessed by many rituals that marks the point of transformation of the ritual actors where they step toward "creating a future that will not be like the past." See Tamar Frankiel, "Prospects in Ritual Studies," *Religion* 31 (2001): 76–77.

65. Namura, *Onna chōhōki,* 32. He uses the terms *tsubone* and *jorō* for such women in this escort role. Historically these were titles for women serving the court and the *bakufu,* as well as sobriquets for courtesans, but here they apply to older and trusted women closely tied to the bride, while also indicating the guides' roots in elite culture.

66. For other examples from lifestyle texts, see Emori Ichirō, ed., *Edo jidai josei seikatsu ezu daijiten* (Tokyo: Ōzorasha, 1996), 7:61–62.

67. For a study of these records and the ritual and occupational changes they indicate, see Kosaka Natsuko, "Kinsei ni okeru katsurame no jitsuzō to sono yuisho," *Joseishigaku* 14 (2004): 51–65.

68. Ema Tsutomu, *Kekkon no rekishi* (Tokyo: Yūzankaku Shuppan, 1971), 96.

69. See excerpts from seventeenth-century ritual guides in Kosaka, "Kinsei ni okeru katsurame no jitsuzō to sono yuisho," 52.

70. For a description of some of these figures, see Nishiyama, *Edo Culture*, 113–124.

71. Ise Sadatake, *Teijō zakki* [1763], vol. 1, ed. Shimada Isao, *Tōyō Bunko* 444 (Tokyo: Heibonsha, 1985), 23.

72. Ibid.

73. *Kogo daijiten*, vol.1, ed. Nakamura Yukihiko, Okami Masao, Sakakura Atsuyoshi (Tokyo: Kadokawa Shoten, 1982–1984), s.v. "amagatsu."

74. For a discussion of dolls as ritual substitutes in Japan, see Law, *Puppets of Nostalgia*, 32–38.

75. Namura, *Onna chōhōki,* 111.

76. Yokoyama, "Joshi kyōyōsho kōka-han *Onna chōhōki* to Takai Ranzan," 107.

77. Seigle, *Yoshiwara*, 228.

78. *Yoshiwara taizen* [1768], in *Yoshiwara fūzoku shiryō* [1930], ed. Sobu Rokurō (Tokyo: Nihon Tosho Sentā, 1978), 156.

79. While festivals, with their surging energy and wild popularity, were typical examples of *misemono*, other types also existed, such as spontaneous pilgrimage, traveling entertainers, and brash displays of individual wealth that taunted sumptuary laws. Events and people that broke with the ordinary—ordinary time, behavior, rules, and expectations—were all *misemono*.

80. Seigle, *Yoshiwara*, 228.

81. For a diagram depicting the position and title of each participant in a large *dōchū*, see Nakamura Shikaku, *Yūkaku no seikatsu* (Tokyo: Hyōronsha, 1976), 78; and Seigle, *Yoshiwara*, 226.

82. Seigle, *Yoshiwara*, 225.

83. Ise, *Teijō zakki*, 1:24.

84. Namura, *Onna chōhōki*, 34.

85. Ema, *Kekkon no rekishi*, 139.

86. Takagi Tadashi, *Mikudarihan to enkiridera* (Tokyo: Kōdansha, 1992), 112, 222–223.

87. *Onna daigaku*, 205.

88. Namura, *Onna chōhōki*, 111.

89. Yokoyama, "Joshi kyōyōsho kōka-han *Onna chōhōki* to Takai Ranzan," 106.

90. See eighteenth-century illustrations and origin story in Emori, ed., *Edo jidai josei seikatsu ezu*, 4:322–325.

91. Nakamura Masahiro, "Kaiawase," in *Sekai daihyakka jiten* (Tokyo: Heibonsha, 1990), 499.

92. Nishiyama Matsunosuke employs the term *yūgei* to refer to such arts and crafts that blossomed among commoners due to their economic rise and the diffusion of elite culture. See Gerald Groemer, "Translator's Introduction," in *Edo Culture: Daily Life and Diversions in Urban Japan, 1600–1868* (Honolulu: University of Hawai'i Press, 1997), 5.

93. Today such shells and other traditional aesthetic craftwork may be purchased in department stores.

94. Harunobu's courtesan series is titled *Yoshiwara seirō bijin awase* [1770]. See his illustration in Hanasaki Kazuo, *Ō Edo monoshiri zukan* (Tokyo: Shufu to Seikatsusha, 2000), 352.

95. Sasama Yoshihiko, *Kōshoku engo jiten* (Tokyo: Yūzankaku Shuppan, 1989), 89.

96. Although Namura does not describe an action of transfer, one procedure among warrior families may have called for a representative of the bride's family to pass the *kaioke* to the groom's representative with a set phrase such as, "May you have long life. I humbly pass to you this *kaioke*." Taking possession of the container, the groom's representative would respond, "May you have long life. I humbly accept this *kaioke*." See Ema, *Kekkon no rekishi*, 148.

97. Typically the husband's household received either all the children or the boys, but ultimately these decisions were made on a case by case basis. See Steenstrup, *A History of Law*, 130.

98. Ise Sadatake, *Teijō zakki* [1763], vol. 2, ed. Shimada Isao, *Tōyō Bunko* 446 (Tokyo: Heibonsha, 1985), 189–190.

99. Ibid., 190.

100. Ise, *Teijō zakki*, 1:23

101. Namura, *Onna chōhōki*, 38.

102. Ema, *Kekkon no rekishi*, 154.

103. Yamakawa Kikue, *Women of the Mito Domain: Recollections of Samurai Family Life,* trans. Kate Wildmon Nakai (Tokyo: University of Tokyo Press, 1992), 105.

104. Namura, *Onna chōhōki,* 38.

105. Ibid., 41.

106. Maeda Isamu, ed., *Edo go no jiten,* s.v. "toko sakazuki" (Tokyo: Kodansha, 1979).

107. Ise, *Teijō zakki,* 1:25.

108. Namura, *Onna chōhōki,* 44.

109. Ibid.

110. Ema, *Kekkon no rekishi,* 148.

111. Quoted from Arima, Wakasugi, and Nishigaki, "Kaisetsu," 74.

112. Seigle, *Yoshiwara,* 187.

113. According to Seigle, seven days marked the span of celebrations for the presenting of a new courtesan in the Yoshiwara. In Saikaku's contemporary description of a Shimabara debut, he describes it as an affair of nine days. In each quarter, however, long before these days of public parading in her first *dōchū,* a debutante would practice the choreography of footwork with her senior courtesan.

114. *Yoshiwara taizen,* 149.

115. See Seigle, *Yoshiwara,* 188. Festival days included celebrations for a quarter's tutelary deity, which in the Yoshiwara was the fox deity Inari. Other fete days for the transfer of bedding were the five annual festivals of national religious life called *gosekku.*

116. Mitani, *Edo Yoshiwara zushū,* 221.

117. Sone, "Prostitution and Public Authority," 180.

118. Donald Keene, "Introduction," in *Four Major Plays of Chikamatsu* (New York: Columbia University Press, 1964), 24–25.

119. Morita Kōichi, "Kaidai," in *Edo jidai josei bunko* (Tokyo: Ōzorasha, 1994), 31:5.

120. Many of the Shimabara's rites, such as debut, were considered elegant standards for other quarters to emulate. Its location in the aristocratic capital of Kyoto made it renowned for taste and elegance.

121. The memorial service, called *mieiku,* annually commemorates the death of Kūkai, the founder of the Shingon sect and abbot of Tōji, in 835. On this anniversary large numbers of people visited Tōji to hear sermons and make offerings to a carved image of Kūkai reputably sculpted by the founder himself.

122. Ihara, *Kōshoku ichidai otoko,* 295.

123. Ibid., 295–296.

124. Seigle, *Yoshiwara,* 66.

125. Kenji Hamada, *Life of an Amorous Man,* 204, takes Saikaku's descriptive allusion of the courtesan as a goddess and explicitly translates the comparison. For the original, see Ihara, *Kōshoku ichidai otoko,* 296.

126. Pierre Bourdieu, *Outline of a Theory of Practice,* trans. Richard Nice (Cambridge: Cambridge University Press, 1984), 94. Here I am following the lead of Bell, *Ritual Theory, Ritual Practice,* who raises this insight by Bourdieu to speak of the ritual body several times in her work.

127. Ihara, *Kōshoku ichidai otoko,* 296.

128. Seigle, *Yoshiwara,* 66, points out that in the latter years of the Yoshiwara actual consumption of wine during first-meeting rites was not practiced, and a courtesan and her partner "only pretended to take a sip" of sake as they made their vows.

129. For Jippensha Ikku's (1765–1831) humorous detailing of the public humiliation of a wayward Yoshiwara client, see Jippensha Ikku and Kitagawa Utamaro, *Yoshiwara seirō nenjū gyōji* [1804], in *Yoshiwara fūzoku shiryō* [1930], ed. Sobu Rokurō (Tokyo: Nihon Tosho Sentā, 1978), 414–415. For English excerpt, see Seigle, *Yoshiwara*, 111–112.

130. Ihara, *Kōshoku ichidai otoko*, 296.

131. Ibid.

132. Mitani, *Edo Yoshiwara zushū*, 38.

4. Placement

1. For such an examination, especially in the context of Tokugawa religious thought, see William R. Lafleur, *Liquid Life: Abortion and Buddhism in Japan* (Princeton, N.J.: Princeton University Press, 1992), 89–102.

2. For this discussion on deliberate and unconscious forms of controlling fertility, see Laurel L. Cornell, "Infanticide in Early Modern Japan? Demography, Culture, and Population Growth," *Journal of Asian Studies* 55 (1996): 45–46.

3. Akira Hayami, "Rural Migration and Fertility in Tokugawa Japan: The Village of Nishijo, 1773–1868," in *Family and Population in East Asian History*, ed. Susan B. Hanley and Arthur P. Wolf (Stanford, Calif.: Stanford University Press, 1985), 122–123.

4. Sakurai Yuki, "Mabiki to datai," in *Nihon no kinsei*, ed. Hayashi Reiko (Tokyo: Chūō Kōronsha, 1993), 15:100.

5. Ingredients could include cherry root, lye, red chili, pomegranate skin and root, and burdock root. See ibid.

6. The Chūjō School of Obstetrics, or at least its name, was synonymous with abortion techniques and services during the Tokugawa period.

7. See passage in Tatsukawa Shōji, *Kinsei yamai no sōshi* (Heibonsha, 1979), 253.

8. For a study of such rhetoric and measures in the domain of Tsuyama, see Sawayama Mikako, "The 'Birthing Body' and the Regulation of Conception of Childbirth in the Edo Period," trans. Elizabeth A. Leicester, *U.S.-Japan Women's Journal* 24 (2003): 10–34.

9. Helen Hardacre, *Marketing the Menacing Fetus in Japan* (Berkeley: University of California Press, 1997), 25.

10. See Giten, *Sutego kyōkai no uta* [1861], in *Edo jidai josei bunko*, vol. 57, ed. Sakurai Yuki (Tokyo: Ōzorasha, 1996). LaFleur, *Liquid Life*, 105–111, presents examples of anti-infanticide rhetoric from the pens of nineteenth-century Confucian and Shinto nativist critics. Giten's contribution to the genre indicates that some Buddhist leaders also took public stands against infanticide.

11. See Sakurai Yuki, "Kaidai," in *Edo jidai josei bunko*, (Tokyo: Ōzorasha, 1996), 57:3. In spite of this karmic warning there is no evidence to suggest that the fate of infanticide fell disproportionately on female babies. On this point, see Susan L. Burns, "The Body as Text: Confucianism, Reproduction, and Gender in Tokugawa Japan," in *Rethinking Confucianism: Past and Present in China, Japan, Korea, and Vietnam*, ed. Benjamin A. Elman, John B. Duncan, and Herman Ooms (Los Angeles: UCLA Asian Pacific Monograph Series, 2002), 212.

12. For a late-period study of the name Takao and its women, see Ōta Nampo and Santō Kyōzan, *Takao kō* [ca. early 1800s], in *Enseki jisshu*, vol. 1 (Tokyo: Chūō Kōronsha, 1979).

13. Kamiya Jirō, "Jinbutsu shōden," in *Zusetsu jinbutsu Nihon no joseishi,* ed. Sōga Tetsuo (Tokyo: Shōgakkan, 1980), 8:154.

14. Ōta and Santō, *Takao kō,* 48.

15. This form of contraception was also a tactical method for avoiding clients for whom a courtesan did not want to provide services. Since many men found the sensation of the paper during intercourse unpleasant and used it as an excuse to take their leave, a woman might choose this method when she found her client disagreeable and wanted to discourage a return visit. Likewise, she could forego this contraceptive to show particular favor toward a man she liked. See Sasama, *Kōshoku engo jiten,* 292–293; Mitani, *Edo Yoshiwara zushū,* 197.

16. Mitani, *Edo Yoshiwara zushū,* 196, 263. Kaibara Ekken also recommends the second month for periodic moxa treatment to protect the body from a host of potential ills. See Kaibara Ekken, *Yōjōkun* [1713], in *Yōjōkun to Wazoku dōjikun,* ed. Ishikawa Ken (Tokyo: Iwanami Shoten, 2000), 171.

17. For this poem and a discussion of birth in the Yoshiwara, see Kiyoshi Hiromi, "Yoshiwara zankoku monogatari," in *Senryū Yoshiwara fūzoku ezu,* ed. Satō Yōjin (Tokyo: Shibundō, 1973), 296–297.

18. Ibid., 296.

19. *Kogo daijiten,* vol. 4, s.v. "Minowa."

20. Nishiyama Matsunosuke, Komori Takayoshi, and Miyamoto Yukiko, *Yūjo* (Tokyo: Kondō Shuppansha, 1979), 168–169.

21. Raifū Sanjin, *Ichi no mori* [1775], in *Shinpon taikei,* ed. Mutō Sadao (Tokyo: Tōkyōdō Shuppan, 1979), 10:113. This anecdote depicts a period of time around the mid-1700s where there existed, among the trends of the day that were intensely cultivated in the quarters and theater, a craze for this shade of green. See Okitsu Kaname, *Edo Yoshiwara shi* (Tokyo: Sakuhinsha, 1984), 141.

22. The highest-skilled courtesans typically spent their childhood years in the quarters as *kamuro.* See Donald Keene, "A Note on Prostitution in Chikamatsu's Plays," in *Four Major Plays of Chikamatsu* (New York: Columbia University Press, 1964), 210.

23. Mitani, *Edo Yoshiwara zushū,* 269.

24. Ibid.

25. Yoshida Hidehiro, *Nihon baishunshi kō* (Tokyo: Jiyūsha, 2000), 87.

26. Namura, *Onna chōhōki,* 60.

27. Ibid.

28. Ibid.

29. Ibid., 67.

30. This notion is expressed in proverbs such as "Until a child is seven it is with the gods" *(Nana sai made wa kami no uchi).*

31. LaFleur, *Liquid Life,* 33–37, offers a good discussion of the liminality of the child and of being "returned" to the gods. Also see the important research of Kuroda Hideo, *Kyōkai no chūsei shōchō no chūsei* (Tokyo: Tōkyō Daigaku Shuppankai, 1986), 185–230.

32. Completing the pantheon of thirteen are Ashuku, Dainichi, and Kokūzō.

33. For a discussion of a version of this tale in its medieval context, see Hank Glassman, "The Religious Construction of Motherhood in Medieval Japan," Ph.D. dissertation, Stanford University, 2001, 151–158. For original story, see *Kumano no gohonji,* in *Sekkyō seibonshū,* ed. Yokoyama Shigeru (Tokyo: Kadokawa Shoten, 1968), 1:133–148; illus., 500.

34. This text is also titled *Three Worlds in a Single Mind (Sangai isshinki)*.

35. For this textual history, see Steven F. Teiser, *The Scripture of the Ten Kings and the Making of Purgatory in Medieval Chinese Buddhism,* Kuroda Institute Studies in East Asian Buddhism, no. 9 (Honolulu: University of Hawai'i Press, 1994), 58–60.

36. Mark Teeuwen and Fabio Rambelli, "Introduction: Combinatory Religion and the *Honji suijaku* Paradigm in Pre-Modern Japan," in *Buddhas and Kami in Japan:* Honji Suijaku *as a Combinatory Paradigm,* ed. Mark Teeuwen and Fabio Rambelli (London: Routledge Courzon, 2003), 14.

37. Teiser, *Scripture of the Ten Kings,* 60.

38. Where there are only ten months of fetal development, there are thirteen stages of death memorial. In the same position as with gestation, the first ten divinities (followed by the closing three) and their time markers are: Fudō, first seven days; Shaka, second seven days; Monju, third seven days; Fugen, fourth seven days; Jizō, fifth seven days; Miroku, sixth seven days; Yakushi, seventh seven days; Kannon, one-hundredth day; Seishi, first anniversary; Amida, third anniversary; Ashuku, seventh anniversary; Dainichi, thirteenth anniversary; and Kokūzō, thirty-third anniversary.

39. Ishikawa Matsutarō, Miyata Noboru, and Sakamoto Kaname, eds., *Edo jijō: Seikatsu hen* (Tokyo: Yūzankaku Shuppan, 1991), 102.

40. Robert J. Smith, *Ancestor Worship in Contemporary Japan* (Stanford, Calif.: Stanford University Press, 1974), 22.

41. Nakamura Hiroko, "Shussan to tanjō," in *Onna no me de miru minzokugaku,* ed. Nakamura Hiroko et al. (Tokyo: Kōbunken, 1999), 71.

42. For major studies of these paradigms, see Jacqueline I. Stone, *Original Enlightenment and the Transformation of Medieval Japanese Buddhism,* Kuroda Institute Studies in East Asian Buddhism, no. 12 (Honolulu: University of Hawai'i Press, 1999); and Mark Teeuwen and Fabio Rambelli, eds., *Buddhas and Kami in Japan:* Honji Suijaku *as a Combinatory Paradigm* (London: Routledge Courzon, 2003).

43. For a comparative discussion of womb depictions from *Essentials of Medicine* to later Tokugawa versions, see Kunimoto Keikichi, *San'ikushi: O-san to kosodate no rekishi* (Morioka City, Japan: Morioka Taimisusha, 1996), 205–232.

44. The date and authorship of *Unity of the Three Wisdoms* are problematic. A 1649 edition, which I use, dates the original year of composition as 1317. This date inscription is in a different style of print from the rest of the text, and, further, another version of the text that is considered older than the 1649 edition does not include the 1317 date at all. The 1649 text is attributed to a monk, Dairyū, of whom we know almost nothing, although Sanford identifies him as a Zen master affiliated with Daitokuji in Kyoto. See James H. Sanford, "Wind, Waters, Stupas, Mandalas: Fetal Buddhahood in Shingon," *Japanese Journal of Religious Studies* 24 (1997): 25. For problems of date and authorship, see Nakamura Kazumoto, "'Tainai totsuki no zu' no shisō shiteki tenkai," *Iwate Daigaku kyōiku gakubu kenkyū nenpō* 50 (1990): 23–24.

45. Sanford, "Wind, Water, Stupas, Mandalas," 1.

46. Washio Junkei, ed., *Sanken itchi sho* (also *Sangai isshinki*), in *Nihon shisō tōsō shiryō* (Tokyo: Tōhō Shoen), 5:503.

47. The text's varied motifs of sexual union as a unifying experience with the divine and its spiritualizing of the womb have led some to consider links between it and the Tachikawa School of Shingon. For these considerations, see Susan Blakeley Klein, "Allegories of Desire: Poetry and Eroticism in *Ise Monogatari,*" *Monumenta Nipponica* 52

(1997): 441–465; Nakamura, "'Tainai totsuki no zu' no shisō shiteki tenkai," 30–31; and James H. Sanford, "The Abominable Tachikawa Skull Ritual," *Monumenta Nipponica* 46 (1991): 1–20.

48. Washio, *Sanken itchi sho*, 525–527.

49. For this coloring, see Stone, *Original Enlightenment*, 39–46.

50. William R. LaFleur, *The Karma of Words: Buddhism and the Literary Arts in Medieval Japan* (Berkeley: University of California Press, 1983), 15.

51. Stone, *Original Enlightenment*, 357.

52. Susan Blakeley Klein, "Wild Words and Syncretic Deities: *Kyōgen Kigo* and *Honji Suijaku* in Medieval Literary Allegoresis," in *Buddhas and Kami in Japan: Honji Suijaku as a Combinatory Paradigm*, ed. Mark Teeuwen and Fabio Rambelli (London and New York: Routledge Courzon, 2003), 188.

53. On this point, see ibid., 193.

54. Stone, *Original Enlightenment*, 125.

55. Washio, *Sanken itchi sho*, 525.

56. Ibid.

57. Ibid., 531.

58. Ibid., 530.

59. Sanford, "Wind, Water, Stupas, Mandalas,"29.

60. Washio, *Sanken itchi sho*, 531.

61. Ibid.

62. For a discussion of the symbolism of ritual objects in medieval Buddhism, including the staff, see Bernard Faure, *Visions of Power: Imagining Medieval Japanese Buddhism* (Princeton, N.J.: Princeton University Press, 1996), 231–236. Also see Stanford, "Wind, Water, Stupas, Mandalas," 15, for the symbolism of *vajra*.

63. Namura, *Onna chōhōki*, 65.

64. Ibid.

65. Ibid., 65–66.

66. For an examination of these critiques, see James Edward Ketelaar, *Of Heretics and Martyrs in Meiji Japan: Buddhism and Its Persecution* (Princeton, N.J.: Princeton University Press, 1990), 3–42.

67. Quoted in Yokoyama, "Joshi kyōyōsho kōka-han *Onna chōhōki* to Takai Ranzan,"108.

68. See illustrations in Tanaka Chitako and Tanaka Hatsuo, eds., *Kaseigaku bunken shūsei zokuhen Edoki* (Tokyo: Watanabe Shoten, 1970), 8:173–174.

69. Timon Screech, *The Western Scientific Gaze in Later Edo Japan: The Lens within the Heart* (Cambridge, Cambridge University Press, 1996), 88.

70. Ochiai Emiko, "The Reproductive Revolution at the End of the Tokugawa Period," trans. Mariko Asano Tamanoi, in *Women and Class in Japanese History*, ed. Hitomi Tonomura, Anne Walthall, and Haruko Wakita (Ann Arbor: Center for Japanese Studies, University of Michigan, 1999), 187–215.

71. For a brief review of this position, see Burns, "The Body as Text," 197–198.

72. For these texts, see Kagawa Genetsu, *Sanron* [1765], in *Nihon sanka sōsho*, ed. Kure Shūzō and Fujikawa Yū (Tokyo: Shibunkaku, 1971); and Kagawa Genteki, *Sanronyoku* [1775], in *Nihon sanka sōsho*, ed. Kure Shūzō and Fujikawa Yū (Tokyo: Shibunkaku, 1971).

73. Ochiai, "The Reproductive Revolution at the End of the Tokugawa Period," 198.

74. See illustrations and excerpts of text in Emori, ed., *Edo jidai josei seikatsu ezu*, 6:236–249.

75. For a study of how early Tokugawa concepts of the body were employed in late-Tokugawa medical and reproduction discourses, see Burns, "The Body as Text," 178–219.

76. Morris, *Life of an Amorous Woman*, 194.

77. Ihara Saikaku, *Kōshoku ichidai onna* [1682], in *Nihon koten bungaku zenshū*, ed. Teruoka Yasutaka and Higashi Akimasa (Tokyo: Shōgakkan, 1971), 38:571.

78. See print in Ochiai, "The Reproductive Revolution at the End of the Tokugawa Period," 199.

79. Burns, "The Body as Text," 178–219.

80. J. Smith, "The Bare Facts of Ritual," 124–125.

81. Other names include *iwata obi* and *yūhada obi*.

82. Quoted from Yokoyama, "Joshi kyōyōsho kōka-han *Onna chōhōki* to Takai Ranzan," 108–109.

83. For these insights on wrapping and Japanese culture, see Joy Hendry, "The Sacred Power of Wrapping," in *Religion in Japan: Arrows to Heaven and Earth*, ed. P. F. Kornicki and I. M. McMullen (Cambridge: University of Cambridge Press, 1996), 287–303.

84. Some of the items are strips of dried abalone, an obi, drawing paper, incense, powdered medicine, and a legging string for use in falconry. See Namura, *Onna chōhōki*, 132–136.

85. Mitani, *Edo Yoshiwara zushū*, 197.

86. See this and similar shrine regulations in Narikiyo Hirokazu, *Josei to kegare no rekishi* (Tokyo: Kakushobō, 2003), 166–173.

87. The day of the dog is considered highly auspicious to begin wearing the belly wrap. This practice, which is still a part of the pregnancy experience for many women in Japan today, is based in part on the perception that dogs give birth with relative ease.

88. Katsuki, *Fujin kotobuki gusa*, 83.

89. Sawayama Mikako, *Shussan to shintai no kinsei* (Tokyo: Keisōshobō, 1998), 151.

90. Nakamura, "'Tainai totsuki no zu' no shisō shiteki tenkai," 29.

91. Ōbayashi Michiko, "O-san ima mukashi," in *Hahatachi no minzokushi*, ed. Ōtō Yuki (Tokyo: Iwada Shoin, 1999), 27.

92. The textile industry was one of the largest employers of women outside of prostitution, and for income generation, silk cultivation was economically on par with specialized cash products such as tobacco, spun thread, and woven cloth. See Hitomi Tonomura and Anne Walthall, "Introduction," in *Women and Class in Japanese History*, ed. Hitomi Tonomura, Anne Walthall, and Haruko Wakita (Ann Arbor: Center for Japanese Studies, University of Michigan, 1999), 12. Also see Uno, "Women and Changes in the Household Division of Labor," 27.

93. Aston, ed. and trans., *Nihongi*, 21. For Japanese, see *Nihon shoki*, 89.

94. Aston, ed. and trans., *Nihongi*, 347. For Japanese, see *Nihon shoki*, 472–473.

95. Namura, *Onna chōhōki*, 66, states that receiving an obi from one's husband is good form, but he also recommends receiving one from a woman who has given birth to many children. A midwife often took responsibility for presenting the belly obi as a gift to a young, newly married woman whom she would serve later during the woman's

delivery. See Sugitatsu Yoshikazu, *O-san no rekishi* (Tokyo: Shūeisha Shinsho, 2002), 114–115.

96. For examples of such diaries, see Minakawa Mieko, "Kinsei makki no *Kuwana nikki, Kashiwazaki nikki* ni mirareru yōiku bunka," in *Bunka to josei, Nihon joseishi ronshū,* ed. Umemura Keiko and Katakura Hisako (Tokyo: Yoshikawa Kōbunkan, 1998), 7:148–168.

97. Anna Meigs, "Food as a Cultural Construction," in *Food and Culture: A Reader,* ed. Carole Counihan and Penny Van Esterik (New York: Routledge, 1997), 97.

98. Namura, *Onna chōhōki,* 62–63.

99. For magic and other "sensibilities" of ritual, see Grimes, *Beginnings in Ritual Studies,* 35–52.

100. Namura, *Onna chōhōki,* 62–63, lists several other examples of foods to avoid so as not to produce a particular consequence.

101. Grimes, *Beginnings in Ritual Studies,* 46.

102. Namura, *Onna chōhōki,* 63. Kaibara Ekken, too, advises that one should hold the storming power of the heavens in prudent awe. When storms strike at night, he cautions, one should change clothes, sit up, and avoid lying down until the storm passes. See Kaibara, *Yōjōkun to Wazoku dōjikun,* 56.

103. Burns, "The Body as Text," 199–202, also notes that this logic still drove latter-period medical discourses. Although some advocates, for example, dismissed food taboos as superstitious, they still viewed intercourse and other behaviors through the lens of logic believing that in a responsive, interconnected universe, present behaviors entail future benefits and risks to the body's health.

104. Namura, *Onna chōhōki,* 73.

105. Ibid.

106. For these criticisms, see Shinmura Taku, *Shussan to seishokukan no rekishi* (Tokyo: Hōsei Daigaku Shuppankyoku 1996), 188–189.

107. Burns, "The Body as Text," 193–202.

108. The popularity of midwives was grounded in things other than their skills. They were present at the birth of a child, and they often developed symbolic and ritually expressed relationships with the children they helped bring into the world. Hardacre, for example, relates a variety of customs showing the relationship between midwife and child, such as having the woman sew the baby's first clothes or even name the child. See Hardacre, *Marketing the Menacing Fetus in Japan,* 23–24.

109. Namura, *Onna chōhōki,* 73.

110. Ibid. *Unity of the Three Wisdoms* offers the same etymological analysis of the characters "Sei-Shi" that make up the name of the deity of the ninth month of gestation. See Washio, *Sanken itchi sho,* 530. Also see Sanford, "Wind, Waters, Stupas, Mandalas," 29, for his translation of the "Sei-Shi" allegoresis.

111. Klein, "Wild Words and Syncretic Deities," 188–191. For an important study of the *Ise monogatari* with reference to various interpretations of "I-Se" and their commentators, see Richard Bowring, "The *Ise monogatari*: A Short Cultural History," *Harvard Journal of Asiatic Studies* 52 (1992): 401–480.

112. Namura, *Onna chōhōki,* 73.

113. Ibid., 74.

114. See this reference in Arima, Wakasugi, and Nishigaki, *Onna chōhōki: Chūkaihen,* 138.

115. Namura, *Onna chōhōki,* 74.

116. Ibid.

5. Exit

1. Ema, *Kekkon no rekishi,* 134–135.

2. Diana Wright, "Severing the Karmic Ties that Bind: The 'Divorce Temple' Mantokuji," *Monumenta Nipponica* 52 (1997): 368.

3. Arima Sumiko and Nishigaki Yoshiko, "Genroku no hanayome: Edo shomin no kekkon," *Josei bunka kenkyūjo kiyō* 2 (1993): 104–105.

4. Ibid., 104.

5. Ibid.

6. Entering into marriage on one's own accord is a constitutional right. Article 24 of the Constitution states the following: "Marriage shall be based only on the mutual consent of both sexes and it shall be maintained through mutual cooperation with the equal rights of husband and wife as a basis. With regard to choice of spouse, property rights, inheritance, choice of domicile, divorce and other matters pertaining to marriage and the family, laws shall be enacted from the standpoint of individual dignity and the essential equality of the sexes." Excerpted from Augustinus Yoshisuke Kōno, *The Evolution of the Concept of Matrimonial Consent in Japanese Law* (Tokyo: Monumenta Nipponica, 1970), 91.

7. Arima and Nishigaki, "Genroku no hanayome," 105.

8. Namura, *Onna chōhōki,* 32.

9. Ibid.

10. Masuda Toshimi, "Nōson josei no kekkon," in *Nihon no kinsei,* ed. Hayashi Reiko (Tokyo: Chūō Kōronsha, 1993), 15:181–182.

11. This is one of the many interesting points that Suzuki Noriko makes in her study of makeup and beauty consciousness in the Tokugawa period. See Suzuki Noriko, "Edo jidai no keshō to biyō ishiki," *Joseishigaku* 13 (2003): 1–17.

12. Namura, *Onna chōhōki,* 25.

13. Ibid., 32.

14. Ibid., 132–133.

15. Ibid., 32

16. Masuda, "Nōson josei no kekkon," 181.

17. Namura, *Onna chōhōki,* 32. With its bright crimson body and high price, bream (called *tai* in Japanese) has been ubiquitous in Japanese celebrations centering around life, success, and prosperity. The popular god of prosperity Ebisu is typically depicted with flapping bream in hand. *Medetai,* the term for congratulations or noting an auspicious event, appropriately forms a pun suggesting one of the fish's most prominent feature—its large, protruding, glassy eyes—by combining the sound *tai* with *me* (eyes) and *de* (protrude).

18. Ibid.

19. Takayama Naoko, "Awabi no rekishi," in *Zenshū Nihon no shokubunka,* ed. Haga Noboru and Ishikawa Hiroko (Tokyo: Yuzankaku, 1997), 4:74.

20. Ibid., 75.

21. *Juga,* celebrations of long life, are particularly noted on the sixty-first, seventy-seventh, and eighty-eighth years of life.

22. Masuda, "Nōson josei no kekkon," 181.

23. Arima, Wakasugi, and Nishigaki, *Onna chōhōki: Chūkaihen,* 290. Dried abalone was also attached to gifts as a decorative sign of the auspicious occasion. Participants in modern weddings no longer use dried abalone to mark presents, instead using celebratory gift paper and envelopes made more eye catching with a special mark or tassel that acts as a contemporary substitute for the older role of *noshi awabi.* See Edwards, *Modern Japan through Its Weddings,* 107.

24. Ema, *Kekkon no rekishi,* 137.

25. Ise, *Teijō zakki,* 1:23.

26. Ibid.

27. Namura, *Onna chōhōki,* 31.

28. Ibid.

29. Ibid.

30. Yoshikawa Keizō, ed., *Koji ruien: Reishikibu* (Tokyo: Yoshikawa Kōbunkan, 1979), 33:981.

31. Namura, *Onna chōhōki,* 31.

32. Ibid.

33. Ibid.

34. Ibid.

35. Ise, *Teijō zakki,* 1:23–24.

36. Ibid., 1:24.

37. Ibid.

38. The custom of a return visit was essential to commoner and warrior families alike. Further, a return visit to the natal home was also part of the *mukotori* (matrilocal) marriage pattern wherein the adopted son-in-law left to visit his family. See Emori Itsuo, *Nihon no kon'in: Sono rekishi to minzoku* (Tokyo: Kōbundō 1986), 302.

39. Namura, *Onna chōhōki,* 31.

40. See Yasu's contract in Ishii, *Edo no yūjo,* 154–157.

41. It was not unusual for a ranking woman to delay her retirement for a year or more in order to pay off any extra debt she incurred to her bordello in outfitting herself and her entourage, which were expenses that signified both her high standing and her need to borrow money from her owner in order to maintain that standing. See Seigle, *Yoshiwara,* 182–183.

42. Ishii, *Edo no yūjo,* 159.

43. As the decades passed, the style of wooden sandals changed, gradually becoming higher and heavier until, near the end of the period, they had reached an unparalleled height and heaviness.

44. Yamakawa, *Women of the Mito Domain,* 43.

45. Ishii, *Edo no yūjo,* 159. In Buddhist lexicon, *shaba* denotes this present world of defilement in which we live and into which the Buddha was born. In the vernacular it means mundane society in opposition to other restrictive social experiences such as monasticism and the pleasure quarters.

46. See print in Suzuki, "Edo jidai no keshō to biyō ishiki," 1.

47. Namura, *Onna chōhōki,* 111.

48. Fujimoto Kizan, *Shikidō ōkagami* [1678], ed. Noma Kōshin (Kyoto: Yūzan Bunko, 1961), 86–87.

49. Ibid., 87.

50. Suzuki, "Edo jidai no keshō to biyō ishiki," 8–10.

51. Fujimoto, *Shikidō ōkagami,* 146.

52. Raymond Firth, *Symbols: Public and Private* (Ithaca, N.Y.: Cornell University Press, 1973), 288.

53. For a study of nuns and hair, see Katsuura Noriko, "Amasogi kō: Kamigata kara mita ama no sonzai keitai," in *Ama to amadera,* Shiriizu josei to Bukkyō, vol. 1, ed. Ōsumi Kazuo and Nishiguchi Junko (Tokyo: Heibonsha, 1989), 11–42. For English, see Katsuura Noriko, "Tonsure Forms for Nuns: Classification of Nuns According to Hairstyle," trans. Virginia Skord Waters, in *Engendering Faith: Women and Buddhism in Premodern Japan,* ed. Barbara Ruch (Ann Arbor: Center for Japanese Studies, University of Michigan, 2002), 109–129.

54. This caution about—and generalization of—hair symbolism comes from C. R. Hallpike, "Social Hair," *Man* 4 (1969): 260–261.

55. Fujimoto, *Shikidō ōkagami,* 146.

56. Ibid., 145. According to Seigle, *Yoshiwara,* 183, a Yoshiwara patron always outfitted the woman whose contract he redeemed.

57. Fujimoto, *Shikidō ōkagami,* 146.

58. Ishii, *Edo no yūjo,* 155, 157.

59. For this and other details of her contract, see ibid., 154–157.

60. Fujimoto, *Shikidō ōkagami,* 145.

61. *Kogo daijiten,* vol. 5, s.v. "wataboshi."

62. Seigle, *Yoshiwara,* 183.

63. Masuda, "Nōson josei no kekkon," 182.

64. Namura, *Onna chōhōki,* 111.

65. Ritual changing of footwear that is attentive to the notion of pollution is often referred to as *hakimono sute,* which means "abandoning one's footwear." It has been practiced in circumstances other than marriage. Funerals are one example where in some localities participants throw away their footwear before returning home from the service. In some places, during an inauspicious year of one's life, it is wise, upon returning from a New Year's visit to a shrine or temple, to toss away footwear worn to the holy site and change into new ones. See Emori Itsuo, *Nihon no kon'in,* 233–234.

66. The social meanings and classifications of unclean things as foundational to social order is found most fully and originally in Mary Douglas, *Purity and Danger: An Analysis of the Concepts of Pollution and Taboo* (London: Routledge, 1966).

67. Takagi Tadashi, *Enkiridera Mantokuji no kenkyū* (Tokyo: Seibundō, 1990), 185.

68. In the museum on the original grounds of Mantokuji there is a large reproduction of this painting. In addition, one may sit and watch an animated short feature describing the history and divorce procedures of the temple. The animation opens with a woman running toward Mantokuji, panting heavily and pleading for help. With her husband nearing, she flings her sandals into the open gate, thus initiating her divorce suit. For a reprint of the painting, see Diana E. Wright, "Mantokuji: More than a 'Divorce Temple,'" in *Engendering Faith: Women and Buddhism in Premodern Japan,* ed. Barbara Ruch, (Ann Arbor: Center for Japanese Studies, University of Michigan, 2002), 251.

69. Emori Itsuo, *Nihon no kon'in,* 275.

70. For an examination of the social and political reality of *hinin,* see Ooms, *Tokugawa Village Practice,* 243–311. Ooms shows how the status of outcast was defined, applied, and used in village practices and in *bakufu* policies of social control. Also see Gerald Groemer, "The Creation of the Edo Outcaste Order," *The Journal of Japanese Studies* 27 (2001):

263–293. Groemer argues that the status of outcast (or "outcaste," as he puts it, because it became a legally codified status in the Tokugawa period) may have begun in the medieval period based on religious notions of purity and pollution and various taboos, but it took on social reality in the Tokugawa only through political, legal, and economic policies designed to maintain social control.

71. Tōkeiji was a "household word" in the Tokugawa period. This is not surprising, given its fame in securing divorces. Its familiarity was also enhanced by its Kamakura location. It was close to Edo and located on an important road for commerce, travel, and pilgrimage, which it shared with large and popular temples such as Engakuji. The other divorce nunnery, Mantokuji, lying in the province of Kōzuke (largely present-day Gumma Prefecture), never found a place in the popular Tokugawa imagination. Although located near an important highway, the Nakasendō, it was still relatively far from Edo and did not enjoy the proximity of popular pilgrimage centers, as did Tōkeiji. See Kaneko Sachiko and Robert E. Morrell, "Sanctuary: Kamakura's Tōkeiji Convent," *Japanese Journal of Religious Studies* 10 (1983): 196; and Wright, "Severing the Karmic Ties that Bind," 365.

72. Grimes, *Reading, Writing, and Ritualizing,* 24.

73. Ian Reader has picked up on this last element in his study on the primacy of action and results in Japanese religion. This is reflected in a "try it and see" attitude that many Japanese bring with them into religious practice, most notably in times of crisis and when trying out the promises of a religious group and its ritual life. See Ian Reader, *Religion in Contemporary Japan* (Honolulu: University of Hawai'i Press, 1991), 15–20.

74. Anne Dutton, "Temple Divorce in Tokugawa Japan: A Survey of Documentation on Tōkeiji and Mantokuji," in *Engendering Faith: Women and Buddhism in Premodern Japan,* ed. Barbara Ruch (Ann Arbor: Center for Japanese Studies, University of Michigan, 2002), 211.

75. For a wealth of divorce notices and the variety of reasons individuals and households gave for ending marriages, see Takagi Tadashi, *Mikudarihan: Edo no rikon to joseitachi* (Tokyo: Heibonsha, 1987).

76. The economic strength of rising commoner daughters and their families must be factored, as Wright suggests, into any discussion on the profitable charity of divorce temples to mediate divorce. See Wright, "Mantokuji: More than a 'Divorce Temple,'" 250.

77. For an extended historical study of Tōkeiji that focuses on the convent's sectarian history and relationships with important Zen centers, most notably Engakuji, see Sachiko Kaneko and Robert E. Morrell, *Zen Sanctuary of Purple Robes: Japan's Tōkeiji Convent since 1285* (Albany N.Y.: State University of New York Press, 2006).

78. Ibid., 256–268.

79. See Wright's "Severing the Karmic Ties that Bind," 360–362, and "Mantokuji: More than a 'Divorce Temple,'" 248–249.

80. Tōkeiji and Matokuji's close relationship to Tokugawa power worked against them once the *bakufu* was swept away. Tōkeiji lost the use of two of its five halls, and several facilities tied to the temple fell into disuse. It also lost its convent status and became a male-administered temple. By the late Meiji period, it made something of a comeback through the energy of its second abbot, Shaku Sōen (1859–1919), who was a central figure in raising the profile of Zen among the cultural elite of Japan and also a world traveler and advocate of Buddhism on the international stage. See Kaneko and Morrell, "Sanctuary: Kamakura's Tōkeiji Convent," 223. Today Tōkeiji is also famous

for its cemetery. Some tombstones read like a Who's Who of popular Zen (e.g., Nishida Kitaro, D. T. Suzuki, and R. H. Blythe). Mantokuji suffered a worse fate for its deep connection to the Tokugawa power structure. Its nuns were laicized in 1872, and its devotional and ritual paraphernalia, including Tokugawa funerary tablets and the temple's images, were confiscated and redistributed throughout the vicinity among other temples and shrines. See Wright, "Severing the Karmic Ties that Bind," 363–364.

81. Dutton, "Temple Divorce in Tokugawa Japan," 225.

82. Wright, "Severing the Karmic Ties that Bind," 375. In addition, a woman at Mantokuji could leave at any time once her husband finally agreed to execute a writ of divorce, but at Tōkeiji a woman had to finish her time of service once the process of extracting a letter from an intractable husband was out of its hands and had become a matter for the magistrate.

83. Takagi, *Mikudarihan: Edo no rikon to joseitachi*, 53. In another study, Takagi further argues that there were a variety of such institutions, including nunneries and retainer homes, in western Japan. However, much research needs to be done to uncover these institutions. See Takagi, *Mikudarihan to enkiridera*, 187–189.

84. See Dutton, "Temple Divorce in Tokugawa Japan," 217; Wright, "Severing the Karmic Ties that Bind," 357.

85. Michel Foucault, "The Subject and Power," in *Michel Foucault: Beyond Structuralism and Hermeneutics*, 2d ed., ed. Hubert L. Dreyfus and Paul Rabinow (Chicago: University of Chicago Press, 1983), 220–221.

86. Ooms, *Tokugawa Village Practice*, 312.

87. Bourdieu, *Outline of a Theory of Practice*, 72–87.

88. Dutton, "Temple Divorce in Tokugawa Japan," 209, touches upon these kinds of peripheral power loci.

89. Wright, "Severing the Karmic Ties that Bind," 379–380, relates that in the vicinity of Mantokuji two samurai families acted as centers of local power through which some women made divorce claims.

90. Surviving documents indicate that the vast majority of requests for divorce were eventually granted. Others ended in women "reuniting" (*fuku-en, ki-en*) with their husbands, while some women were expelled and sent back to their husbands' homes for poor behavior, dishonest representation during negotiations, or illness. For a list of all results of extant cases from Tōkeiji, see Takagi Tadashi, *Enkiri Tōkeiji shiryō* (Tokyo: Heibonsha, 1997), 846–877. The only full, extant record is for the year 1866, which shows that twenty-one cases ended in divorce, three ended in reconciliation, four were under adjudication, and three petitioners were expelled. One of the latter three, Tori, was dismissed when investigators found she was using her brother-in-law to pose as her husband in negotiations. See Tamamuro Fumio, "Tera ni kakekomu onnatachi," in *Nihon joseishi*, ed. Kasahara Kazuo (Tokyo: Hyōronsha, 1973), 5:97–99.

91. See Takagi, *Mikudarihan to enkiridera*, 131, for a review and charting of the steps required to sue for divorce. Also see Kaneko and Morrell, "Sanctuary: Kamakura's Tōkeiji Convent," 217, for a review of steps at Tōkeiji.

92. For a translation of Kane's letter, see Kaneko and Morrell, "Sanctuary: Kamakura's Tōkeiji Convent," 219–220. For all documents related to the case, including Kanjirō's accusations, see Takagi, *Enkiridera Tōkeiji shiryō*, documents 221–228, 916, and 917.

93. Takagi, *Mikudarihan: Edo no rikon to joseitachi*, 157.

94. Ibid., 157.

95. See Takagi Tadashi, *Enkiridera Mantokuji no kenkyū* (Tokyo: Seibundō, 1990), 475–477. Also see Wright, "Severing the Karmic Ties that Bind," 379.

96. Wright, "Severing the Karmic Ties that Bind," 374.

97. See Steenstrup, *A History of Law in Japan until 1868*, 130.

98. Takagi, *Mikudarihan: Edo no rikon to joseitachi*, 211–212.

99. See pertinent documents pertaining to this case in Takagi, *Enkiridera Mantokuji no kenkyū*, 714–716. Also see Wright, "Severing the Karmic Ties that Bind," 375.

100. This was not an unusual practice in making out divorce notices in some localities. See Takagi, *Mikudarihan: Edo no rikon to joseitachi*, 211–212.

101. Dutton, "Temple Divorce in Tokugawa Japan," 209–210.

102. Takagi, *Enkiridera Tōkeiji shiryō*, 256; Kaneko and Morrell, "Sanctuary: Kamakura's Tōkeiji Convent," 220.

103. Takagi, *Mikudarihan: Edo no rikon to joseitachi*, 51–53.

104. See passage in Anzai Ikuo, "Jihō enkiri kō," *Josei bunka kenkyūjo kiyō* 3 (1994): 83.

105. Nagasawa Toshiaki, *Edo Tōkyō no shomin shinkō* (Tokyo: Miyai, 1996), 133–134.

106. Not all imperial wedding parties chose to detour when drawing near the Nakasendō nettle tree. The 1861 party of Princess Kazumiya proceeded onward past the tree, disregarding its reputation. Perhaps a likely cause for the group's resolute action, however, was that the tree had been concealed from trunk to branches with straw matting. See Nagasawa, *Edo Tōkyō no shomin shinkō*, 134–135.

107. Igarashi Tomio, *Kakekomidera* (Tokyo: Kakushobō, 1989), 253.

108. Clothey, *Rhythm and Intent*, 13.

109. For images of Meiji divorce *ema*, see Ishiko Junzō, *Ko-ema zufu: Fūjikomerareta minshū no inori* (Tokyo: Hōga Shoten, 1972), 62–63, 78–79. For a study of *ema* and their religious function, see Ian Reader, "Letters to the Gods: The Form and Meaning of *Ema*," *Japanese Journal of Religious Studies* 18 (1991): 23–50.

110. Takagi, *Mikudarihan: Edo no rikon to joseitachi*, 19. The poem plays on the phrase *namaki saku*, which literally means "to split a living tree," but figuratively means actions meant to split a couple apart.

111. Ibid.

112. Kaneko Sachiko and Robert E. Morrell, "Tōkeiji: Kamakura's 'Divorce Temple' in Edo Popular Verse," in *Religions of Japan in Practice*, ed. George J. Tanabe (Princeton, N.J.: Princeton University Press, 1999), 509.

113. Igarashi, *Kakekomidera*, 253.

114. Smyers, *Fox and the Jewel*, 19–20.

115. Bitō, "Thought and Religion," 391.

116. This founding myth appears in several period sources. See Hayakawa Junzaburō, ed., *Kinsei bungei sosho*, in *Fūzokuhen* (Tokyo: Kokusho Kankōkai, 1911), 10:204–205; Saitō Gesshin, *Tōto saijiki* [1838], ed. Asakura Haruhiko, *Tōyō Bunko* 159 (Tokyo: Heibonsha, 1970), 1:168; and *Yoshiwara taizen*, 161.

117. Smyers, *Fox and the Jewel*, 15.

118. For a discussion on the links between foxes and Inari, see ibid., 75–86.

119. *Yoshiwara taizen*, 161.

120. According to the *Yoshiwara taizen*, 162, the title came into existence shortly after the quarter's relocation after the 1657 fire; however, it leaves the event undated and

gives no details. For account in the *Kiyū shoran*, see Kitamura Nobuyo, *Kiyū shōran* [1816], in *Nihon zuihitsu taisei* (Tokyo: Nihon Zuihitsu Taisei, 1979), 2:254.

121. Takigawa, *Yoshiwara no shiki*, 269.

122. *Yoshiwara taizen*, 160–161.

123. For an interesting discussion of Jizō and the phallus motif combined as *dōsojin*, see LaFleur, *Liquid Life*, 122–126.

124. Although writing was a professional obligation for a courtesan, it allowed her client to enjoy the play of romance and of being needed emotionally. Writing a letter was simply the most common and innocuous way of playing the game of love and desire. Other forms existed for a courtesan to "prove" her love, and these were mainly sacrificial actions done upon the body, ranging from tattooing the client's name on her skin to cutting her hair, pulling a nail, and, at the extreme, severing a finger. See Lawrence Rogers, "She Loves Me, She Loves Me Not: Shinjū and *Shikidō ōkagami*," *Monumenta Nipponica* 49 (1994): 31–60.

125. Smyers, *Fox and the Jewel*, 184.

126. Ibid., 75–78, 131–138.

127. With the Meiji push to create an organized Shinto, Kurosuke's shrine and the three other Inari shrines were consolidated and renamed Yoshiwara Jinja.

128. Saitō, *Tōto saijiki*, 1:164.

129. See list of shrines and their events in Hagiwara Tatsuo, "Edo no Inari," in *Inari shinkō*, ed. Naoe Hiroji (Tokyo: Yūzankaku Shuppan, 1983), 151–154.

130. Saitō, *Tōto saijiki*, 1:164.

131. This apt phrase comes from Hur's study of Sensōji and its centering of religion and popular culture. See Nam-lin Hur, *Prayer and Play in Late Tokugawa Japan: Asakusa Sensōji and Edo Society* (Cambridge, Mass.: Harvard University Asia Center, Harvard University Press, 2000).

132. Takigawa, *Yoshiwara no shiki*, 270.

133. Seigle, *Yoshiwara*, 108.

134. See list of the Yoshiwara's festival days in Mitani, *Edo Yoshiwara zushū*, 273–274.

135. Seigle, *Yoshiwara*, 106.

136. Anne Walthall, "Peripheries: Rural Culture in Tokugawa Japan," *Monumenta Nipponica* 39 (1984): 372–373.

137. Seigle, *Yoshiwara*, 108. The creation of massive floats was just one form of festivity that the Yoshiwara most avidly copied from Kyoto's famed Gion festival. See Takigawa, *Yoshiwara no shiki*, 269.

138. Saitō Gesshin notes that the parade of courtesans clad in white kimono was a popular draw and explains its origins in the late seventeenth-century life of a *tayū* named Takahashi. An extremely popular courtesan, she fell ill one day with fever. Her many faithful clients came to visit and wish her well. Despite her condition she insisted on meeting them all and socializing with them in a teahouse while dressed in white kimono. It is from her original behavior, Saitō concludes, that courtesans have come to wear white on the Yoshiwara's biggest fete day. See Saitō Gesshin, *Tōto saijiki* [1838], ed. Asakura Haruhiko. *Tōyō Bunko* 177 (Tokyo: Heibonsha, 1971), 2:200. The story is surely legendary. It casts Takahashi as the perfect *tayū*: unselfish, giving, and so charming and skilled in the art of social talk that she can visit and flirt even while in the throes of illness. Most likely the Yoshiwara borrowed this practice of wearing white on the first day

of the eighth month from the shogunate's women's quarters of Edo Castle. Palace women donned white outer robes on this date as part of the celebrations memorializing Tokugawa Ieyasu's entrance into Edo on the same day in 1590. See Miyata, *Edo no saijiki*, 128–129.

139. For other *monbi* and festival days that were a regular part of the Yoshiwara's calendar, see Mitani, *Edo Yoshiwara zushū*, 273–274.

140. Seigle, *Yoshiwara*, 110.

141. Winston Davis, *Dōjō: Magic and Exorcism in Modern Japan* (Stanford, Calif.: Stanford University Press, 1980), 177–178.

142. Smyers, *Fox and the Jewel*, 135.

143. Takigawa, *Yoshiwara no shiki*, 267.

144. Ishii, *Edo no yūjo*, 154, 156.

145. Takigawa, *Yoshiwara no shiki*, 267.

146. Hamada Giichirō, *Edo senryū jiten* (Tokyo: Tōkyōdō Shuppan, 1968), 149.

147. Ibid.

148. Seigle, *Yoshiwara*, 181.

149. Amino Yoshihiko and Miyata Noboru, *Rekishi no naka de katararete konakatta koto* (Tokyo: Yōsensha, 1998), 50.

150. Ishii, *Edo no yūjo*, 155, 157.

151. Seigle, *Yoshiwara*, 181.

152. Hamada Giichirō, *Edo senryū jiten*, 149.

153. Ibid.

6. Conclusion

1. Moore, *A Passion for Difference*, 6.

2. "Ritual density" comes from Bell's discussion of typologies that attempt to classify societies in terms of their historical reliance on ritual. See Catherine Bell, *Ritual: Perspectives and Dimensions* (Oxford: Oxford University Press, 1997), 173–209.

3. Bourdieu, *Outline of a Theory of Practice*, 168.

4. This is a general description of the phenomenon. For specific cases from the Okayama domain and analysis, see Mega, *Hankachō no naka no onnatachi*, 50–93.

5. Jonathan Z. Smith, *Map Is Not Territory: Studies in the History of Religion*. (Chicago: University of Chicago Press, 1993), 295–296.

6. Peter L. Berger, *The Sacred Canopy: Elements of a Sociological Theory of Religion* (Garden City, N.Y.: Anchor Books, 1969), 4–14.

Primary Sources

Asai Ryōi. *Tōkaidō meishoki* [1662]. Vols. 1 and 2, ed. Asakura Haruhiko. *Tōyō Bunko* 346 and 361. Tokyo: Heibonsha, 1979.

Buyō Inshi. *Seji kenbunroku* [1816], ed. Hanjō Eijirō. Tokyo: Seiabō, 2001.

Chikamatsu Monzaemon. *Shinjū yoi kōshin machi* [1722]. In *Chikamatsu Monzaemon zenshū, Nihon koten bungaku zenshū*. Vol. 44, ed. Torigoe Bunzō. Tokyo: Shōgakkan, 1975.

―――. *Yūgiri awa no naruto* [1712]. In *Chikamatsu zenshū*. Vol. 9, ed. Fujii Otoo. Osaka: Asahi Shimbunsha, 1927.

―――. *Yūgiri sanzesō* [1686]. In *Chikamatsu zenshū*. Vol. 2, ed. Fujii Otoo. Osaka: Asahi Shimbunsha, 1925.

Egawa Tanan [aka Egawa Tarōzaemon]. *Shinpu ni atauru sho*. In *Kinsei joshi kyōiku shisō, Nihon kyōiku shisō taikei*. Vol. 16, ed. Umezawa Seiichi. Tokyo: Nihon Tosho Sentā, 1980.

Fujimoto Kizan. *Shikidō ōkagami* [1678], ed. Noma Kōshin. Kyoto: Yūzan Bunko, 1961.

Giten. *Sutego kyōkai no uta* [1861]. In *Edo jidai josei bunko*. Vol. 57, ed. Sakurai Yuki. Tokyo: Ōzorasha, 1996.

Hayakawa Junzaburō, ed. *Kinsei bungei sōsho*. Vol. 10. In *Fūzokuhen*. Tokyo: Kokusho Kankōkai, 1911.

Ihara Saikaku. *Kōshoku ichidai onna* [1686]. In *Nihon koten bungaku zenshū*. Vol. 38, ed. Teruoka Yasutaka and Higashi Akimasa. Tokyo: Shōgakkan, 1971.

―――. *Kōshoku ichidai otoko* [1682]. In *Nihon koten bungaku zenshū*. Vol. 38, ed. Teruoka Yasutaka and Higashi Akimasa. Tokyo: Shōgakkan, 1971.

―――. *Kōshoku nidai otoko* [1684]. In *Shin Nihon koten bungaku taikei*. Vol. 76, ed. Fuji Akio, Inoue Toshiyuki, and Satake Akihiro. Tokyo: Iwanami Shoten, 1991.

Ise Sadatake. *Teijō zakki* [1763]. Vol. 1, ed. Shimada Isao. *Tōyō Bunko* 444. Tokyo: Heibonsha, 1985.

―――. *Teijō zakki* [1763]. Vol. 2, ed. Shimada Isao. *Tōyō Bunko* 446. Tokyo: Heibonsha, 1985.

Jippensha Ikku and Kitagawa Utamaro. *Yoshiwara seirō nenjū gyōji* [1804]. In *Yoshiwara fūzoku shiryō* [1930], ed. Sobu Rokurō. Tokyo: Nihon Tosho Sentā, 1978.

Kagawa Genetsu. *Sanron* [1765]. In *Nihon sanka sōsho,* ed. Kure Shūzō and Fujikawa Yū. Tokyo: Shibunkaku, 1971.

Kagawa Genteki. *Sanronyoku* [1775]. In *Nihon sanka sōsho,* ed. Kure Shūzō and Fujikawa Yū. Tokyo: Shibunkaku, 1971.

Kaibara Ekken. *Yōjōkun* [1713]. In *Yōjōkun to Wazoku dōjikun,* ed. Ishikawa Ken. Tokyo: Iwanami Shoten, 2000.

Katsuki Gyūzan. *Fujin kotobuki gusa* [1692]. In *Nihon sanka sōsho,* ed. Kure Shūzō and Fujikawa Yū. Tokyo: Shibunkaku, 1971.

Kitamura Nobuyo. *Kiyū shōran* [1816]. In *Nihon zuihitsu taisei.* 4 Vols. Tokyo: Nihon Zuihitsu Taisei, 1979.

Kojiki. In *Nihon shisō taikei.* Vol. 1, ed. Aoki Kazuo et al. Tokyo: Iwanami Shoten, 1982.

Kumano no gohonji. In *Sekkyō seibonshū.* Vol. 1, ed. Yokoyama Shigeru. Tokyo: Kadokawa Shoten, 1968.

Kuruwa bunshō [1808]. In *Meisaku kabuki zenshū.* Vol. 7, ed. Toita Yasuji. Tokyo: Tokyo Sōgen Shinsha, 1969.

Masuho Zankō. *Endō tsugan* [1715]. In *Kinsei shikidōron, Nihon shisō taikei.* Vol. 60, ed. Noma Kōshin. Tokyo: Iwanami Shoten, 1976.

Namura Jōhaku. *Nan chōhōki* [1693]. In *Onna chōhōki Nan chōhōki, Nihon shigaku kyōiku kenkyūjo chōsa shiryō,* no. 122, ed. Namae Yoshio, Sekishita Toshihide, and Saitō Junkichi. Tokyo: Nihon Shigaku Kyōiku Kenkyūjo, 1985.

———. *Onna chōhōki* [1692]. In *E-iri Onna chōhōki: Honbunhen,* ed. Arima Sumiko, Wakasugi Tetsuo, and Nishigaki Yoshiko. Tokyo: Tōyoko Gakuen Joshi Tanki Daigaku Josei Bunka Kenkyūjo, 1989.

Nihon shoki. In *Nihon koten bungaku taikei.* Vol. 67, ed. Sakamoto Tarō et al. Tokyo: Iwanami Shoten, 1967.

Okuda Shohakken. *Joyō kunmō zui* [1687]. In *Kaseigaku bunken shūsei zokuhen Edoki.* Vol. 8, ed. Tanaka Chitako and Tanaka Hatsuo. Tokyo: Watanabe Shoten, 1970.

Onna daigaku [ca. early 1700s]. In *Kaibara Ekken Muro Kyūsō.* In *Nihon shisō taikei.* Vol. 34, ed. Araki Kengo and Inoue Tadashi. Tokyo: Iwanami Shoten, 1970.

Ōta Nampo and Santō Kyōzan. *Takao kō* [ca. early 1800s]. In *Zoku enseki jisshu.* Vol. 1. Tokyo: Chūō Kōronsha, 1980.

Raifū Sanjin. *Ichi no mori* [1775]. In *Shinpon taikei.* Vol. 10, ed. Mutō Sadao. Tokyo: Tōkyōdō Shuppan, 1979.

Saitō Gesshin. *Edo meisho zue* [1834–1836]. 6 Vols, ed. Ichiko Natsuo and Suzuki Kenichi. Tokyo: Chikuma Shobō, 1997.

———. *Tōto saijiki* [1838]. Vol. 1, ed. Asakura Haruhiko. *Tōyō Bunko* 159. Tokyo: Heibonsha, 1970.

———. *Tōto saijiki* [1838]. Vol. 2, ed. Asakura Haruhiko. *Tōyō Bunko* 177. Tokyo: Heibonsha, 1971.

Sawada Kichi. *Onna imagawa* [1700]. In *Edo jidai josei seikatsu ezu daijiten.* Vol. 1, ed. Emori Ichirō. Tokyo: Ōzorasha, 1993.

Shikitei Sanba and Ryūtei Rijō. *Ukiyodoko* [1813–1823]. In *Edo no fūzoku shiryō.* Vol. 5, ed. Ono Takeo. Tokyo: Tenbōsha, 1974.

Shōji Katsutomi. *Ihon dōbō goen* [1720]. In *Enseki jisshu.* Vol. 5. Tokyo: Chūō Kōronsha, 1980.

Takai Ranzan. *Onna chōhōki* [1847]. In *Kaseigaku bunken shūsei zokuhen Edoki*. Vol. 8, ed. Tanaka Chitako and Tanaka Hatsuō. Tokyo: Watanabe Shoten, 1970.

Uesugi Yōzan. *Momo no wakaba* [1808]. In *Jokun sōsho*. Vol. 5, ed. Ōbayashi Tokutarō. Tokyo: Shiritsu Takanawa Shukujo Gakkō, 1912.

Yashiro Hirotaka. *Tsuma ni ataru sho*. In *Kinsei joshi kyōiku shisō, Nihon kyōiku shisō taikei*. Vol. 16, ed. Umezawa Seiichi. Tokyo: Nihon Tosho Sentā, 1980.

Yoshikawa Keizō, ed. *Koji ruien: Reishikibu*. Vol. 33. Tokyo: Yoshikawa Kōbunkan, 1979.

Yoshiwara taizen [1768]. In *Yoshiwara fūzoku shiryō* [1930], ed. Sobu Rokurō. Tokyo: Nihon Tosho Sentā, 1978.

Yūjo daigaku [1807]. In *Edo jidai josei bunko*. Vol. 31, ed. Morita Kōichi. Tokyo: Ōzorasha, 1995.

Washio Junkei, ed. *Sanken itchi sho* (also *Sangai isshinki*). In *Nihon shisō tōsō shiryō*. Vol. 5. Tokyo: Tōhō Shoen.

Secondary Sources

Amino Yoshihiko and Miyata Noboru. *Rekishi no naka de katararete konakatta koto*. Tokyo: Yōsensha, 1998.

Anzai Ikuo. "Jihō enkiri kō." *Josei bunka kenkyūjo kiyō* 3 (1994): 83–99.

Arima Sumiko and Nishigaki Yoshiko. "Edoki josei no seikatsu ni kansuru kenkyū: *Onna chōhōki* ni miru shorei to kikkyō." *Tōyō gakuen joshi tanki daigaku kiyō* 26 (1991): 43–66.

———. "Edoki josei no seikatsu ni kansuru kenkyū: *Onna chōhōki* ni miru shussan to byōki." *Tōyō gakuen joshi tanki daigaku kiyō* 25 (1990): 1–28.

———. "Genroku no hanayome: Edo shomin no kekkon." *Josei bunka kenkyūjo kiyō* 2 (1993):103–146.

———. "*Onna chōhōki* ni miru Genroku no joseizō." *Josei bunka kenkyūjo kiyō* 1 (1992): 213–248.

Arima Sumiko, Wakasugi Tetsuo, and Nishigaki Yoshiko. "Kaisetsu." In *E-iri Onna chōhōki: Honbunhen*, ed. Arima Sumiko, Wakasugi Tetsuo, and Nishigaki Yoshiko. Tokyo: Tōyoko Gakuen Joshi Tanki Daigaku Josei Bunka Kenkyūjo, 1989, 142–177.

———. *Onna chōhōki: Chūkaihen*. Tokyo: Josei Bunka Kenkyūjo, 1989.

Aston, W. G., ed. and trans. *Nihongi*. London: George Allen & Unwin, Ltd., 1956.

Baird, Robert D. *Category Formation and the History of Religions*. 2d ed. Berlin: Mouton de Gruyter, 1991.

Barthes, Roland. *Mythologies*, trans. Annette Lavers. New York: Hill and Wang, 1972.

Bell, Catherine. *Ritual: Perspectives and Dimensions*. Oxford: Oxford University Press, 1997.

———. *Ritual Theory, Ritual Practice*. Oxford: Oxford University Press, 1992.

Berger, Peter L. *The Sacred Canopy: Elements of a Sociological Theory of Religion*. Garden City, N.Y.: Anchor Books, 1969.

Bernheimer, Charles. *Figures of Ill Repute: Representing Prostitution in Nineteenth-Century France*. Cambridge, Mass.: Harvard University Press, 1989.

Bernstein, Gail Lee, ed. *Recreating Japanese Women, 1600–1945*. Berkeley: University of California Press, 1991.

Bitō Masahide. "Thought and Religion: 1550–1700," trans. Kate Wildmon Nakai. In

The Cambridge History of Japan. Vol. 4, ed. John Whitney Hall. Cambridge: Cambridge University Press, 1991, 373–424.

Bouchy, Anne. "The Chisel of the Women Divers and the Bow of the Feudal Lords of the Sea: The Dual Structure of Labor and Village Organization in Women Divers' Society—A Case Study of the Town of Ijika," trans. John Davis. In *Gender and Japanese History.* Vol. 2, ed. Haruko Wakita, Anne Bouchy, and Chizuko Ueno. Osaka: Osaka University Press, 1999, 349–390.

Bourdieu, Pierre. *Outline of a Theory of Practice,* trans. Richard Nice. Cambridge: Cambridge University Press, 1984.

Bowring, Richard. "The *Ise monogatari:* A Short Cultural History." *Harvard Journal of Asiatic Studies* 52 (1992): 401–480.

Brandon, James R. *Kabuki: Five Classic Plays.* Honolulu: University of Hawai'i Press, 1992.

Burns, Susan L. "The Body as Text: Confucianism, Reproduction, and Gender in Tokugawa Japan." In *Rethinking Confucianism: Past and Present in China, Japan, Korea, and Vietnam,* ed. Benjamin A. Elman, John B. Duncan, and Herman Ooms. Los Angeles: UCLA Asian Pacific Monograph Series, 2002, 178–219.

Cassirer, Ernst. *An Essay on Man.* New Haven, Conn.: Yale University Press, 1944.

Chamberlain, Basil Hall. "Educational Literature for Japanese Women." *The Journal of the Royal Asiatic Society* 10 (1878), 325–343.

———. *Women and Wisdom of Japan.* London: John Murray, 1905.

Chapkis, Wendy. *Live Sex Acts: Women Performing Erotic Labour.* London: Cassell, 1997.

Cherry, Kittredge. *Womansword: What Japanese Words Say about Women.* Tokyo: Kodansha International, 1987.

Clothey, Fred W. *Rhythm and Intent: Ritual Studies from South Asia.* Madras, India: Blackie and Son Publishers, 1983.

Comaroff, Jean. *Body of Power, Spirit of Resistance.* Chicago: University of Chicago Press, 1985.

Cornell, Laurel L. "Infanticide in Early Modern Japan? Demography, Culture, and Population Growth." *The Journal of Asian Studies* 55 (1996): 22–50.

———. "Peasant Family and Inheritance in a Japanese Community: 1671–1980." Ph.D. dissertation, The Johns Hopkins University, 1981.

Davis, Winston. *Dōjō: Magic and Exorcism in Modern Japan.* Stanford, Calif.: Stanford University Press, 1980.

———. *Japanese Religion and Society: Paradigms of Structure and Change.* Albany: State University of New York Press, 1992.

de Bary, Wm. Theodore, ed. *Sources of Japanese Tradition.* Vol. 1. New York: Columbia University Press, 1958.

de Becker, J. E. *The Nightless City, or the History of the Yoshiwara Yūkwaku* [1899]. New York: ICG Muse, Inc., 2000.

Dobbins, James C. *Letters of the Nun Eshinni: Images of Pure Land Buddhism in Medieval Japan.* Honolulu: University of Hawai'i Press, 2004.

Douglas, Mary. *Purity and Danger: An Analysis of the Concepts of Pollution and Taboo.* London: Routlege, 1966.

Durkheim, Emile. *The Elementary Forms of Religious Life* [1912], trans. Karen E. Fields. New York: The Free Press, 1995.

Dutton, Anne. "Temple Divorce in Tokugawa Japan: A Survey of Documentation on

Tōkeiji and Mantokuji." In *Engendering Faith: Women and Buddhism in Premodern Japan,* ed. Barbara Ruch. Ann Arbor: Center for Japanese Studies, University of Michigan, 2002, 209–245.

Edwards, Walter. *Modern Japan through Its Weddings.* Stanford, Calif.: Stanford University Press, 1989.

Eliade, Mircea. *The Sacred and The Profane: The Nature of Religion,* trans. Willard R. Trask. San Diego: Harcourt Brace Jovanovich, 1959.

Ema Tsutomu. *Kekkon no rekishi.* Tokyo: Yūzankaku Shuppan, 1971.

Emori Ichirō, ed. *Edo jidai josei seikatsu ezu daijiten.* Vols. 1–9. Tokyo: Ōzorasha, 1992–1996.

Emori Ichirō and Koizumi Yoshinaga. "*Ezu daijiten* no henshū kōki." In *Edo jidai josei seikatsu kenkyū* (Supplement to *Edo jidai josei seikatsu ezu daijiten*), ed. Emori Ichirō. Tokyo: Ōzorasha, 1994.

Emori Itsuo. *Nihon no kon'in: Sono rekishi to minzoku.* Tokyo: Kōbundō, 1986.

Faure, Bernard. *Visions of Power: Imagining Medieval Japanese Buddhism.* Princeton, N.J.: Princeton University Press, 1996.

Firth, Raymond. *Symbols: Public and Private.* Ithaca, N.Y.: Cornell University Press, 1973.

Foucault, Michel. "The Subject and Power." In *Michel Foucault: Beyond Structuralism and Hermeneutics.* 2d ed., ed. Hubert L. Dreyfus and Paul Rabinow. Chicago: University of Chicago Press, 1983. 208–226.

Frankiel, Tamar. "Prospects in Ritual Studies." *Religion* 31 (2001): 75–87.

Geertz, Clifford. *The Interpretation of Cultures.* New York: Basic Books, 1973.

Gerstle, Andrew C., ed. and trans. *Chikamatsu: 5 Late Plays.* New York: Columbia University Press, 2001.

Glassman, Hank. "The Religious Construction of Motherhood in Mediveal Japan." Ph.D. dissertation, Stanford University, 2001.

Grapard, Allan G. "The Shinto of Yoshida Kanemoto." *Monumenta Nipponica* 47 (1992): 27–58.

Grimes, Ronald L. *Beginnings in Ritual Studies.* Washington, D.C.: University Press of America, 1982.

———. *Reading, Writing, and Ritualizing: Ritual in Fictive, Liturgical, and Public Places.* Washington, D.C.: The Pastoral Press, 1993.

Groemer, Gerald. "The Creation of the Edo Outcaste Order." *The Journal of Japanese Studies* 27 (2001): 263–293.

———. "Translator's Introduction." In *Edo Culture: Daily Life and Diversions in Urban Japan, 1600–1868.* Honolulu: University of Hawai'i Press, 1997, 1–19.

Hagiwara Tatsuo. "Edo no Inari." In *Inari shinkō,* ed. Naoe Hiroji. Tokyo: Yūzankaku Shuppan, 1983, 151–164.

———. "The Tokugawa Shogunate and Religion: Shinto under the Shogunate." In *A History of Japanese Religion,* ed. Kasahara Kazuo, trans. Paul McCarthy and Gaynor Sekimori. Tokyo: Kosei, 2000, 345–355.

Hallpike, C. R. "Social Hair." *Man* 4 (1969): 256–264.

Hamada Giichirō. *Edo senryū jiten.* Tokyo: Tōkyōdō Shuppan, 1973.

Hamada, Kenji, trans. *The Life of an Amorous Man.* Rutland, Vt.: Charles E. Tuttle Company, 1963.

Hanasaki Kazuo. *Ō Edo monoshiri zukan.* Tokyo: Shufu to Seikatsusha, 2000.

Hane, Mikiso. *Premodern Japan: A Historical Survey.* Boulder, Colo.: Westview Press, 1991.

Hanley, Susan B. *Everyday Things in Premodern Japan: The Hidden Legacy of Material Culture.* Berkeley: University of California Press, 1997.

———. "Family and Fertility in Four Tokugawa Villages." In *Family and Population in East Asian History,* ed. Susan B. Hanley and Arthur P. Wolf. Stanford, Calif.: Stanford University Press, 1985, 196–228.

———. "Tokugawa Society: Material Culture, Standard of Living, and Life-Styles." In *The Cambridge History of Japan.* Vol. 4, ed. John Whitney Hall. Cambridge: Cambridge University Press, 1991, 660–705.

Hardacre, Helen. *Marketing the Menacing Fetus in Japan.* Berkeley: University of California Press, 1997.

———. *Shintō and the State: 1868 to the Present.* Princeton, N.J.: Princeton University Press, 1988.

Harootunian, H. D. *Things Seen and Unseen: Discourse and Ideology in Tokugawa Nativism.* Chicago: University of Chicago Press, 1988.

Hashimoto Katsusaburō. *Edo no hyakujo jiten.* Tokyo: Shinchō Sensho, 1997.

Hayami, Akira. "Rural Migration and Fertility in Tokugawa Japan: The Village of Nishijo, 1773–1868." In *Family and Population in East Asian History,* ed. Susan B. Hanley and Arthur P. Wolf. Stanford, Calif.: Stanford University Press, 1985, 110–132.

Hendry, Joy. "The Sacred Power of Wrapping." In *Religion in Japan: Arrows to Heaven and Earth,* ed. P. F. Kornicki and I. M. McMullen. Cambridge: University of Cambridge Press, 1996, 287–303.

Holloway, Wendy. "Gender Difference and the Production of Subjectivity." In *Changing the Subject: Psychology, Social Regulation and Subjectivity,* ed. Julian Henriques et al. London: Methuen, 1984, 227–263.

Hubbard, Jamie. "Premodern, Modern, and Postmodern: Doctrine and the Study of Japanese Religion." *Japanese Journal of Religious Studies* 19 (1992): 3–28.

Huizinga, Johan. *Homo Luden: A Study of the Play Element in Culture.* Boston: Beacon Press, 1955.

Hur, Nam-lin. *Prayer and Play in Late Tokugawa Japan: Asakusa Sensōji and Edo Society.* Harvard East Asian Monographs. Cambridge, Mass.: Harvard University Asia Center, Havard University Press, 2000.

Igarashi Tomio. *Kakekomidera.* Tokyo: Kakushobō, 1989.

Inoue Zenjō. *Tōkeiji to kakekomi onna.* Tokyo: Yūrin Shinsho, 1995.

Ishii Ryōsuke. *Edo no yūjo.* Tokyo: Akashi, 1989.

Ishikawa Matsutarō, Miyata Noboru, and Sakamoto Kaname, eds. *Edo jijō: Seikatsu hen.* Tokyo: Yūzankaku Shuppan, 1991.

Ishiko Junzō. *Ko-ema zufu: Fūjikomerareta minshū no inori.* Tokyo: Hōga Shoten, 1972.

Jansen, Marius B. *The Making of Modern Japan.* Cambridge, Mass.: The Belknap Press of Harvard University Press, 2000.

———. "The Meiji Restoration." In *The Cambridge History of Japan.* Vol. 5, ed. Marius B. Jansen. Cambridge: Cambridge University Press, 1989, 308–366.

Jinnai Hidenobu. *Tokyo: A Spatial Anthropology,* trans. Kimiko Nishimura. Berkeley: University of California Press, 1995.

———. "The Spatial Structure of Edo," trans. J. Victor Koschmann. In *Tokugawa Japan: The Social and Economic Antecedents of Modern Japan,* ed. Nakane Chie and Ōishi Shinzaburō. Tokyo: University of Tokyo Press, 1990, 124–146.

Kalland, Arne. *Fishing Villages in Tokugawa Japan.* Honolulu: University of Hawai'i Press, 1995.

Kamiya Jirō. "Jinbutsu shōden." In *Zusetsu jinbutsu Nihon no joseishi.* Vol. 8, ed. Sōga Tetsuo. Tokyo: Shōgakkan, 1980, 150–163.

Kaneko Sachiko and Robert E. Morrell. "Sanctuary: Kamakura's Tōkeiji Convent." *Japanese Journal of Religious Studies* 10 (1983): 195–228.

———. "Tōkeiji: Kamakura's 'Divorce Temple' in Edo Popular Verse." In *Religions of Japan in Practice,* ed. George J. Tanabe. Princeton, N.J.: Princeton University Press, 1999, 523–550.

———. *Zen Sanctuary of Purple Robes: Japan's Tōkeiji Convent since 1285.* Albany, N.Y.: State University of New York Press, 2006.

Katsuura Noriko. "Amasogi kō: Kamigata kara mita ama no sonzai keitai." In *Ama to amadera.* Shiriizu josei to Bukkyō. Vol. 1, ed. Ōsumi Kazuo and Nishiguchi Junko. Tokyo: Heibonsha, 1989, 11–42.

———. "Tonsure Forms for Nuns: Classification of Nuns According to Hairstyle," trans. Virginia Skord Waters. In *Engendering Faith: Women and Buddhism in Premodern Japan,* ed. Barbara Ruch. Ann Arbor: Center for Japanese Studies, University of Michigan, 2002, 109–129.

Keene, Donald, trans. *Chūshingura: The Treasury of Loyal Retainers.* New York: Columbia University Press, 1971.

———. *Four Major Plays of Chikamatsu.* New York: Columbia University Press, 1964.

———. "Introduction." In *Four Major Plays of Chikamatsu.* New York: Columbia University Press, 1964, 1–38.

———. "A Note on Prostitution in Chikamatsu's Plays." In *Four Major Plays of Chikamatsu.* New York: Columbia University Press, 1964, 209–211.

———. *World Within Walls.* New York: Holt, Rinehart, and Winston, 1976.

Kelleher, Theresa. "Confucianism." In *Women in World Religions,* ed. Arvind Sharma. Albany: State University of New York Press, 1987, 135–159.

Kendall, Laurel. *Getting Married in Korea: Of Gender, Morality, and Modernity.* Berkeley: University of California Press, 1996.

Ketelaar, James Edward. *Of Heretics and Martyrs in Meiji Japan: Buddhism and Its Persecution.* Princeton, N.J.: Princeton University Press, 1990.

Kitagawa, Joseph M. *On Understanding Japanese Religion.* Princeton, N.J.: Princeton University Press, 1987.

Kiyoshi Hiromi. "Yoshiwara zankkoku monogatari." In *Senryū Yoshiwara fūzoku ezu,* ed. Satō Yōjin. Tokyo: Shibundō, 1973, 291–304.

Klein, Susan Blakeley. "Allegories of Desire: Poetry and Eroticism in *Ise Monogatari.*" *Monumenta Nipponica* 52 (1997)441–465.

———. "Wild Words and Syncretic Deities: *Kyōgen kigo* and *Honji suijaku* in Medieval Literary Allegoresis." In *Buddhas and Kami in Japan:* Honji Suijaku *as a Combinatory Paradigm,* ed. Mark Teeuwen and Fabio Rambelli. London: Routledge Courzon, 2003, 177–203.

Ko, Dorothy, JaHyun Kim Haboush, and Joan R. Piggott, eds. *Women and Confucian Cultures in Premodern China, Korea, and Japan.* Berkeley: University of California Press, 2003.

Kobayashi Junji. "Kinsei Nihon ni okeru koi to jendā: Masuho Zankō *Endō tsugan* ni okeru dansei no imēji." *Josei shigaku* 8 (1998): 1–13.

Kogo daijiten, ed. Nakamura Yukihiko, Okami Masao, and Sakakura Atsuyoshi. 5 Vols. Tokyo: Kakukawa Shoten, 1982–1984.

Koizumi Eitarō. *Wakan yaku-kō.* Tokyo: Asakaya Shoten, 1891.

Kornicki, Peter. *The Book in Japan: A Cultural History from the Beginnings to the Nineteenth Century.* Honolulu: University of Hawai'i Press, 2001.

Kosaka Natsuko. "Kinsei ni okeru katsurame no jitsuzō to sono yuisho." *Joseishigaku* 14 (2004): 51–65.

Kubo Noritada. *Kōshin shinkō kenkyū.* Vols. 1 and 2. Tokyo: Daiichi Shobō, 1996.

Kuki Shūzō. *Iki no kōzō.* Tokyo: Iwanami Shoten, 1930.

Kunimoto Keikichi. *San'ikushi: O-san to kosodate no rekishi.* Morioka City, Japan: Morioka Taimisusha, 1996.

Kurachi Katsunao. *Sei to karada no kinseishi.* Tokyo: Tōkyō Daigaku Shuppankai, 1998.

———. "Seikatsu shisō ni okeru seiishiki." In *Nihon josei seikatsu-shi: Kinsei.* Vol. 3, ed. Miyashita Michiko and Kurachi Katsunao. Tokyo: Tōkyō Daigaku Shuppankai, 1990, 203–226.

Kuroda Hideo. *Kyōkai no chūsei shōchō no chūsei.* Tokyo: Tōkyō Daigaku Shuppankai, 1986.

Kōno, Augustinus Yoshisuke. *The Evolution of the Concept of Matrimonial Consent in Japanese Law.* Tokyo: Monumenta Nipponica, 1970.

LaFleur, William R. *The Karma of Words: Buddhism and the Literary Arts in Medieval Japan.* Berkeley: University of California Press, 1983.

———. *Liquid Life: Abortion and Buddhism in Japan.* Princeton, N.J.: Princeton University Press, 1992.

Lane, Richard. *Images from the Floating World: The Japanese Print.* New York: Konecky and Konecky, 1978.

Langer, Susanne K. *Philosophy in a New Key: A Study in the Symbolism of Reason, Rite, and Art.* Cambridge, Mass.: Harvard University Press, 1942.

Law, Jane Marie. *Puppets of Nostalgia: The Life, Death, and Rebirth of the Japanese Awaji Ningyō Tradition.* Princeton, N.J.: Princeton University Press, 1997.

Leach, Edmund. *Culture and Communication: The Logic by which Symbols are Connected.* Cambridge: Cambridge University Press, 1976.

Lebra, Joyce Chapman. "Women in an All-Male Industry: The Case of Sake Brewer Tatsu'uma Kiyo." In *Recreating Japanese Women, 1600–1945,* ed. Gail Lee Bernstein. Berkeley: University of California Press, 1991, 131–148.

Leupp, Gary P. *Male Colors: The Construction of Homosexuality in Tokugawa Japan.* Berkeley: University of California Press, 1995.

———. *Servants, Shophands, and Laborers in the Cities of Tokugawa Japan.* Princeton, N.J.: Princeton University Press, 1992.

Maeda Isamu, ed. *Edo go no jiten.* Tokyo: Kōdansha, 1979.

Mass, Jeffrey P. *Lordship and Inheritance in Early Medieval Japan.* Stanford, Calif.: Stanford University Press, 1989.

Masuda Toshimi. "Nōson josei no kekkon." In *Nihon no kinsei.* Vol. 15, ed. Hayashi Reiko. Tokyo: Chūō Kōronsha, 1993, 167–190.

Matsunaga, Daigan, and Alice Matsunaga. *Foundation of Japanese Buddhism.* Vol. 2. Los Angeles: Buddhist Books International, 1984.

McCullough, William H. "Japanese Marriage Institutions in the Heian Period." *Harvard Journal of Asiatic Studies* 27 (1967): 103–167.

McMullin, Neil. "Historical and Historiographical Issues in the Study of Pre-Modern Japanese Religions." *Japanese Journal of Religious Studies* 16 (1989): 3–40.

———. "Which Doctrine? Whose 'Religion'?—A Rejoinder." *Japanese Journal of Religious Studies* 19 (1992): 29–40.

McVeigh, Brian J. "The Vitalistic Conception of Salvation as Expressed in Sūkyō Mahikari." *Japanese Journal of Religious Studies* 19 (1992): 41–68.

———. *Wearing Ideology: State, Schooling, and Self-Presentation in Japan.* Oxford: Berg, 2000.

Mega Atsuko. *Hankachō no naka no onnatachi.* Tokyo: Heibonsha, 1995.

Meigs, Anna. "Food as a Cultural Construction." In *Food and Culture: A Reader,* ed. Carole Counihan and Penny Van Esterik. New York: Routledge, 1997, 95–106.

Minakawa Mieko. "Kinsei makki no *Kuwana nikki, Kashiwazaki nikki* ni mirareru yōiku bunka." In *Bunka to josei, Nihon joseishi ronshū.* Vol. 7, ed. Umemura Keiko and Katakura Hisako. Tokyo: Yoshikawa Kōbunkan, 1998, 148–168.

Mitani Kazuma. *Edo Yoshiwara zushū.* Tokyo: Rippū Shobō, 1977.

Miyake Hitoshi. *Shugendō: Essays on the Structure of Japanese Folk Religion,* ed. H. Byron Earhart. Ann Arbor: Center for Japanese Studies, University of Michigan, 2001.

Miyamoto Yukiko. "Kuruwa to shukuba." In *Nihon joseishi,* ed. Wakita Haruko, Hayashi Reiko, and Nagahara Kazuko. Tokyo: Yoshikawa Kōbunkan, 1987, 128–135.

Miyata Noboru. *Edo saijiki.* Tokyo: Yoshikawa Kōbunkan, 1981.

Moore, Henrietta L. *A Passion for Difference: Essays in Anthropology and Gender.* Bloomington: Indiana University Press, 1994.

Morita Kōichi. "Kaidai." In *Edo jidai josei bunko.* Vol. 31. Tokyo: Ōzorasha, 1995, 1–6.

Morris, Ivan, ed. and trans. *The Life of an Amorous Woman.* New York: New Directions Books, 1969.

Murao Yoshie. "Kekkon girei ni miru 'sahō' no eikyō." *Nihon minzokugaku* 235 (2003): 65–99.

Nagano Hiroko. "Bakuhansei kokka to shomin josei." In *Nihon joseishi,* ed. Wakita Haruko, Hayashi Reiko, and Nagahara Kazuko. Tokyo: Yoshikawa Kōbunkan, 1987, 122–128.

Nagasawa Toshiaki. *Edo Tōkyō no shomin shinkō.* Tokyo: Miyai, 1996.

Nakai, Nobuhiko, and James L. McClain. "Commercial Change and Urban Growth in Early Modern Japan." In *The Cambridge History of Japan.* Vol. 4, ed. John Whitney Hall. Cambridge: Cambridge University Press, 1991, 519–595.

Nakamura Hiroko. "Shussan to tanjō." In *Onna no me de miru minzokugaku,* ed. Nakamura Hiroko et al. Tokyo: Kōbunken, 1999, 54–83.

Nakamura Kazumoto. "'Tainai totsuki no zu' no shisō shiteki tenkai." *Iwate Daigaku kyōiku gakubu kenkyū nenpō* 50 (1990): 23–36.

Nakamura Masahiro. "Kaiawase." In *Sekai daihyakka jiten.* Tokyo: Heibonsha, 1990, 499.

Nakamura Shikaku. *Yūkaku no seikatsu.* Tokyo: Hyōronsha, 1976.

Nakane Chie. "Tokugawa Society," trans. Susan Murata. In *Tokugawa Japan: The Social and Economic Antecedents of Modern Japan,* ed. Nakane Chie and Ōishi Shinzaburō. Tokyo: University of Tokyo Press, 1990, 213–231.

Nakano Hajimu. "Kuki Shūzō and the Structure of *Iki.*" In *Culture and Identity: Japanese Intellectuals during the Interwar Years,* ed. J. Thomas Rimer. Princeton, N.J.: Princeton University Press, 1990, 261–272.

Nakayama Tarō. *Baishō sanzennen-shi*. Tokyo: Parutosusha, 1984.

Narikiyo Hirokazu. *Josei to kegare no rekishi*. Tokyo: Kakushobō, 2003.

Nickerson, Peter. "The Meaning of Matrilocality: Kinship, Property, and Politics in Mid-Heian." *Monumenta Nipponica* 48 (1993): 429–467.

Nishiyama Matsunosuke. *Edo Culture: Daily Life and Diversions in Urban Japan, 1600–1868*, trans. and ed. Gerald Groemer. Honolulu: University of Hawai'i Press, 1997.

Nishiyama Matsunosuke, Komori Takayoshi, and Miyamoto Yukiko. *Yūjo*. Tokyo: Kondō Shuppansha, 1979.

Nosco, Peter. "Masuho Zankō (1655–1742): A Shinto Popularizer between Nativism and National Learning." In *Confucianism and Tokugawa Culture*, ed. Peter Nosco. Princeton, N.J.: Princeton University Press, 1984, 166–187.

Ōbayashi Michiko. "O-san ima mukashi." In *Hahatachi no minzokushi*, ed. Ōtō Yuki. Tokyo: Iwada Shoin, 1999, 25–42.

Ochiai Emiko. "The Reproductive Revolution at the End of the Tokugawa Period." In *Women and Class in Japanese History*, ed. Hitomi Tonomura, Anne Walthall, and Haruko Wakita. Ann Arbor: Center for Japanese Studies, University of Michigan, 1999, 187–215.

Ōguchi Yūjirō. "Kinsei nōson ni okeru josei sōzokunin." In *Ie-Shinzoku no seikatsu bunka, Nihon rekishi minzoku ronshū*. Vol. 3, ed. Fukuta Ajio and Tsukamoto Manabu. Tokyo: Yoshikawa Kōbunkan, 1993: 119–151.

Okitsu Kaname. *Edo Yoshiwara shi*. Tokyo: Sakuhinsha, 1984.

Ooms, Herman. *Tokugawa Village Practice: Class, Status, Power, Law*. Berkeley: University of California Press, 1996.

Ōtō Yuki. *Kodomo no minzokugaku: ichininmae ni sodateru*. Tokyo: Sōdo Bunka, 1982.

Philippi, Donald L., ed. and trans. *Kojiki*. Tokyo: University of Tokyo Press, 1968.

Reader, Ian. "Letters to the Gods: The Form and Meaning of Ema." *Japanese Journal of Religious Studies* 18 (1991): 23–50.

———. *Religion in Contemporary Japan*. Honolulu: University of Hawai'i Press, 1991.

Reader, Ian, and George Tanabe. *Practically Religious: Worldy Benefits and the Common Religion of Japan*. Honolulu: University of Hawai'i Press, 1998.

Richie, Donald. "Foreword to the Facsimile Edition." In *The Nightless City, or the History of the Yoshiwara Yūkwaku*. New York: IMG Muse, Inc., 2000, xi–xxvi.

Robertson, Jennifer. "The Shingaku Woman: Straight from the Heart." In *Recreating Japanese Women, 1600–1945*, ed. Gail Lee Berstein. Berkeley: University of California Press, 1991, 88–107.

Rogers, Lawrence. "She Loves Me, She Loves Me Not: Shinjū and *Shikidō ōkagami*." *Monumenta Nipponica* 49 (1994): 31–60.

Rozman, Gilbert. *Urban Networks in Ch'ing China and Tokugawa Japan*. Princeton, N.J.: Princeton University Press, 1973.

Saeki Junko. *Yūjo no bunkashi*. Tokyo: Chūkō Kōronsha, 1990.

Sakurai Yuki. "Kaidai." In *Edo jidai josei bunko*. Vol. 57. Tokyo: Ōzorasha, 1996, 1–6.

———. "Mabiki to datai." In *Nihon no kinsei*. Vol. 15, ed. Hayashi Reiko. Tokyo: Chūō Kōronsha, 1993, 97–128.

Sanford, James H. "The Abominable Tachikawa Skull Ritual." *Monumenta Nipponica* 46 (1991):1–20.

———. "Wind, Waters, Stupas, Mandalas: Fetal Buddhahood in Shingon." *Japanese Journal of Religious Studies* 24 (1997): 1–38.

Sasama Yoshihiko. *Kōshoku engo jiten.* Tokyo: Yūzankaku Shuppan, 1989.

Sawayama Mikako. "The 'Birthing Body' and the Regulation of Conception and Child-birth in the Edo Period," trans. Elizabeth A. Leicester. *U.S.-Japan Women's Journal* 24 (2003): 10–34.

———. *Shussan to shintai no kinsei.* Tokyo: Keisōshobō, 1998.

Screech, Timon. *The Western Scientific Gaze and Popular Imagery in Later Edo Japan: The Lens within the Heart.* Cambridge: Cambridge University Press, 1996.

Seigle, Cecilia Segawa. *Yoshiwara: The Glittering World of the Japanese Courtesan.* Honolulu: University of Hawai'i Press, 1993.

Sharf, Robert. "Sanbōkyōdan: Zen and the New Religions." *Japanese Journal of Religious Studies* 22 (1995): 417–458.

Shimada Isao. "Kaisetsu." In *Teijō zakki.* Vol. 1, ed. Shimada Isao. *Tōyō Bunko* 444. Tokyo: Heibonsha, 1985, 305–348.

Shinmura Taku. *Shussan to seishokukan no rekishi.* Tokyo: Hōsei Daigaku Shuppankyoku, 1996.

Shively, Donald H. "*Bakufu* versus *Kabuki.*" In *Studies in the Institutional History of Early Modern Japan,* ed. John W. Hall and Marius B. Jansen. Princeton, N.J.: Princeton University Press, 1968, 231–261.

———. "Popular Culture." In *The Cambridge History of Japan.* Vol. 4, ed. John Whitney Hall. Cambridge: Cambridge University Press, 1991, 706–769.

Smith, Jonathan Z. "The Bare Facts of Ritual." *Journal of the History of Religions* 20 (1980): 112–127.

———. *Map Is Not Territory: Studies in the History of Religion.* Chicago: University of Chicago Press, 1993.

———. *To Take Place: Toward Theory in Ritual.* Chicago: University of Chicago Press, 1987.

Smith, Robert J. *Ancestor Worship in Contemporary Japan.* Stanford, Calif.: Stanford University Press, 1974.

Smith, Thomas C. "The Japanese Village in the Seventeenth Century." In *Studies in the Institutional History of Early Modern Japan,* ed. John W. Hall and Marius B. Jansen. Princeton, N.J.: Princeton University Press, 1968, 263–282.

Smyers, Karen A. *The Fox and the Jewel: Shared and Private Meanings in Contemporary Japanese Inari Worship.* Honolulu: University of Hawai'i Press, 1999.

Sone Hiromi. "'Baita' kō." In *Nihon josei seikatsu-shi: Chūsei.* Vol. 3, ed. Miyashita Michiko and Kurachi Katsunao. Tokyo: Tōkyō Daigaku Shuppankai, 1990, 111–141.

———. "Joseishi to fueminizumu—Ueno Chizuko cho *Rekishigaku to fueminizumu* ni yosete." *Joseishigaku* 6 (1996): 73–82.

———. "Prostitution and Public Authority in Early Modern Japan," trans. Akiko Terashima and Anne Walthall. In *Women and Class in Japanese History,* ed. Hitomi Tonomura, Anne Walthall, and Haruko Wakita. Ann Arbor: Center for Japanese Studies, University of Michigan, 1999, 169–185.

Sperber, Dan. *Rethinking Symbolism.* Cambridge: Cambridge University Press, 1974.

Spiro, Melford E. "Religion: Problems of Definition and Explanation." In *Culture and Human Nature: Theoretical Papers of Melford E. Spiro,* ed. Benjamin Kilborne and L. L. Langness. Chicago: University of Chicago Press, 1986, 187–212.

Steenstrup, Carl. *A History of Law in Japan until 1868.* Leiden: E. J. Brill, 1996.

————. "The Imagawa Letter: A Muromachi Warrior's Code of Conduct Which Became a Tokugawa Schoolbook." *Monumenta Nipponica* 28 (1973): 295–316.

Stone, Jacqueline I. *Original Enlightenment and the Transformation of Medieval Japanese Buddhism.* Kuroda Institute Studies in East Asian Buddhism, no. 12. Honolulu: University of Hawai'i Press, 1999.

Sugano, Noriko. "State Indoctrination of Filial Piety in Tokugawa Japan: Sons and Daughters in the *Offical Records of Filial Piety.*" In *Women and Confucian Cultures in Premodern China, Korea, and Japan,* ed. Dorothy Ko, JaHyun Kim Haboush, and Joan R. Piggott. Berkeley: University of California Press, 2003, 170–189.

Sugitatsu Yoshikazu. *O-san no rekishi.* Tokyo: Shūeisha Shinsho, 2002.

Suzuki Noriko. "Edo jidai no keshō to biyō ishiki." *Joseishigaku* 13 (2003): 1–17.

Tabata Yasuko. *Nihon chūsei no josei.* Tokyo: Yoshikawa Kōbunkan, 1987.

Tadenuma Yasuko. "Samazama na kon'in." In *Onna no me de miru minzokugaku,* ed. Nakamura Hiroko et al. Tokyo: Kōbunken, 1999, 24–52.

Takagi Tadashi. *Enkiridera Mantokuji no kenkyū.* Tokyo: Seibundō, 1990.

————. *Enkiridera Tōkeiji shiryō.* Tokyo: Heibonsha, 1997.

————. *Mikudarihan: Edo no rikon to joseitachi.* Tokyo: Heibonsha, 1987.

————. *Mikudarihan to enkiridera.* Tokyo: Kōdansha, 1992.

Takamure Itsue. *Nihon kon'in shi.* In *Takamure Itsue zenshū.* Vol. 6, ed. Takamure Itsue and Hashimoto Kenzō. Tokyo: Rironsha, 1966.

Takayama Naoko. "Awabi no rekishi." In *Zenshu Nihon no shokubunka.* Vol. 4, ed. Haga Noboru and Ishikawa Hiroko. Tokyo: Yūzankaku Shuppan, 1997, 65–80.

Takigawa Masajirō. *Yoshiwara no shiki.* Tokyo: Seiabō, 1971.

————. *Yūjo no rekishi.* Tokyo: Shibundō, 1967.

Tamamuro Fumio. "Tera ni kakekomu onnatachi." In *Nihon josei-shi.* Vol. 5, ed. Kasahara Kazuo. Tokyo: Hyōronsha, 1973, 59–114.

Tanaka Chitako and Tanakao Hatsuo, eds. *Kaseigaku bunken shūse zokuhen Edoki.* Vol 8. Tokyo: Watanabe Shoten, 1970.

Tatsukawa Shōji. *Kinsei yamai no sōshi.* Tokyo: Heibonsha Sensho, 1979.

Teeuwen, Mark, and Fabio Rambelli, eds. *Buddhas and Kami in Japan:* Honji Suijaku *as a Combinatory Paradigm.* London: Routledge Courzon, 2003.

————. "Introduction: Combinatory Religion and the *Honji suijaku* Paradigm in Pre-Modern Japan." In *Buddhas and Kami in Japan:* Honji Suijaku *as a Combinatory Paradigm,* ed. Mark Teeuwen and Fabio Rambelli. London: Routledge Courzon, 2003, 1–53.

Teiser, Steven F. *The Scripture of the Ten Kings and the Making of Purgatory in Medieval Chinese Buddhism.* Kuroda Institute, Studies in East Buddhism, no. 9. Honolulu: University of Hawai'i Press, 1994.

Teruoka Yasutaka. "Pleasure Quarters and Tokugawa Culture," trans. C. Andrew Gerstle. In *18th Century Japan,* ed. C. Andrew Gerstle. Sydney: Allen and Unwin, 1989, 3–32.

Thornbury, Barbara E. *Sukeroku's Double Identity: The Dramatic Structure of Edo Kabuki.* Ann Arbor: Center for Japanese Studies, University of Michigan, 1982.

Tocco, Martha C. "Norms and Texts for Women's Education in Tokugawa Japan." In *Women and Confucian Cultures in Premodern China, Korea, and Japan,* ed, Dorothy Ko, JaHyun Kim Haboush, and Joan R. Piggott. Berkeley: University of California Press, 2003, 193–218.

Tonomura, Hitomi. "Re-envisioning Women in the Post-Kamakura Age." In *The Ori-*

gins of Japan's Mediveal World, ed. Jeffrey P. Mass. Stanford, Calif.: Stanford University Press, 1997, 138–169.

———. "Women and Inheritance in Japan's Early Warrior Society." Comparative Studies in Society and History 32 (1990): 592–623.

Tonomura, Hitomi, and Anne Walthall. "Introduction." In Women and Class in Japanese History, ed. Hitomi Tonomura, Anne Walthall, and Haruko Wakita. Ann Arbor: Center for Japanese Studies, University of Michigan, 1999, 1–16.

Tucker, John Allen. Itō Jinsai's Gomō Jigi and the Philosophical Definition of Early Modern Japan. Leiden: Brill, 1998.

Turner, Victor. The Forest of Symbols: Aspects of Ndembu Ritual. Ithaca, N.Y.: Cornell University Press, 1967.

———. The Ritual Process: Structure and Anti-Structure. Ithaca, N.Y.: Cornell University Press, 1977.

Ueno Chizuko. "Modern Patriarchy and the Formation of the Japanese Nation State." In Multicultural Japan: Paleolithic to Postmodern, ed. Donald Denoon et al. Cambridge: Cambridge University Press, 1996, 215–223.

Uno, Kathleen S. "Women and Changes in the Household Division of Labor." In Recreating Japanese Women, 1600–1945, ed. Gail Lee Bernstein. Berkeley: University of California Press, 1991, 17–41.

Unoda Shoya. "Kinsei jokunsho ni okeru shomotsu to dokusha—Onna shōgaku wo tegakari toshite." Joseishigaku 11 (2001): 15–31.

Varley, H Paul. A Chronical of Gods and Sovereigns: Jinnō shōtōki of Kitabatake Chikafusa. New York: Columbia University Press, 1980.

Wakita Haruko. "Marriage and Property in Premodern Japan from the Perspective of Women's History," trans. Suzanne Gay. Journal of Japanese Studies 10 (1984): 73–99.

———. "The Medieval Household and Gender Roles within the Imperial Family, Nobility, Merchants, and Commoners," trans. Gary P. Leupp. In Women and Class in Japanese History, ed. Hitomi Tonomura, Anne Walthall, and Haruko Wakita. Ann Arbor: Center for Japanese Studies, University of Michigan, 1994, 81–97.

Walthall, Anne. "The Life Cycle of Farm Women in Tokugawa Japan." In Recreating Japanese Women, 1600–1945, ed. Gail Lee Bernstein. Berkeley: University of California Press, 1991, 42–70.

———. "Peripheries: Rural Culture in Tokugawa Japan. Monumenta Nipponica 39 (1984): 371–392.

———. The Weak Body of a Useless Woman: Matsuo Taseko and the Meiji Restoration. Chicago: University of Chicago Press, 1998.

Woolf, Virginia. "Professions for Women." In The Death of the Moth and Other Essays. New York: Harcourt, Brace, and Company, 1942, 235–242.

Wright, Diana E. "Mantokuji: More than a 'Divorce Temple.'" In Engendering Faith: Women and Buddhism in Premodern Japan, ed. Barbara Ruch. Ann Arbor: Center for Japanese Studies, University of Michigan, 2002, 247–276.

———. "Severing the Karmic Ties that Bind: The 'Divorce Temple' Mantokuji." Monumenta Nipponica 52 (1997): 357–380.

Yamaguchi Keizaburō and Asano Shūgō, eds. Genshoku ukiyoe daihyakka jiten. Vol. 6. Tokyo: Taishūkan Shoten, 1982.

Yamakawa Kikue. Women of the Mito Domain: Recollections of Samurai Family Life, trans. Kate Wildmon Nakai. Tokyo: University of Tokyo Press, 1992.

Yokota Fuyuhiko. "Imagining Working Women in Early Modern Japan," trans. Mariko Asano Tamanoi. In *Women and Class in Japanese History,* ed. Hitomi Tonomura, Anne Walthall, and Haruko Wakita. Ann Arbor: Center for Japanese Studies, University of Michigan, 1999, 153–167.

Yokoyama Manabu. "Joshi kyōyōsho kōka-han *Onna chōhōki* to Takai Ranzan." In *Edo jidai josei seikatsu kenkyū* (Supplement to *Edo jidai josei seikatsu ezu daijiten*), ed. Emori Ichirō. Tokyo: Ōzorasha, 1994, 100–114.

Yonemoto, Marcia. *Mapping Early Modern Japan: Space, Place, and Culture in the Tokugawa Period (1603–1868).* Berkeley: University of California Press, 2003.

Yoshida Hidehiro. *Nihon baishunshi kō.* Tokyo: Jiyūsha, 2000.

ABOUT THE AUTHOR

WILLIAM LINDSEY, who received his doctorate in religious studies from the University of Pittsburgh, is currently assistant professor of religious studies at the University of Kansas. Among his publications are "Motive, Myth, and Metaphor: Religion and the Good Life in a Tokugawa Female Lifestyle Guide," in the *Journal of Japanese Religious Studies,* and "Ninpu no karada o gishiki no kankyō ni suru koto—girei kenkyū kara mita Edo jidai no ninshin," in *Hikaku minzoku kenkyū. Fertility and Pleasure* is his first book.

Production Notes for LINDSEY / FERTILITY AND PLEASURE

Cover and interior designed by Liz Demeter
with text in Bembo and display in Bliss

Composition by Josie Herr

Printing and binding by The Maple-Vail Book
Manufacturing Group

Printed on 60# Text White Opaque, 426 ppi